CONTENTS

	Introduction	1
Chapter 1	**What is Entrepreneurship?**	**5**
	Introduction	5
	Personality Traits	7
	Entrepreneurial Background	9
	Behavioural Aspects of Entrepreneurship	12
	Management Approaches to Entrepreneurship	12
	Entrepreneurship as a Process	14
	Research Trends in Entrepreneurship	15
	Conclusion	17
Chapter 2	**Finding the Business Idea**	**21**
	Introduction	21
	Key Concepts	23
	Structured Techniques for Idea Generation	26
	Where to Find Business Ideas	31
	Transforming Ideas into Realisable Opportunities	33
	Conclusion	35
Chapter 3	**The Business Plan Process**	**38**
	Introduction	38
	Process and Output	40
	The New Venture Creation Process	40
	Key Questions	41
	Business Planning	44
	The Structure of a Business Plan	46

	A Starting Point	47
	Conclusion	50
Chapter 4	**Marketing Research**	**52**
	Introduction	52
	Definitions of Market Research	53
	Why is Marketing Research Essential?	54
	The Marketing Research Process	56
	Stage 1 – Problem Definition	57
	Stage 2 – Choose a Research Design	58
	Stage 3 – Planning the Data Collection	
	Method(s) & Instrument(s)	60
	Stage 4 – Sampling	70
	Stage 5 – Fieldwork, Gathering the Required	
	Information	72
	Stage 6 – Analysis of the Data	72
	Stage 7 – Presentation of the Results and Findings	73
	Conclusion	75
Chapter 5	**Intellectual Property**	**78**
	Introduction	78
	Patents	79
	Trade Marks	82
	Copyright	85
	Registered Designs	87
	Conclusion	89
Chapter 6	**Legal Issues**	**92**
	Introduction	92
	Legal Trading Structures	93
	Employment Law	99
	Health and Safety	103
	Contract Law	105
	Conclusion	109
Chapter 7	**Managing the New Venture**	**111**
	Introduction	111
	Management in the Small Firm Context	113
	New Venture Growth – The Management Issues	116

	Balancing Entrepreneurial and Professional Management	119
	Management Functions Applied to the New Venture	122
	Conclusion	127

Chapter 8	**Marketing in the Entrepreneurial New Venture**	**131**
	Introduction	132
	The Marketing/Entrepreneurship Interface	132
	The Marketing Advantages of an Entrepreneurial New Venture	133
	Developing a Marketing Plan for an ENV	134
	Marketing Planning in the ENV	135
	Maintaining the ENV's Entrepreneurial Effort	144
	Conclusion	145

Chapter 9	**Operations – Designing the Process**	**148**
	Introduction	148
	Operations Design in Context	149
	Defining the Process of Making	150
	Transformation Process	151
	Process	153
	Location	157
	Conclusion	160

Chapter 10	**Human Resource Management**	**163**
	Introduction	163
	Recruitment and Selection Practices	165
	Training and Development Practices	168
	Building an Employee Involvement Culture	169
	Performance Management Practices	171
	Conclusion	172

Chapter 11	**Finance for New Ventures**	**175**
	Introduction	175
	The Role of Finance in New Venture Creation	177
	Types and Sources of Finance	180
	Estimating Financing Needs	190
	Financial Management	194
	Conclusion	196

Chapter 12   Planning for Growth   **203**
                Introduction   203
                Theoretical Background   204
                "Stages-of-Growth" Models   205
                Barriers to Growth   208
                Strategic Characteristics of High Growth Ventures   210
                Practical Information on Development of
                Businesses in Ireland   212
                Conclusion   218

Chapter 13   Reviewing the Business Plan   **222**
                Introduction   222
                Financial Projections   223
                Reviewing the Process   224
                Reviewing the Output   229
                Tailoring the Plan for the Reader   235
                Conclusion   236

Chapter 14   Entrepreneurship in Different Contexts   **243**
                Introduction   243
                Corporate Entrepreneurship (Intrapreneurship)   245
                Mediated Entrepreneurship   249
                Public Sector Entrepreneurship   251
                Social Entrepreneurship   254
                Conclusion   257

Chapter 15   Entrepreneurship and the Role of the State   **260**
                Introduction   260
                The Role of State Agencies   261
                Ireland's Entrepreneurial Future   262
                Key Interests   263
                Conclusion   264

TABLES

Table 1.1:   Attributes of Successful Entrepreneurs   8

Table 4.1:   Choosing a Research Design   59

Table 4.2:   Distinctions Between Secondary and Primary Data   60

Table 4.3:   Strengths and Weaknesses of Principal Survey
             Methods   68

Table 4.4:   Summary of the Marketing Research Process   74

Table 6.1:   Contrasting the Different Legal Structures for
             Business   98

Table 7.1:   Government Agencies, Professional Associations,
             Universities and Institiutes of Technology   129

Table 8.1:   The Marketing Planning Process   136

Table 10.1: The Predictive Power of Selection Methods   167

Table 10.2: Five Level Evaluation Framework for a
             Training Programme   169

Table 11.1: Investment Activity Venture Capital Funds
             1996 to 2000   187

Table 13.1: Critical Questions, Answers and Evidence   231

FIGURES

Figure 3.1   SPOTcheck Factor   49

Figure 4.1: The Marketing Research Process   57
Figure 4.2: Research Designs   58

Figure 7.1: Business Environment   118
Figure 7.2: Management Functions   123

Figure 9.1: Supply Chain Management   152
Figure 9.2: The Transformation Process   152

Figure 10.1: The Recruitment Process   165

Figure 11.1: Types of Finance   181

Figure 13.1: Projected Profit & Loss Account   238
Figure 13.2: Projected Balance Sheet   239
Figure 13.3: Initial Investment Summary   240
Figure 13.4: Investment Investment – Sources of Funding   241
Figure 13.5: How Ratios Combine   227
Figure 13.6: The Business Life Cycle   234

ABOUT THE EDITORS

Dr Thomas M. Cooney BComm, MBA, PhD, MMII, MCIM, MIBA is a lecturer in entrepreneurship and marketing at the Dublin Institute of Technology and a director of Optimum Results (SME Training and Consultancy). His work incorporates teaching, researching, writing, mentoring, training, and consulting on the issues of new venture creation, small business management, and marketing. He has co-founded two enterprises and was a Director of the Bolton Trust. He has also been a Visiting Research Scholar at Babson College (USA) and at the Foundation for SME Development at the University of Durham (UK).

Shane Hill DMS, MBA, MMII, is a lecturer in entrepreneurship and marketing at Dundalk Institute of Technology. He has published widely within the field of entrepreneurship and entrepreneurship education over the last number of years. His current research interests include entrepreneurship education and training, high-technology entrepreneurship and entrepreneurship within the community sector.

ABOUT THE AUTHORS

Naomi Birdthistle is a junior lecturer in entrepreneurship and management at the University of Limerick.

Thomas M. Cooney is a lecturer in entrepreneurship and marketing at the Dublin Institute of Technology and a director of Optimum Results.

Sinéad Dunne is a patent specialist and trade mark attorney with Tomkins & Co.

Declan Fleming is a lecturer in marketing at the Department of Marketing, National University of Ireland, Galway.

Dan Flinter is chief executive officer of Enterprise Ireland.

Anthony Foley is a senior lecturer in economics and enterprise at Dublin City University Business School.

Shane Hill is a lecturer in entrepreneurship and marketing at the Dundalk Institute of Technology.

Briga Hynes is a lecturer in entrepreneurship and management at the University of Limerick.

Ron Immink is new business director of Oak Tree Press.

Cathal Lane is a European, Irish and UK patent attorney with Tomkins & Co.

Martina Lordan is managing director of Lordan & Associates and a visiting lecturer with the Entrepreneurship Unit at the University of Lancaster.

Pauric McGowan is a lecturer in entrepreneurship and marketing at the University of Ulster.

Bill O'Gorman is a lecturer in entrepreneurship, operations and management at University College Cork.

Colm O'Gorman is a lecturer in entrepreneurship at UCD Business School, University College Dublin.

Brian O'Kane is managing director of Oak Tree Press.

Michael Purtill is a barrister-at-law.

Niall Rooney is a solicitor and European trade mark attorney with Tomkins & Co.

Dermot Rush is a director of The Performance Partnership, a Human Resource Management consultancy based in Galway.

INTRODUCTION

The notion of securing a "job for life" no longer holds the promising allure of days past. The pace of economic change has quickened to such a degree that managers need to be able to react far more quickly than ever before by adapting their markets, their products, and their people. Employees are being asked to update their skills more frequently, so that they will continue to offer benefit to an enterprise. If employees are unwilling or unable to change, they may no longer have a job within the organisation. However, there are also an increasing number of people who simply do not wish to work for one company throughout their career and instead find greater reward in moving across companies and industries. They pursue opportunities that improve their own position and long-term loyalty to the firm is sacrificed to personal ambition. In essence, the idea of job security has altered and individuals are increasingly looking at their career in terms of personal development and independence rather than organisational development and dependence.

In addition to the growth in personal career development, there has also been a significant expansion over the past decade in entrepreneurship as a career option. The economic boom of the late 1990s offered many business opportunities that Irish people willingly accepted. The high-profile success of Irish entrepreneurs in building profitable businesses that have traded on international stock exchanges has offered local role models to those considering business ownership as a career option. Instead of entrepreneurs being viewed as "gangsters or chancers", they are now recognised for their role in the development of the Irish economy. Government policies and State support agencies have sought to engender entrepreneurship through a wide variety of initiatives and assistance for new venture creation is now more accessible than at any time in the history of the State. The current economic, social, and cultural environments in Ireland promote entrepreneurial endeavour more proactively than previously was perceptible.

The positive change in mood towards entrepreneurship has also cascaded through the Irish education system. Initially, third-level colleges provided occasional modules in entrepreneurship as an option for those considering self-employment. But, increasingly, these modules became available as core subjects, as well as options, across a widening range of courses. No longer do students take third-level courses only to enter existing businesses but many now seek greater independence through self-employment. A decade ago, students considering starting their own business were advised to get at least 10 years' work experience before establishing their own venture. Today, a significant and increasing number of students graduate to create their own venture immediately after graduation, most frequently in the area of e-commerce. Entrepreneurship is now seen as a viable career option and not simply something that could happen in later years.

A student taking a course in Entrepreneurship will not suddenly become an entrepreneur, having been struck by some bolt of enlightenment like Saul on the road to Damascus. A course in Entrepreneurship (or New Venture Creation) should achieve two goals for a student. First, it should provoke in the student an entrepreneurial mindset and a sense of entrepreneurial behaviour that can be used in many different environments. Second, it should provide a toolbox into which the student can delve whenever the prospect of becoming an entrepreneur arises. It is the contention of the editors that every person considers entrepreneurship at least once in their life, even if it is a fleeting occurrence. Early exposure to the process of new venture creation should ensure that a person considers entrepreneurship more positively when that opportunity arises and that they would have a better awareness of what issues to consider when making a decision on the matter. Having completed the course in Entrepreneurship, a student will be familiar with the key areas that need examination regarding new venture creation.

New Venture Creation in Ireland has been designed to provide the reader with the fundamental questions – and answers – that must be considered when establishing a business. It breaks down the elements of business planning through the different chapters. By reviewing the literature on many of the elements, a contextual background is offered that explains how that topic has developed through the years. Each chapter gives a practical guide to the issues that need to be addressed and explains where further information can be ascertained through appropriate websites.

This mix of theory and practice is reflected in the fact that the book brings together academics and practitioners as subject authors, people who are experts in their specialist area. It is interesting to note the different styles of writing that such a combination uncovers, and how each author presents their knowledge. The book does not deal with issues such as e-commerce, female entrepreneurship, family businesses, or a range of other topics on an individual basis but rather views all types of entrepreneurial activity under the same general process.

We hope that *New Venture Creation in Ireland* excites you on the wonderful journey that is entrepreneurship and strongly suggest that the principal barrier to new venture creation is not knowledge, ability, or the environment, but one's own mindset. If you believe in yourself, then you can make it happen.

Enjoy the course and the book. We look forward to reading some day about your success as an entrepreneur. Best of luck!

Thomas M. Cooney
Shane Hill
September 2002

CHAPTER 1

WHAT IS ENTREPRENEURSHIP?

Shane Hill[*]

LEARNING OBJECTIVES

- To give readers an overview of the field of entrepreneurship and provide the necessary background for further development in subsequent chapters
- To explore some of the approaches to studying entrepreneurship
- To develop an understanding of who entrepreneurs are and what it is that they do
- To understand some of the issues involved in contemporary entrepreneurship research.

INTRODUCTION

Entrepreneurship is a term used globally in a variety of different circumstances by scholars, governments, business people, financial institutions, community activists, minority groups, and the public at large. Many regard entrepreneurship as a key constituent in the stimulation and wealth development of an economy. Wennekers and Thurik (1999), for example, argued that the importance of entrepreneurship in modern open economies in terms of economic

---

[*] Shane Hill is a lecturer in entrepreneurship and marketing at the Dundalk Institute of Technology.

growth is greater than ever. Fiet (2000) suggested a growing interest in entrepreneurship which reflects a new economic environment altered by changes in the corporate world, new technological developments, and emerging world markets. Within the context of today's global marketplace, a focused and proactive entrepreneurial approach in terms of constantly pursuing innovation, opportunity, change and flexibility seems not only to be desirable but a necessity for survival and growth within many sectors. This applies equally to the new venture and to established concerns. The central importance of entrepreneurship is now well acknowledged by many scholars. For example, Anderson and Jack (2001) talk of the prevalence of the "Enterprise Culture", and the widespread acceptance that entrepreneurship is the "engine" that drives the economy of many countries.

Over the past four decades, there has been much academic consideration as to who entrepreneurs are and what entrepreneurship really means. Kilby (1971) famously drew the analogy between efforts to understand the entrepreneur and the fictional characters *Heffalumps* (from "Winnie the Pooh"), creatures that are difficult to describe. Thirty years later, Nodoushani and Nodoushani (2000) point out that, despite the "entrepreneurial explosion" of the 1980s, we are still struggling to define the term entrepreneurship. Entrepreneurship theory has many different facets and perspectives that purport to contribute to furthering our understanding of the individual person behind entrepreneurship and what it is they do. Numerous models that claim to explain entrepreneurship have been proposed but, as yet, no definitive paradigm has been commonly accepted. A number of scholars, however, have attempted to provide an overview of the major contributions to the field. Notable among these are works by Cunningham and Lischeron (1991) and Carson *et al* (1995).

Cunningham and Lischeron (1991) suggested six distinct schools of thought on entrepreneurship: the "Great Person" School, the Psychological Characteristics School, The Classical School, The Management School, the Leadership School, and the Intrapreneurship School. Carson *et al* (1995), in their examination of the concept of entrepreneurship, refer to trait approaches, the social psychological approach, behavioural approaches, entrepreneurship as a process, and entrepreneurial managers.

This chapter reviews some of the varied research contributions that attempt to explore entrepreneurship. It begins by looking at some of the research carried out in the area of identifying entrepreneurial personality attributes and qualities. This is followed by highlighting some of the entrepreneurial background factors that are important in the entrepreneurial development of the individual. Behavioural and managerial aspects of entrepreneurship are then explored before entrepreneurship as a process is discussed and, finally, some of the recent research trends within the field are investigated. Through a brief overview of the rationale behind some of the major propositions, the reader will gain insight into the complex world of entrepreneurship and the principal characteristics of an entrepreneur.

PERSONALITY TRAITS

The major proposition within this genre of entrepreneurship research is that the entrepreneur is an individual with unique personality characteristics, qualities and attributes that somehow explain their entrepreneurial actions and motivations. It holds that, if one could somehow understand the person behind entrepreneurship and, in particular, their personality characteristics, then it would lead to a greater understanding about entrepreneurship and why some individuals become entrepreneurs.

The trait approach to entrepreneurship has involved significant research deliberations among scholars over the past 40 years. Their work has resulted in a very wide range of varying traits that attempt to understand further the individual entrepreneur. McClelland (1987), for example, refers to lists of personal characteristics needed for successful entrepreneurship containing 32, and even 42, different traits. As yet, no definitive checklist of required entrepreneurial attributes has been agreed. However, Vesper (1996), in his comprehensive examination of the characteristics of entrepreneurs, observes that decades of scholarly work by researchers has given some degree of indication as to the personal determinants of entrepreneurial potential. He cites work by Mitton (1989) and Kunze (1990), who identified the attributes of successful entrepreneurs highlighted in **Table 1.1** below. These lists, ranging from a need for control and appetite for uncertainty, to impatience and obsession, go some way to illustrating the contrasting variety of traits associated with successful entrepreneurship.

Gasse (1985) concluded that research findings into the various characteristics of entrepreneurs can be broken down into the need for achievement, creativity and initiative, risk-taking, objective-setting, self-confidence, strong internal locus of control, need for independence and autonomy, and motivation, energy and commitment. One can readily appreciate how many of these might be applied to the start-up or growth-led entrepreneurial practitioner. Such people will likely possess an enormous need to achieve, an ability to confront diversity, and a will to overcome the plethora of challenges associated with new venture formation, survival and growth. They will probably be creative and demonstrate initiative through their constant pursuance of new ideas, change, and the continual improvement of all aspects of their venture. Entrepreneurs must be capable of dealing with the various aspects of venture risk and uncertainty while, at the same time, constantly seeking out information and establishing clear objectives for the future. They will need a firm belief and confidence in themselves and in their new venture proposition (especially when things do not go to plan). They may also possess a personal desire for control, independence and autonomy that might contribute to their drivel, constant commitment, and the extreme energy necessary for entrepreneurial start-up, survival and growth.

TABLE 1.1: ATTRIBUTES OF SUCCESSFUL ENTREPRENEURS

Mitton (1989)
A big-picture perspective
An ability to spot unique business opportunities
A tendency to commit totally to a cause
A need for complete control
A utilitarian view of what is right
An appetite for uncertainty
A tendency to use contacts and connections
An attitude that embraces high competence
Special know-how.

Kunze (1990)
Daring
Single-minded
Egocentric
Disenchanted with the *status quo*
Impatient
Obsessive.

Source: **Vesper (1996)**

Interestingly, some of these issues are taken up by Kets de Vries (1996), who somewhat shatters the stereotypical image of the entrepreneur as a supremely confident person. He suggested that many entrepreneurs are individuals who respond to feelings of low self-esteem, inferiority, and helplessness, and that many of them are "allergic" to authority.

There is little doubt that the substantial body of entrepreneurial trait research conducted over the last number of decades has made significant efforts to augment our understanding, appreciation, and awareness of entrepreneurship and the individual entrepreneur. The trait approach, in taking the individual entrepreneur as the main focus of study, offers insight into the personality behind entrepreneurial types and has resulted in much debate as to the central qualities required for successful entrepreneurship. It is not, however, without critics.

Gartner (1988), for example, observed four vulnerabilities concerning the trait approach:

- Numerous and varied definitions of the entrepreneur seem to be used in many trait research contributions
- Relatively few studies use the same definition
- There appears to be a certain lack of homogeneity among entrepreneurs chosen in research deliberations
- The number of traits associated with the entrepreneur portray an individual of contradictions and a larger-than-life character.

As with the definition of entrepreneurship, there is little agreement on the principal traits of an entrepreneur. As a result, many researchers work with the attitude that, while they cannot define an entrepreneur, they will recognise one when they see one. Such an approach obviously leads to inconsistencies in research and means that scholars are not always comparing like with like.

ENTREPRENEURIAL BACKGROUND

The entrepreneurial background approach proposes that entrepreneurship can be explained through the exploration of a range of social issues and external considerations that appear to stimulate entrepreneurial action. The focus here moves away somewhat from innate personality and draws more on the society and environment that entrepreneurs experience and develop within. Carson *et al* (1995) talk of the social psychological approach to entrepreneurship and refer to specific issues including family circumstances and social background, exposure to education, religion, culture, work and general life experiences.

A significant amount of research suggests a linkage between entrepreneurship and various aspects of the entrepreneur's family and social background. Some scholars refer to the possibility that, within a family unit, first-born children are more likely to follow entrepreneurial career paths than their younger brothers and sisters. For example, Hisrich and Ó Cinnéide (1986), in their survey of Irish entrepreneurs, established that 32% were first-born. Why should the birth order of children be a factor in entrepreneurship? The rationale for this includes such possibilities as the eldest siblings having a greater degree of adult interaction from an early age, having increased levels of self-belief due to being given greater responsibility than younger siblings, and being first in their family to reach important life-cycle events such as attending school, college, and entering the world of work. However, Hisrich and Peters (1998) point out that the first-born effect has not been present in a number of studies and suggest that further research is required to emphatically establish its relationship to entrepreneurial decisions.

Other studies indicate a link between entrepreneurship and parental occupations, suggesting that children with an entrepreneurial parent receive a unique insight into the entrepreneurial way of life, which may result in the child seeing such a career as "the norm" and one to which to aspire and emulate. Cooper and Dunkelberg (1987) suggested that business ownership within a family exposes the young to "role models" and, in a broadly-based survey of 890 entrepreneurs, explain that half were from families where the parents or guardians owned a business enterprise.

The formal education received by entrepreneurs is another area that has been explored by researchers. Garavan and Ó Cinnéide (1994) indicated that the literature suggests that it is desirable to have two successful entrepreneurial parents, adequate education levels, and work experience. Gasse (1982) argues that, while there may have been a perception that entrepreneurs were less educated than the general population, this has now changed, and studies imply that entrepreneurs actually achieve more education than that of the general population. However, evidence of the relationship between the amount of formal education obtained by entrepreneurs and the subsequent success of their business propositions is, as yet, not totally conclusive. For example, Cooper and Gascon (1992), in a comprehensive examination of 17 studies linking education and venture performance, point out that a positive relationship was established in only 10 studies.

Religion and culture are two further considerations often outlined as possible stimuli for individuals to act in an entrepreneurial fashion. Wickham (2001) suggests that religion is central to culture in that it facilitates people in developing a certain perspective of the world, which, in turn, influences their approach to entrepreneurship. Bridge *et al* (1998) alluded to "the Protestant work ethic", which seems to link an attitude to business with certain religious convictions. They outline, however, that there has been comparatively little written about the impact of religion on enterprise and observe that, in general, it is probably impossible to separate the influence of religion from that of culture as they are so interlinked.

Work and life experiences are also said to play a role sometimes in determining entrepreneurial action. Timmons (1990) refers to the fact that successful entrepreneurs often go through an "apprenticeship", where they gain business experience and knowledge in pursuance of their entrepreneurial careers. Hisrich and Peters (1998) propose that, once the decision to launch a venture is taken, prior technical and sector specific experience is of critical importance, as is managerial experience once the enterprise is established. They also believe that previous entrepreneurial experience is central to potential success and outline that many established entrepreneurs believe that their most significant venture was not their first.

It is beyond doubt that the social and environmental circumstances and situations in which individuals find themselves have a major influence on their perceptions and views towards entrepreneurship. Factors such as parents and family background, schooling, religion and culture and work and life experience all contribute to moulding a person – who they are, how they see things, and their approach to pursuing their dreams and aspirations. But whether a common background to entrepreneurs can be established is questionable. Increasingly, entrepreneurs are coming from a wider variety of backgrounds and experiences. Their only commonality is their desire to establish a successful new venture and their belief that they will achieve their objectives.

BEHAVIOURAL ASPECTS OF ENTREPRENEURSHIP

Behavioural approaches to understanding entrepreneurship attempt to explore what it is that entrepreneurs actually do. The rationale is that a better understanding of entrepreneurship and the individual entrepreneur can be obtained by exploring the behaviour of entrepreneurs and not just their individual characteristics. For this approach, it is what the entrepreneur does that is the main focus of study.

Gartner (1989) believed that this approach to entrepreneurship views the creation of a venture as the main issue of examination and that the personality traits and characteristics of the individual are somewhat secondary to their behaviours. He suggested that research activity should focus on the actions of the entrepreneur and that researchers must observe entrepreneurs in the process of creating organisations, and identify the skills, roles, and activities involved.

O'Gorman and Cunningham (1997) asserted that this approach to entrepreneurship facilitates entrepreneurial behaviour being classified by, for example, an entrepreneur's problem-solving and delegation abilities. Likewise, Timmons (1990) observed that entrepreneurship is not just personality analysis, but rather it is a question of exploring what it is entrepreneurs do within the context of establishing and developing ventures. He proposes that entrepreneurs are born and made better and that certain attitudes and behaviours can be obtained, refined and practiced through a combination of study and experience.

MANAGEMENT APPROACHES TO ENTREPRENEURSHIP

The management approach to entrepreneurship views the entrepreneurial person as one who conducts managerial tasks within new and developing entrepreneurial ventures. Entrepreneurs, if they are to be successful, must attempt to manage their concerns in a manner that continually identifies opportunities and ultimately leads to survival and growth. There is little doubt about the enormous managerial challenges faced by entrepreneurs. Even the smallest of enterprises requires planning, co-ordination, and control of important functions such as research and development, quality, production, marketing, human resource management and financial management.

Garavan, Ó Cinnéide and Fleming *et al* (1997) suggested that, according to the management approach, entrepreneurship is a series of learned activities that integrates the functional areas of management into a framework, which is applied during new venture development and growth. They suggest managerial experience and prowess are not always central at the formative stages of a new enterprise but, when the entity reaches the rapid growth stage, effective managerial ability is critical. They pointed out that entrepreneurs could find it difficult to adjust managerially from the relative informality of the start-up venture to the necessarily-changing arrangements of the growing concern.

Cunningham and Lischeron (1991) explained managerial approaches to entrepreneurship in terms of the entrepreneur organising an initiative and taking risk while, at the same time, being involved in managerial functions such as supervising, controlling and providing entrepreneurial leadership. They suggested that the managerial approach holds that entrepreneurship can be taught, since an individual's managerial ability can be improved through the development of their rational, analytical, and cause-and-effect orientation.

Carson *et al* (1995) discussed the concept of entrepreneurial managers who manage new and existing concerns in a fashion that continually attempts to pursue newness, innovation, and change. These individuals are opportunity-focused, calculated risk-takers, effective leaders, team-builders, negotiators and networkers.

Hisrich and Peters (1998) proposed that the skills required by entrepreneurs could be classified into three areas:
- Technical skills include such activities as writing, team-building, organising, and listening
- Business management skills include important entrepreneurial tasks like planning and goal setting, control, negotiation, marketing, and finance
- Personal entrepreneurial skills involve activities such as leadership, change management, risk-taking, and innovation.

Again, many of these can be learned, and oppose the view that entrepreneurs are born and not made.

The importance of effective management is obvious when it comes to the ultimate survival of entrepreneurial ventures. Regardless of the technical brilliance of the founding entrepreneur(s), or indeed the merits

of the product or service being offered, start-ups frequently face
challenges when managerial expertise is low. Managerial issues and how
they relate to the entrepreneurial venture are discussed in **Chapter 7**.

ENTREPRENEURSHIP AS A PROCESS

Another means of attempting to comprehend further the diverse and
complex issues involved in entrepreneurship has been through process
approaches. These approaches to entrepreneurship endeavour to explain
the overall process involved in the creation of a new venture.

Van Slyke *et al* (1992) believed that entrepreneurship is a process of
bringing together a unique set of resources in pursuance of a particular
opportunity. They propose a start-up process that embodies six core
issues in the creation of a new venture:

* Evaluating the opportunity
* Developing the business concept
* Assessing the required resources
* Acquiring the necessary resources
* Managing the venture
* Harvesting and distributing value.

The process starts with an idea or opportunity. A key challenge here is to
attempt to establish the extent of opportunity for the new proposition.
Subsequently, the entrepreneurial team must contemplate a business
concept or strategy that will, hopefully, maximise the identified
opportunity and consider the resources that must be put in place to
make it a reality. The next stage in the process is acquiring these
necessary resources and managing the resulting entity, the new venture.
Finally, once the venture is established, value is created and
consideration must be given to realising and distributing this added
value. For example, harvesting value that has been created may mean
selling the company.

Barrow (1998) noted that, each year, many small business founders
decide to part with their ventures for reasons ranging from retirement,
to a desire to get into something different, to a decision to capitalise on
the value already generated, or a realisation that the venture might need
an association with a more substantial business enterprise.

Hisrich and Peters (1998) proposed that the process of creating a new venture could be outlined within a four-stage entrepreneurial process. The stages involved were:

- Identifying and evaluating an opportunity
- Developing a business plan
- Determining the resources required
- Managing the resultant entity.

They suggested that new entrepreneurial ventures begin with an opportunity, the extent of which has to be considered. Consequently, a business plan is written, which puts the idea down on paper and highlights important issues such as the rationale, facts, figures and implications of pursuing the opportunity. Thereafter, the entrepreneurial team can consider the resources they possess, those that they need and how the missing resources might be acquired. Finally, once the new venture is created, it must be managed in a way that enables it to achieve the objectives of the founders.

It is logical that new venture creation can be explained through a process of related issues that must be considered by both the aspiring and experienced entrepreneur alike. However, it can be argued that potential entrepreneurs do not think in terms of sequential processes but prefer to concentrate on those activities that can be undertaken immediately.

RESEARCH TRENDS IN ENTREPRENEURSHIP

Entrepreneurship as an academic discipline is enjoying unprecedented deliberation by researchers internationally. Wortman (1987) suggested that entrepreneurship is one of the newest fields of research in management. He alluded to a number of trends that have improved entrepreneurship research, including the movement towards defining the boundaries of the field, a division between individual and corporate entrepreneurship, more robust research designs, methods, statistical techniques, larger data samples and databases, and a movement from exploratory to causal research. However, entrepreneurship research is not without its challenges.

Harrison and Leitch (1994), while supporting the view that entrepreneurship as a field of study is coming of age, stressed that it does not yet have a clearly defined philosophical, theoretical and methodological core. They argued in favour of the benefits of a closer relationship between entrepreneurship and leadership studies and highlighted two important issues. Firstly, they proposed that, within both areas, there is increasing focus afforded to the role of the team as opposed to the "heroic" individual. Secondly, they suggested that increasingly dynamic business environments have resulted in renewed attention being given to the development of human capital and continuous learning in organisations as the means for achieving competitive advantage, survival and growth.

Frank *et al* (1997), in their comprehensive examination of entrepreneurship and small business research in Europe, revealed a growing interest in many countries. Their findings demonstrated significantly increased interest in the following areas of research: entrepreneurship/start ups, internationalisation, innovation/technology transfer, and networks/exchange relations. They reported that research into entrepreneurship and start-ups addresses a number of core issues including national and regional aspects of firm foundation patterns and closure, new venture growth, strategy, the start-up process, assistance systems for new ventures, and psychological and educational aspects of entrepreneurship. Studies on internationalisation focus on issues relating to the internationalisation process such as the decision to export, entry modes, barriers to exporting, and the importance of networks in assisting the internationalisation process for small ventures. Scholars working on themes relating to innovation and technology transfer are exploring such things as sources and barriers to innovation, the impact of networking/co-operation and public assistance programmes, high-tech start-ups, and organisational innovation. Finally, Frank *et al* highlighted that research within the general area of networks and exchange relations included studies into the network concept and how it relates to entrepreneurial start-ups, innovation, and internationalisation.

Significant progress has been made within the field of entrepreneurship over the last number of decades. This has added to our understanding of the entrepreneur and the business venture that they create. However, there are many issues remaining that warrant further research and deliberation. Vesper (2001), for example, suggested a number of diverse areas for further research, including legal aspects, service *versus* product companies, contrasting start-up types, the control and management of cash flow, business plans, and the degree of fit between the entrepreneur and the particular venture. Much has been achieved but there remains a great deal of work to be done before entrepreneurs and entrepreneurship can be understood more fully.

CONCLUSION

The objective of this chapter has been to introduce the reader to some of the differing ways of viewing, understanding, and studying entrepreneurship. No one approach has all the definitive answers. Entrepreneurship is highly complex, both in nature and practice, and, to understand it better, one needs to have some insight and appreciation of all of the perspectives highlighted above. There is little doubt that each approach adds to our comprehension, insight, and empathy of what it is to be an entrepreneur. It is from this initial awareness of the world of entrepreneurship that subsequent chapters of this book will build. Through exploration of many of the key aspects of new venture creation in Ireland, the reader will gain an insight into the opportunities and challenges faced by an entrepreneur.

All good entrepreneurial ventures commence with an idea and this process is featured in **Chapter 2**. Before an idea becomes a business reality, the aspiring entrepreneur needs to be aware of the importance of the business plan (**Chapters 3** and **13**), the critical need for good market research (**Chapter 4**), and a broad understanding of legal issues and intellectual property (**Chapters 5** and **6**). The reader must also grasp the managerial aspects of the new venture (**Chapter 7**), marketing (**Chapter 8**), operations (**Chapter 9**), human resources management (**Chapter 10**), finance (**Chapter 11**), and growth (**Chapter 12**).

If establishing a new entrepreneurial venture is equated to an entrepreneur undertaking a journey, then this book provides a rich source of landmarks to be considered along the way, where these landmarks feature, and how they might be negotiated. As with all challenging journeys, information, planning and preparation (and perhaps a degree of luck!) are key to success.

QUESTIONS

1. "Entrepreneurs are born and not made." Discuss.
2. Discuss the difference between the terms entrepreneur, entrepreneurship, and entrepreneurial.

3. Evaluate the trait, background, and behavioural approaches to entrepreneurship and assess their contribution to furthering our understanding of entrepreneurship.
4. Conduct a detailed literature review into one of the approaches to entrepreneurship. Present your findings to class colleagues.
5. Write a case study on a high profile entrepreneur of your choice. What skills and abilities does this person exhibit?
6. Interview an entrepreneur of your choice. What entrepreneurial traits and behaviours have they exhibited in their career to date?
7. Entrepreneurship research should not explore the individual entrepreneur but rather should focus on what they do. Discuss.

USEFUL WEBSITES

www.smallbusinessportal.co.uk

CHECKLIST FOR CHAPTER

After reading this chapter, check that you understand and appreciate:
• The importance of entrepreneurship
• The approaches to studying entrepreneurship presented in the chapter
• Who entrepreneurs are and what it is they do
• Some of the issues involved in contemporary entrepreneurship research.

REFERENCES

Anderson, A.R., and Jack, S.L. (2001) - Entrepreneurship Education Within the Enterprise Culture: Producing Reflective Practitioners - *Enterprise and Learning* (Edited by Anderson, A.R., and Jack, S.L.) Centre for Entrepreneurship Research, University of Aberdeen, p 332.
Barrow, C. (1998) - *The Essence of Small Business* – 2nd Edition, Prentice Hall Europe, p 159.
Bridge, S.; O'Neill, K. and Cromie, S. (1998) - *Understanding Enterprise, Entrepreneurship and Small Business* - Macmillan Business, p 78.
Carson, D.; Cromie, S.; McGowan, P. and Hill, J. (1995) - *Marketing and Entrepreneurship in SMEs: An Innovative Approach* - Prentice Hall International (UK) Limited, pp 49-59.

Cooper, A. and Gascon, J. (1992) - Entrepreneurs, Processes of Founding, and New Firm Performance - *State of the Art of Entrepreneurship Research* (Edited by Sexton, D., and Kasda, J.) Boston, MA: PWS-Kent.

Cooper, A.C. and Dunkelberg, W.C. (1987) - Entrepreneurial Research: Old Questions, New Answers and Methodological Issues - *American Journal of Small Business*, Winter, p 15.

Cunningham, J.B. and Lischeron, J. (1991) - Defining Entrepreneurship - *Journal of Small Business Management*, Vol.29, No.1, pp 45-61.

Fiet, J.O. (2000) - The Pedagogical Side of Entrepreneurship Theory - *Journal of Business Venturing*, Vol.16, pp 101-117.

Frank, H. and Landstrom, H. (1997) - Entrepreneurship and Small Business Research in Europe: Analysis and Reflections - *Entrepreneurship and Small Business Research in Europe: An ECSB Survey* (Edited by Landstrom, H.; Frank, H., and Veciana, J.M.) Avebury, pp 382-395.

Garavan, T .N. and Ó Cinnéide, B. (1994) - Entrepreneurship Education and Training Programmes: A Review and Evaluation - *Journal of Industrial Training*, Vol. 18, No.8, pp 3-12.

Garavan, T.N.; Ó Cinnéide, B. and Fleming, P. (with McCarthy, B. and Downey, A.) (1997) - *Entrepreneurship and Business Start-Ups in Ireland, Volume 1, An Overview* – Cork: Oak Tree Press, pp 25-63.

Gartner, W.B. (1989) - "Who Is an Entrepreneur?" Is the Wrong Question - *Entrepreneurship Theory and Practice*, Summer, pp 47-68.

Gasse, Y. (1982) - Elaborations on the Psychology of the Entrepreneur - *Encyclopaedia of Entrepreneurship* (Edited by Kent, C.A. and Sexton, D.L.), Prentice Hall, pp 57-67.

Gasse, Y. (1985) - A Strategy for the Promotion and Identification of Potential Entrepreneurs at Secondary School Level - *Frontiers of Entrepreneurial Research*, Babson College, Wellesley, MA, pp 538-559.

Harrison, R.T. and Leitch, C.M. (1994) - Entrepreneurship and Leadership: The Implications for Education and Development - *Entrepreneurship & Regional Development*, Vol.6, pp 111-125.

Hisrich, R.D. and Ó Cinnéide, B. (1986) - The Irish Entrepreneur: Characteristics, Problems and Future Successes - *Proceedings of Conference on Entrepreneurship*, April, Dublin.

Hisrich, R.D. and Peters, M.P. (1998) – *Entrepreneurship* - Irwin McGraw-Hill, pp 20-74.

Kets de Vries, M.F.R. (1996) - The Anatomy of the Entrepreneur: Clinical Observations - *Human Relations*, Vol.49, No.7, pp 853-884.

Kilby, P. (1971) - *Entrepreneurship and Economic Development* - The Free Press.

Kunze, R.J. (1990) - *Nothing Ventured* – Harper, p 200.

McClelland, D.C. (1987) - Characteristics of Successful Entrepreneurs - *Journal of Creative Behaviour*, Vol.21, No.3, pp 219-233.

Mitton, D.G. (1989) - The Complete Entrepreneur - *Entrepreneurship Theory and Practice*, Vol. 13, No. 3, p 9.

Nodoushani, O. and Nodoushani, P.A. (2000) - Second Thoughts on the
    Entrepreneurial Myth - *Entrepreneurship and Innovation*, February, pp 7-12.
O'Gorman, C. and Cunningham, J. (1997) - *Enterprise in Action: An Introduction to
    Entrepreneurship in an Irish Context* – Cork: Oak Tree Press, pp 1-27.
Timmons, J.A. (with Smollen, L.E. and Dingee, A.L.M.) (1990) - *New Venture
    Creation: Entrepreneurship in the 1990s* - Irwin, p 23, p165.
Van Slyke, J.R.; Stevenson, H.H. and Roberts, M.J. (1992) - The Start-up Process -
    The Entrepreneurial Venture (Readings selected by Sahlman, W.A. and Stevenson,
    H.H.) - Harvard Business School Publications, pp 81-97.
Vesper, K.H. (1996) - *New Venture Experience* - Vector Books, pp 6-7.
Vesper, K.H. (2001) - Missing Links in Entrepreneurship - *Entrepreneurship
    Education: A Global View* (Edited by Brockhaus, R.H.; Hills, G.E.; Klandt, H. and
    Welsch, H.P.) Ashgate, pp 3-16.
Wennekers, S. and Thurik, R. (1999) - Linking Entrepreneurship and Economic
    Growth - *Small Business Economics*, Vol. 13, No. 1, pp 27-55.
Wickham, P. (2001) - *Strategic Entrepreneurship: A Decision-Making Approach to New
    Venture Creation and Management* - Financial Times, Prentice Hall, pp 56-57.
Wortman, M.S. (1987) - Entrepreneurship: An Integrating Typology and
    Evaluation of the Empirical Research in the Field - *Journal of Management*, Vol.
    13, No. 2, pp 259-279.

CHAPTER 2

FINDING THE BUSINESS IDEA

Martina Lordan and Thomas M. Cooney***

LEARNING OBJECTIVES

- To explore the terminology of creativity
- To understand creativity – process and myths
- To develop techniques to improve thinking skills and ideas generation
- To generate criteria for evaluating ideas
- To understand how to screen ideas
- To transform ideas into opportunities.

INTRODUCTION

*Other people see things and say 'Why?'….. But I dream things
that never were and say 'Why not?'*
George Bernard Shaw

One of the great myths of entrepreneurship is that the entrepreneur has to be exceptionally talented or creative in order to find a business idea. Because many people in Irish society believe that they are not creative or

* Martina Lordan is managing director of Lordan & Associates and a visiting lecturer with the Entrepreneurship Unit at the University of Lancaster.
** Thomas M Cooney is a lecturer in entrepreneurship and marketing at the Dublin Institute of Technology and a director of Optimum Results.

innovative, they then also believe that they are not capable of finding an idea to start their own business.

This myth is untrue from a couple of perspectives. Firstly, each person possesses creative abilities but, through a lack of development of the conceptual/right-side of the brain or a positive, encouraging environment, these abilities are not given the opportunity to flourish. Weisberg (1986) observed how society holds a very mythical romantic view of how ideas are found – that creative individuals are perceived to possess some extraordinary intellectual thought-processes in order to discover and achieve what they do. But Weisberg's view is that extraordinary ideas or achievements are not necessarily the result of extraordinary people. Secondly, studies identifying and describing the characteristics of highly-creative people provided information regarding their cognitive and affective characteristics and hence de-mystified the notion of creativity.

The personality attributes of the creative person are (Sternberg, 1988):

- Open-mindedness
- Willingness to surmount obstacles
- Moderate risk-taking
- Intrinsic motivation
- Willingness to grow
- Desire for recognition.

These characteristics are significant in strategies for creating that involve the motivation to commit time, energy, and effort to creative pursuits that can be observed in the personal attributes of an entrepreneur in new venture creation. The majority of entrepreneurs see what is already being done and are willing to commit time, effort and resources so that they can provide similar products faster, cheaper, or better. They may be on holiday abroad and notice something that is not available presently in the Irish market, or they may take an idea that already exists elsewhere within Ireland and make it available within their own locality. It was Plato who described a new idea as the recognition of an old one or the new application of a concept. This chapter explores how individuals can generate ideas from a wide variety of sources or through their own creative capabilities, and then develop these ideas into a business venture.

Studies indicate that 90% or more of founders start their companies in the same market-place, technology, or industry they have been working in (Timmons, 1999). As already stated, most successful entrepreneurial opportunities involve the pursuit of relatively simple ideas or replicating existing ideas in a different geographical area. For example, entrepreneurs have established successful businesses from mass retailing of computers, furniture, and carpets in attractive retail outlets or developing health food shops and gyms for the emerging health conscious populations.

If an area or sector focus has been identified for which an opportunity for a new venture is sought, it is worthwhile to make contact with networks, professionals, consultants, and customers/suppliers in that area. Impact studies of networking have indicated that customer and supplier networks were highly influential in determining how manufacturing firms re-orientate their business in line with the market place and these networks very often provided the stimulus for new product development (Lordan *et al*, 2000). Networking will provide valuable up-to-date facts and business intelligence to assist in identifying gaps in the market or assessing the potential of a proposed idea. Networking and market research also provide a reality check on the potential of ideas for venture creation, which can either highlight difficulties or enhance entrepreneurial confidence in pursuing an idea (Lordan *et al*, 2000a). Such checks may require some creative problem-solving or may indicate that the area is worth exploring further. Saunders (1997) confirms that creativity for new venture creation can be enhanced through increasing an entrepreneur's networks.

To develop one's capabilities in finding a business idea, it is important to initially understand the key terms before examining the techniques that can be employed to generate ideas.

KEY CONCEPTS

To develop a better understanding of how business ideas are found, it is useful first to understand a number of key concepts. This section examines creativity, discovery, invention, innovation and opportunity, and looks at how they are employed in a business context.

Creativity

Creativity is frequently perceived to be associated with the arts or with people of artistic abilities. However, Koestler (1964) defines creativity as the "act of making new relationships from old ideas". Keil (1987) describes creativity as "the ability to look at things differently". With these definitions, distinctive talents are not a prerequisite to creativity. Indeed, Cougar (1996) reviewed over 30 definitions and the two most common characteristics of creativity he identified were "newness or uniqueness" and "value or utility". These characteristics are common among the majority of enterprises where a person brings something new or of value to a geographical area.

Rhodes (1961) reviewed over 60 common definitions of creativity and refined them into four strands:

- *Person*: understanding the traits, characteristics or attributes of the creative personality of the entrepreneur;
- *Process:* describing the stages of thinking or the process creative people use to invent something new and useful;
- *Product*: the qualities of a product/service which make it creative;
- *Press*: the nature of the press or environment that is conducive or inhibitive of creativity.

Rhodes explains how it is more realistic to think of these four strands in relation to each other and operating together rather than in isolation. To observe a potential entrepreneur being creative involves therefore not only considering the mental patterns in finding ideas, but the context in which that person is operating, the desired objective or product idea, as well as the personal characteristics of the person. People may achieve these strands if they are willing to be open to the belief that they have creative abilities and are motivated to commit time and effort in the search for new ideas and in engaging in the principles for transforming ideas into realisable opportunities discussed later in this chapter. Thus, both creativity and entrepreneurship are a way of thinking and behaving in an environment and can be enhanced with development (Lordan, 1988).

Discovery

Discovery is very often associated with finding something unexpectedly, or even by accident, for the first time. For the purposes of discovering new business ideas, research does not support the notion of accidental finding of ideas. Very often discoveries are the result of a careful methodical approach to seeking new ideas or alternative solutions.

Cougar (1996), in his research on creativity, confirms that there is little evidence of discovery happening by accident. Louis Pasteur said that inspiration is the impact of a fact on a well-prepared mind, that very often the discovery takes place when a person has already been focusing or seeking new alternatives or solutions.

Invention

An invention is the solution/outcome to a problem, very often a technical one. Provided the inventor can demonstrate that he or she has been the first to design the technology, and provided it is then judged to be "not obvious to those skilled in the state of the art", the inventor may be granted legal rights over the invention as "intellectual property" by means of a patent. Because the inventive process does not follow a logical and reasoned path from known facts, it is often associated with the process of creativity.

According to Tidd *et al* (2001), it is worthwhile noting that an invention is only a first step in a long process of bringing a good idea to widespread and effective use and is no guarantee of commercial success.

Within the different key concepts being examined, invention is the most difficult for a potential entrepreneur to achieve since it involves the development of a new product or service that currently is not available in the market. It is not taking something that already exists and doing it better but conceptualising and developing something from an original position.

Innovation

Innovation is a *process* whereby new ideas are put into practical use to add value commercially. Drucker (1985) describes innovation as the means by which entrepreneurs exploit change as an opportunity for a different business or service. Porter (1990) describes innovation as a means of enterprises achieving competitive advantage through the adoption of new technologies and new ways of doing things.

However, innovations may take place when non-technological ideas are put into practice. Innovation may include product innovation, process innovation, marketing innovation, or management innovation. Creativity is necessary but not sufficient to lead to innovation.

Opportunity

Opportunities are not characterised as necessarily arising from technological inventions or breakthrough ideas. They can take the form of bringing an existing product to market with an improved set of characteristics that adds value to customers and is profitable to make and sell. It is important that the opportunity has or is able to achieve competitive advantage and the economics of the venture are rewarding and allow significant profit and growth potential.

Timmons (1999) describes an opportunity as having the qualities of being attractive, durable, and timely and being anchored in a product or service that creates or adds value for its buyer or end-user. Muzyka (1997) describes an opportunity as a business concept that, if turned into a tangible product or service, will result in financial profit. The question to be asked with opportunity might be: There is a gap in the market, but is there a market in the gap?

These five key concepts are frequently used interchangeably without much distinction and are very often referred to in mythical terms. For the purposes of seeking new ideas, these concepts have distinct meanings and are worthy of demystification in order to engender in people a greater belief in their own creative abilities. These concepts are not mutually exclusive but they should be understood independently since a discovery is not necessarily an invention or even an opportunity, and an invention may not necessarily be an opportunity.

STRUCTURED TECHNIQUES FOR IDEA GENERATION

Creativity research indicates that creative thinking is a skill that can be enhanced and learned. This is important for entrepreneurs who are continually seeking new ideas. Studies indicate that children in their formative years are more creative in their behaviours but, as a consequence of the emphasis placed on logical and rational behaviour by the educational system, creativity becomes inhibited.

Creative thinking is a skill that improves with practice, according de Bono (1969). De Bono describes the mind as a self-organising system that places knowledge into patterns. This is how one can do routine tasks without much focus (for example, washing teeth). In order to think laterally across these patterns, stimulus tools or provocations are helpful. Creative thinking techniques are tools that assist in breaking routine patterns in thinking in order to generate more novel ideas.

In order to enhance the creative thinking and behaviour of entrepreneurs, this section examines techniques for the enhancement of novel ideas and how to screen ideas for opportunities. The purpose of these techniques is to force people's thinking to consider a broader range of alternatives before applying rational thinking in the evaluation and selection of ideas. A structured process in the search for ideas can be developed in three distinct stages:

- Techniques for generating ideas
- Evaluation and prioritisation of ideas
- Screening ideas for opportunities.

These stages are now examined in detail.

Techniques for Generating or Improving Ideas

The following methods are designed to help break away from routine habits of thinking and to produce more ideas than normal. De Bono (1995) proposed that searching for ideas or alternatives is a process that is not as easy as one might assume and that guidelines in preparing for structured sessions are useful. In generating ideas, it is important that participants are allowed the freedom to be expansive and to suggest any idea that they wish. Remember that, at some meeting somewhere, some person suggested to the assembled group that it would be a wonderful idea to go to the moon. Imagine the immediate reaction to that suggestion, yet it was made possible by those who believed that the only limitations were in the mind.

Guidelines for an idea-finding session include:

- **Select participants:** It is beneficial to have participants with different perspectives and, therefore, a group selection might involve a mix of suppliers, dealers, customers, experts, academics, and potential employees.
- **Have a facilitator:** The facilitator records the ideas and leads the group through a systematic, disciplined process of ideas generation and selection of ideas. The facilitator does not actively participate in ideas generation or evaluation.
- **Task focus:** A sectoral area or task focus of the session is selected for which the group are called upon to generate ideas. The focus may be redefined and change direction as it is explored for opportunities during the session.

The following techniques assist in the process of generating ideas:

- **Brainstorming:** Creativity and ideas generation was generally a haphazard activity until Osborn (1953) presented the brainstorming technique. Osborn observed that better ideas were produced when two principles were followed for more deliberate idea generation: "deferment of judgement" and "quantity breeds quality". Deferment of judgement means that judgement or evaluation of ideas is not allowed during the ideas generation stage, since almost any proposed idea can be criticised. All ideas, however ridiculous, are potentially useful and censorship of ideas must be actively avoided. This encourages a person to come up with more ideas without being fearful of criticism and evaluation. Quantity breeds quality means that, the more ideas generated, the more likely a better solution will be found. This emphasis on quantity increases the number of alternatives from which novel solutions can come to light more freely. The theory supporting this principle is that our more dominant ideas tend to stem from habitual, common thinking, whereas continuing ideas generation beyond this calls for more original thinking. The list of ideas generated during the brainstorming session are evaluated and screened later. Many techniques have been developed using brainstorming as the base and the technique itself has become so popular that people tend to class all creativity techniques by this name.

- **Synectics:** Synectics is "the joining together of different and apparently irrelevant elements" and its theory "applies to the integration of diverse individuals into a problem-stating problem-solving group" (Gordon, 1961). The person seeking ideas plays an active role in describing the problem, his/her power to act in trying to solve it, what efforts have been made, and what would be the ideal solution. In-out listening is encouraged, where participants are encouraged to listen for ideas/images triggered during the session and to record them until an opportunity arises to share them among the group. Exploration of, and redefining of, the problem is considered by the group before the ideas generation stage. To overcome blocks to ideas generation, the facilitator leads the participants on an "excursion" through the use of analogy and metaphor, and where "the strange is made familiar and the familiar strange" to gain new insights for expansion. These new insights from the excursion are "force-fitted" to the real task at hand, where members of the group make connections and a new set of possible solutions are generated. The entrepreneur evaluates each idea generated for its perceived potential, the possibilities suggested by the idea, and any concerns raised. The ideas, potential, possibilities and concerns may need to be explored further to generate a feasible solution.

- **Brainwriting:** Brainwriting differs from brainstorming, in that the ideas generated are recorded individually on a piece of paper. Its advantage over brainstorming is that it reduces inhibitions as ideas can be recorded anonymously and submitted to the group and thus ensures that all participants have an equal opportunity to share ideas.

- **Invitational Stems/Wishful Thinking:** An invitational stem approach for generating ideas is an effective tool for breaking mind-sets. A fantasy, or wishful thinking, mode is invited, which permits the generation of ideas without evaluation. Invitational stems can take the form of:
  ◊ Wouldn't it be wonderful if ...
  ◊ What I really want to do is ...
  ◊ If I didn't have to consider cost ...
  ◊ Wouldn't it be awful if ...
  ◊ I wish ...
  ◊ How to ...

- **Method 635:** This method is easily remembered, since it involves a group of six participants each writing down three ideas within five minutes. The cards are exchanged five times, with each person trying to build and develop on the ideas already generated. This method suits the development of problems where radical solutions are not desired, as there may be less freewheeling.

These methods are all group-based and may not suit the needs of an individual entrepreneur. However, the entrepreneur may invite friends, associates, or experts to join them for a discussion in which a variety of ideas are explored and the entrepreneur acts as facilitator. The willingness to explore a business idea with others should act as a springboard for what could be possible rather than providing reasons for why something either cannot or should not be done. This does not mean that realism is jettisoned in the pursuit of fantasy but that negative thinking is not beneficial to the establishment of a new venture.

Evaluating and Prioritising Ideas

The evaluation stage of modifying, comparing, and assessing of ideas is useful for shortlisting those ideas that should be pursued initially and prioritising more than one business idea for further consideration. The techniques offered below may be used for screening ideas initially and then rejecting options that are not worth considering further:

- **PMI:** Plus, Minus, Interesting is a focused feedback model for screening ideas. **P** is evaluating the advantages or plus about the idea; **M** is the minus, disadvantages or unsuitability of the idea for an opportunity; and **I** is for the interesting or unique points that the idea might offer (De Bono, 1995a).

- **Clustering:** Clustering is a convergent technique that is an attempt to recognise and group ideas according to certain themes or categories. This activity facilitates evaluation, particularly when a large number of ideas have been generated. The clustering of ideas in similar themes or patterns also provides a fuller scope of the possibilities.
- **Batelle Method:** This is a three step evaluation process:
  ◊ Selection criteria are developed
  ◊ Scoring criteria are developed (for example, 10 being excellent and 1 being poor). A weight is assigned to each factor being considered (for example, growth rate might be 7, ROI might be 10). The score is multiplied by the weight to obtain a total for each idea
  ◊ Rating criteria are developed for which a minimum rating is selected and ideas that rate lower than the minimum are eliminated.

What is important about this process is that the entrepreneur decides on criteria for evaluating the ideas that have been generated, in the context of the appropriate market and to ensure that both the advantages and disadvantages of each idea are carefully considered. This will then allow the entrepreneur to prioritise their ideas and to explore further those ideas in a systematic fashion.

Screening the Ideas for Opportunities

A key stage of the entrepreneurial process is the creation and recognition of opportunities from ideas that have been generated. Knowing the difference between a good idea and an opportunity is vital (Timmons, 1989). It is therefore important for an entrepreneur to be able to assess whether serious potential exists in an idea and how much effort and investment is needed for it to be realisable.

In a study of failure of owner-managed businesses (Birley and Niktari, 1995), it was reported that two-thirds of business failure could have been avoided if the opportunity was properly assessed at the concept and business planning stage. Too many potential entrepreneurs have wasted time and money pursuing ideas that were were going nowhere. Anecdotal evidence suggests that, too frequently, potential entrepreneurs decide to establish enterprises based solely on their best friend's opinion of the idea. The decision to create a new venture should be based on solid market research (see **Chapter 4**) and not on the uninformed opinion of a friend.

This stage should examine the size of the market, the strength of potential competitors, market conditions and trends, profit margins, and the source of sales.

Once an idea has been selected for implementation, it is then imperative that a proper business plan be developed (see **Chapter 3**) so that the financial viability of the enterprise can be determined.

WHERE TO FIND BUSINESS IDEAS

While the use of idea generation techniques is highly beneficial in developing potential business opportunities, there are other simpler methods that can also be employed. They involve examining the current business environment to assess whether there is an opening within your geographical area for a new venture creation based on an idea that already exists elsewhere. These methods include:

- **Existing Businesses:** Many businesses ideas are sourced from existing business concepts, whereby a growing market allows for a "me too" product or service through an improvement on what already exists. Being able to offer an existing product or service faster, cheaper and of higher quality is a source of competitive advantage worthy of consideration for a venture. Purchasing an existing business has also frequently proven to be a viable option. Knowledge of the business or networking with customers/suppliers can provide sound business intelligence upon which to base a purchase or business improvement idea (Lordan *et al*, 2000).

- **Franchises:** Franchising is increasingly considered a source of business venture opportunity (see **Chapter 15**). A franchise is a licensed arrangement to sell goods or services as an independent entrepreneur. The advantages, disadvantages and person-fit need to be carefully considered, as well as whether the franchise control and fees are offset by the brand-name, proven track record, and training and guidance provided to franchisees. Some business practices of franchisers are not conducive to franchisees making profits, especially where exclusive territorial rights are not negotiable and the market potential can be diluted by other franchisees in the area.

- **Product Licensing:** Product licensing occurs when an entrepreneur produces and sells an existing product developed by another business within a specific geographical area for an agreed fee. This has become popular in recent years with companies, particularly American software firms, that wish to expand their sales abroad but do not wish to take the risk of exporting from their home base or of establishing an operation in another country. Support agencies such as Enterprise Ireland can help mediate between interested parties in this type of venture.

- **Patents:** Research in the Patents Office can establish what ideas have been patented that may be available to manufacture through agreement with the originator of the patent. Usually this involves paying an immediate fee for the use of the patent and royalties on sales of the product.

- **Networking:** A very useful source of new ideas is networking. By joining associations such as the Chambers of Commerce and meeting with other businesspeople, opportunities may arise that would suit the needs of the potential entrepreneur. The disadvantage of this method is that it is unpredictable and the entrepreneur is not in control of the timeframe, since it may take months before a worthwhile stimulus for a business idea is suggested.

- **Support Agencies:** Support agencies such as Enterprise Ireland frequently maintain a file of business opportunities that they believe may be of interest to Irish entrepreneurs. Many of these opportunities involve "import substitution", the production in Ireland of products currently being imported.

- **Use of the Internet:** A number of websites offer free software tools for creative purposes that take the user through a complete problem-solving process. Typically, the software is designed to keep the user on track in the overall process, offer appropriate techniques at appropriate stages and assist with the logistics of record-keeping of ideas. (Search words for finding such sites are: creativity + tools + idea generation + business.) Some of the more popular websites are listed at the end of this chapter. In searching for new business ideas on the Internet, it is worth noting that what may work in one country may not work in Ireland due to market, social or cultural differences. All ideas, no matter how successful elsewhere, must be explored fully to determine their suitability for the Irish market.

Sourcing of business ideas is rarely a critical problem in new venture creation, since most people have some awareness of current potential opportunities. Key issues are:

- Timing
- Feasibility of the idea
- Suitability of the idea to the circumstances of the potential entrepreneur.

If a potential entrepreneur cannot find an idea, then probably they are not searching hard enough. If they are struggling with this challenge, then maybe they are not suited to the demands of entrepreneurship.

TRANSFORMING IDEAS INTO REALISABLE OPPORTUNITIES

So far, this chapter has examined ways of generating new ideas for a business and where ideas might be found from existing businesses. But finding an idea is only the first step in the process of transforming an idea into a realisable opportunity.

The key principles of this process are:

- **Action-oriented**: The potential entrepreneur must be active in searching for new ideas and in taking action to transform good ideas into opportunities. Realising opportunities requires bias towards action and a sense of urgency as opportunities are usually time-sensitive. *Competing in time* reflects the importance of having the capability to introduce new products to a market faster than one's competitors (Kay, 1993).
- **Focus and pace**: Maintaining focus and pace to mobilise one's knowledge and technological skills to create a new venture is key to success. It is important to have a development and launch schedule in developing an opportunity, since entrepreneurs very often have their "fingers in more than one pie" (Hensman *et al*, 1999).
- **Easy to understand:** If the product, process, or service is easy for people to understand, then it is more likely to be accepted and adopted, particularly for potential investors and customers who need to understand the added value.
- **Networking with the industry:** Networking provides up-to-date business intelligence that can be critical to the development of the opportunity. It also provides an opportunity to learn about the industry while building contacts and capability to deliver a product/service. Networking with customers is key to maintaining a

customer focus on idea development and the delivery of a product/service (Lordan *et al*, 2000).

- **Try, test and revise:** Idea development is a continuous process of gathering data, testing the concept in order to refine it and improving the opportunity potential. Continually reviewing and reformulating the business concept to suit customers and market needs is vital. Birley (1997) observed that most entrepreneurs find that the business that was eventually created bore little resemblance to the one they had originally envisaged.

- **Harnessing competencies and capability**: The fit between the competencies of the lead entrepreneur and the management team in terms of capability and know-how is critical for mobilising resources to transform the opportunity into a viable operating business. Drucker (1985) states that, unless the business opportunity is managed skilfully, it will not survive regardless of how desirable the product is, the investment it attracts, or even how much demand there is for it. Opportunities must be both beneficial and attainable for those on the team, using the resources that are available.

What these principles reinforce is the notion of being proactive. Establishing a new business is not about waiting for something to happen but about making it happen. The principles are concerned with the continual pursuit of developing a sustainable successful business. Having established the business, it is crucial to continue using these principles, so that excellence is always the goal of the enterprise.

A good example of these principles in action in an Irish context is the supermarket chain, Superquinn. Despite its success, this organisation continually seeks to improve upon its operations and its offerings to customers. Constant innovation and renewal, listening to the customer, and success being the responsibility of everyone in the organisation are the key beliefs that the organisation follows ceaselessly.

The mindset of the entrepreneur at the outset of creating a new venture will invariably be the mindset that they will hold throughout the life of the business. If one starts with the correct mindset (proactive and positive), the chances of succeeding in the long-term improve dramatically.

CONCLUSION

That entrepreneurs are exceptional people is a myth. What they see are opportunities that anybody else could see if they were to look more closely. However, it is the willingness to make something happen with ideas that makes the entrepreneur. The well-known quote concerning 1% inspiration and 99% perspiration is what entrepreneurship and creativity is really about. But, for most people, the barrier is their belief that they themselves are not creative, which is usually a fallacy. Every person has some creative abilities, but often they have not been developed over the years and so have become weakened. In trusting one's own ability to be creative (to whatever degree), then a person can open up a whole world of opportunity.

This chapter has sought to debunk some of the myths surrounding entrepreneurs and their creative abilities. It has defined key concepts so as to give the reader a clearer understanding of what these terms mean and how they differ in their operation. The chapter has provided techniques for generating ideas and supplied sources for business ideas. And, finally, the chapter has outlined a series of principles for transforming these ideas into realisable opportunities.

A person wishing to establish their own business should not be deterred because of a misguided belief that they cannot generate a good business idea. It is having the self-belief to transform an idea into a business opportunity that is the real challenge – and which turns a person into an entrepreneur.

QUESTIONS

1. In a group of not more than five people, put together a 10-minute class presentation on anything to do with the arts. You cannot use poetry (too many students take this option as they believe it is easy) and all work must be original to the group. Examples would include painting a picture, putting on a play, or sculpting some work.
2. Discuss the differences between the terms: creativity, discovery, invention, innovation, and opportunity.
3. In a group of not more than five people, use one of the techniques for generating ideas mentioned in the chapter to develop a business idea to be implemented within your college.

4. Using the Internet, identify a business opportunity that currently exists abroad but is not available in Ireland.
5. List 10 things that you have done that you consider creative.
6. "I have the same creative abilities as the majority of entrepreneurs." Discuss.

USEFUL WEBSITES

entrepreneurs.about.com/cs/ideas/
entrepreneurs.about.com/library/weekly/1999/aa092799.htm
www.bizplus.ie
www.businesscreativitynetwork.org.uk/tools.htm
www.circle-of-excellence.com
www.cocd.be/eng/index.htm
www.entrepreneur.com
www.irc.net.lu
www.niftybusinessideas.com/
www.planware.org
www.powerhomebiz.com
www.work-at-home-index.net/links/telecommuting.html

CHECKLIST FOR CHAPTER

After reading this chapter, check that you understand and appreciate:
• The differences between the key concepts
• The techniques for generating new ideas
• How to evaluate and prioritise ideas
• Where to find business ideas
• The principles for transforming ideas into realisable opportunities
• That not all entrepreneurs are highly creative
• That everyone has some creative abilities.

REFERENCES

Birley, S (1977) - An Opportunity: But is it Worth it? - *Mastering Enterprise* (Edited by Birley, S. and Muzyka, D.), Pitman Publishing, London.
Birley, S and Niktari, N. (1995) - *The Failure of Owner-Managed Businesses: The Diagnosis of Accountants and Bankers* - ICAEW, London.

Cougar, J.D. (1996) - *Creativity & Innovation in Information Systems Organizations* - Boyd & Fraser, Danvers, MA.

De Bono, E. (1995) - *Serious Creativity* - Harper Collins, London.

De Bono, E. (1962) - *The Mechanism of Mind* - Penguin Books, London.

De Bono, E. (1995a) - *CoRT Thinking* - Advanced Practical Thinking Training, Inc, Des Moines, IA.

De Bono, E. (1969) - *Opportunities: A Handbook of Business Opportunities Search* - Penguin Books, London.

Drucker, P.F. (1985) - *Innovation and Entrepreneurship* - Butterworth Heinemann, Oxford.

Gordon, W.J.J. (1961) – *Synectics* - Harper and Row, New York.

Hensman, N.; Lordan, M.; Duckett, L.; Cave, F. and Ashcroft, G. (1999) - Culture and Process Modification as the Key to Learning in Innovation by SMEs - *Proceedings of 3rd Enterprise and Learning Conference*, University of Paisley, Scotland.

Kay, J (1993) - *Foundations of Corporate Success: How Business Strategies Add Value* - Oxford University Press.

Keil, J.M. (1987) - *The Creative Corporation* - Dow Jones-Irwin, Homewood, IL .

Koestler, A. (1964) - *The Act of Creation* - Macmillan, New York.

Lordan, M (1988) - *Methods of Enhancing Creativity for Engineering Design* -PhD Thesis, University of Manchester Institute of Science and Technology (UMIST), UK.

Lordan, M.; Hensman, N.; Wright, M and Cave, F. (2000) - The Growth and Development of Small Firms as a Result of Participation in Knowledge Networks. - *Proceedings of 3rd ISBA National Small Firms Policy & Research Conference* (Small Firms: Adding the Spark), Robert Gordon University, Aberdeen, Scotland.

Lordan, M.; Hensman, N.; Wright, M. and Cave, F. (2000a) - Business Network Formation: The Impact on Knowledge Transfer and Economic Development of SMEs - *Proceedings of TII 2000 Annual Conference*, Funchal, Maderia.

Muzyka, D. (1997) - Spotting the Market Opportunity - *Mastering Enterprise* (Edited by Birley, S. and Muzyka, D.), Pitman Publishing, London.

Osborn, A.F. (1953) - *Applied Imagination: Principles and Procedures of Creative Problem Solving* - Charles Scribner's Sons, New York.

Porter, M. (1990) - *The Competitive Advantage of Nations* - Macmillan, London.

Rhodes, M. (1961) - *An Analysis of Creativity* - Phi Delta Kappan, Vol. 42, April 1961, pp 305-310.

Saunders, P (1997) - The Search for a Good Idea - *Mastering Enterprise* (Edited by Birley, S. and Muzyka, D.), Pitman Publishing, London.

Sternberg, R.J. (1988) - *The Nature of Creativity: Contemporary Psychological Perspectives* - Cambridge University Press.

Tidd, J.; Bessant, J. and Pavitt, K. (2001) - *Managing Innovation* - Wiley, New York.

Timmons, J. A. (1999) - *New Venture Creation: Entrepreneurship for the 21st Century* - Irwin/McGraw-Hill, Boston.

Timmons, J.A. (1989) - *New Business Opportunities* - Brick House Publishing, Acton, MA.

Weisburg, R. (1986) - *Creativity: Genius and Other Myths* - Freeman & Co, New York.

CHAPTER 3

THE BUSINESS PLAN PROCESS

Brian O'Kane [*] *and Ron Immink* [**]

LEARNING OBJECTIVES

- To understand the reasons for, and benefits of, business planning in the context of new venture creation
- To appreciate the difference between the process of business planning and the output, the business plan;
- To know fully the steps involved in the process of business planning and how they inter-relate
- To comprehend the structure of a typical business plan.

INTRODUCTION

Research and anecdotal evidence both show that an effective business plan is one of the major elements in successful business start-ups. The fact that almost 50% of new businesses world-wide fail within three years of being established, and that 75% of these failures can be shown to be due to lack of planning, emphasises the importance of a structured approach to business planning in the context of new venture creation. It is not enough to know where one wants to go, a potential entrepreneur must also know how they are going to get there. A good business plan offers the entrepreneur a route map to success.

---

[*] Brian O'Kane is managing director of Oak Tree Press.
[**] Ron Immink is new business director at Oak Tree Press.

Business plans have many different and important purposes. Sahlman *et al* (1996) saw them as "a means to explain ideas to others and enlist support and a vehicle for thinking through the complex array of issues involved in starting a new venture". Business plans are also variously defined as "a pathway to profit" (Pinson, 2001), "a written document that predicts the future path of your business" (Simpson *et al*, 1996), and "a vital tool for running a business" (Stutely, 1999). Rich & Gumpert (1999) go so far as to state that "a comprehensive, carefully thought-out business plan is essential to the success of entrepreneurs".

On the other hand, Sahlman (1999a) points out that "business plans rank no higher than 2 – on a scale from 1 to 10 – as a predictor of a new venture's success". Why? Because:

> *... most waste too much ink on numbers and devote too little attention to the information that really matters.*

The benefits of business plans are dependent on how they are used – as live documents that bring clarity of thinking to the actions of the entrepreneur or as something that needs to be written simply to get finance for the start-up. While fund-raising is often a necessary purpose of business planning, it is certainly not the only, or indeed major, purpose. In fact, the main reasons for business planning are:

- To establish the fundamental viability of a project
- To define realistic goals for the business and map out the steps and intermediate targets required in achieving them
- To act as a yardstick for measuring progress against the targets
- To communicate ideas to outsiders, particularly those outsiders the promoters are seeking to persuade to invest in the business.

A business plan offers a potential entrepreneur the opportunity to work through all of the issues involved in new venture creation. It enables them to analyse the business idea more effectively and make more competent judgements on the best way forward. It also assists the entrepreneur in determining what additional information is required for each functional area of the business. The plan acts as a checklist against which knowledge is gathered, assimilated, and used to make better-informed decisions. This chapter highlights the difference between the process and the output, then takes the reader through the steps involved in developing a business plan, and then offers a typical structure for a business plan.

PROCESS AND OUTPUT

Business planning for a new venture is a **process** that defines the goals of the business and the means by which they will be achieved. The process involves a thorough analysis of the major factors involved in achieving success in a new business. The **output** from the process is a formal business plan document that records those goals and factors. This distinction between process (business planning) and output (a business plan) is critical – and, arguably, the business planning (process) is more important than the business plan (output).

The process of business planning is reasonably straightforward (see the Key Questions later in this chapter) but is made complex by its dynamic nature. An entrepreneur will often need to return to earlier information or decisions and revise their plan in the light of new information. The plan is therefore a snapshot of a moment in time while the process needs to be continually worked upon. This means that the business plan should be updated at least once a year. Failure to do this may leave the entrepreneur making decisions based on information that is outdated.

As finance is the language of business, it is particularly important for an entrepreneur to understand the financial implications and consequences of the decisions made during the business planning process. The effects of these are shown in the financial projections – profit and loss account, balance sheet and cash flow – prepared as part of the business plan.

THE NEW VENTURE CREATION PROCESS

The new venture creation process usually results in the establishment of an enterprise, although sometimes the business planning exercise leads to a decision not to proceed. Sahlman (1999b) calls this the "Nike Model": Just Do It! If Not, Just Say No!

The process can be, and often is, relatively informal. People set up businesses every day with little forethought, planning or formality. In Ireland, one can become a sole trader almost simultaneously with the decision to do so – the only inescapable formality is the requirement to register for tax purposes.

However, introducing some structure into the process brings benefits, including:

- The development of managerial/entrepreneurial skills
- The development of an extended personal and business network
- Enhanced and informed decision-making skills.

Entrepreneurship is the dynamic process of creating incremental wealth. This wealth is generated by individuals who assume a risk in terms of equity, time and/or career commitment by providing value for some product or service. The product or service may or may not be new or unique but somehow the entrepreneur must infuse value by securing and allocating the necessary skills and resources in a way that is beneficial to the end-user.

"Securing and allocating the necessary skills and resources" is what the process of business planning is all about. "Resources" in this context is anything that contributes to the venture. The structure of the business planning process proposed in this chapter is based around a number of key questions, so-called because they (or more correctly, their answers) are critical to ensuring the success of a new venture (Immink & O'Kane, 2002).

KEY QUESTIONS

In deciding whether to start a new business, a potential entrepreneur must ask themselves a number of questions. The entrepreneur cannot be an expert in all areas of the business and therefore they should know their own strengths and weaknesses precisely. They should also be familiar with the markets that they are entering, the potential competitors that they may face, and the people who will be their customers. But there are also many more questions to be addressed.

These key questions are:
- Are you the right person to set up and run a business?
- Have you got a feasible idea?
- What formalities must you complete before you start your business?
- What sales do you expect and how will you generate them?
- How, and with what resources, will you meet your planned sales?
- Can you describe the people you will need and how you will organise them?
- How will you fund your business?
- Have you the best plan possible?
- Have you got a document that adequately captures all your strategies, targets and projections?

Although apparently simple, these questions are very powerful. Answering them well (there are no "correct" answers in the real world) leads to a stronger business and one more likely to achieve its aims. This is because they are derived from the viewpoint of a reader, not the writer, of a business plan. In answering these key questions, an entrepreneur answers the questions that will be in the forefront of a reader's mind, be that reader an investor, a lender or potential participant in the new venture.

Are you the right person?

Some people are born entrepreneurs; others could never face the responsibilities involved. The decision to take on self-employment is not one to be made lightly, because of the risks involved. A potential entrepreneur needs to consider themselves, their family and/or dependants, and their personal and financial circumstances before they decide whether self-employment is the right choice for them at that time. If they lack the combination of personal qualities, skills and experience that are essential for entrepreneurship, they should undertake appropriate training to fill the gaps before starting a new business. (See **Chapter 1, What is Entrepreneurship?** and **Chapter 7, The Management Team**.)

Have you got a feasible idea?

Not just an idea, but a *feasible* idea? The marketplace can be cruel, rewarding only a small number of the millions of new products and services that are launched each year. Whether the idea will work in the marketplace is a critical question – and one that is best tested before significant funds are invested in the new venture. Technologists and venture capitalists often call this "proof of concept"; the term "feasibility study" is also used. (See **Chapter 2, Finding the Business Idea** and **Chapter 4, Market Research**.)

What formalities must you complete?

In most countries, businesses are subject to regulation. It is important that an entrepreneur identifies and complies with those regulations that apply to their new business. In addition, through patents and other forms of intellectual property rights (IPR), where appropriate, they should protect their idea or its implementation before exposing it fully to the marketplace. (See **Chapter 5, Intellectual Property** and **Chapter 6, Legal Issues**.)

What sales do you expect?

Sales are the engine of business growth. Without sales, a business has nothing. So the level of sales planned is critical. Equally critical is a clear explanation of what activity is planned to create these sales – since they will not happen of their own accord. Additionally, the entrepreneur will need to know how they will promote the product or service, the price that is to be charged, and how the product will be distributed. (See **Chapter 8, Marketing**.)

How will you meet your planned sales?

Generating sales is not the end of the story. Once a customer has placed an order, they expect that order to be fulfilled – promptly, efficiently, with a product or service that meets their needs, at a price they can afford. Is the business able to do this? How? At what cost? With what resources? (See **Chapter 9, Operations**.)

Can you describe the people you will need?

People are critical to any business. How many people, with what skills and experience and how they are organised for maximum efficiency and effectiveness are all important questions for the entrepreneur to answer. (See **Chapter 7, Management Team** and **Chapter 10, Human Relations Management**.)

How will you fund your business?

The 64-million-dollar question, literally. Many entrepreneurs start here and then try to build their business according to the funds they can raise. A better approach is to plan the business and then seek financing based on a clear, logical and solid business plan document that sets out what funding is needed, what it will be used for and what risk and return can be expected. An understanding of the types of finance needed – and available – is essential. The entrepreneur also needs to understand financial management in order to maintain a positive cash flow for the business. (See **Chapter 11, Raising Finance**.)

Have you the best plan possible?

If not, perhaps more research is needed. A weak business plan can cripple – or kill – a new business. **Chapter 13** explores some of the techniques an entrepreneur can use to review their business plan and make it stronger, providing the opportunity to test a business model before implementing it. (See **Chapter 13, Reviewing the Business Plan**.)

Have you captured your strategies, targets and projections?

As previously stated, a business plan usually serves many purposes. It may need to address a number of audiences and capture the essence of a business – in as few pages as possible. What it says and how it says it will be determined largely by the audience at which it is aimed. But there's a core of information that's essential in any business plan document. (See **Chapter 12, Planning for Growth** and **Chapter 13, Reviewing the Business Plan**.)

Depending on the reader, there may be additional questions. For example, a banker will be concerned about security for a loan and the ability to repay the loan over an agreed period. An investor will want to know what they will get back for their investment and what is the "exit strategy". A support agency providing grants may be concerned with the number of jobs being created. But whatever the background of the reader, each will need to have clear answers to all of the questions posed above. If the entrepreneur cannot provide clarity of thinking in dealing with these questions, then it suggests that the business idea has not been thought through fully and that more work needs to be done. In many ways, answering these questions acts as a safety valve against someone establishing a new business without understanding the requirements of the business.

BUSINESS PLANNING

There is absolutely no doubt that engaging in the process of business planning has a positive effect on the potential for success of a new venture. It identifies the issues, clarifies them, and develops the solutions. Business planning for a new venture is a process that defines the goals of the business, through a thorough definition of values, vision, mission – and, if taking Charles Handy's (2001) advice, a definition of the passion that underlies the business idea. This is followed by allocating the resources to the factors that will enable the business to achieve its stated goals – across the functional areas of people, marketing, process and infrastructure. There are also intrinsic factors, such as family support, entrepreneurial drive, and attitude to growth that are difficult to quantify, but contribute as much (and some would argue more) to achieving the goals set for the new venture. Therefore, the process involves a thorough analysis of all the major factors involved in achieving the success of the new business.

Carried out diligently and objectively, this process will establish the viability (or otherwise) of the new venture. If there is no market for the product, or one that can only be reached at great cost, or the product cannot be made and delivered to the customer through whatever channels of distribution are necessary for the price that the customer is prepared to pay, this will all become evident – and can then be acted upon, before the business risks an entry to the market.

Goals are essential to the achievement of any plan. They set a direction, establish a path, provide an indicator of achievement and help to avoid distractions. Because business success is often a distant target, intermediate targets are useful as milestones. It's often said that "if you don't where you want to go, anywhere will do". Without a clear plan, it can be difficult sometimes in the pressure of day-to-day minutiae to know whether the business is making progress – or even heading in the right direction. Re-reading the business plan can help to set a business back on track again – or confirm that it was on the right path all along.

Where bankers and investors become involved, the communication of a business idea assists people who are going to help achieve the success the entrepreneur desires. How well the entrepreneur communicates their idea will be a major factor in determining the level of support that they will receive and thus, ultimately perhaps, in determining its success. And while bankers and investors may be the most usual groups to whom an entrepreneur will communicate their business idea through a business plan, there are other people with whom a plan may be shared – for example, suppliers who will be extending significant credit or key staff whose confidence and commitment are necessary to win.

In addition, engaging in the process of business planning very often helps to develop the business management capabilities of the entrepreneur and/or their management team. Through the business planning process, the entrepreneur is exposed to a wide range of business topics and disciplines, some of which they may not have had previous experience, but all of which are essential to the development of a sound business and important from a personal skills perspective.

Military planners recognise that the best plans are made worthless, the minute the soldiers go into battle. There are just too many variables with which to cope. But that doesn't make them give up planning. They realise that what helps them win wars is the thinking that has been done in arriving at the plan. Properly thought-through, the plan allows for things going wrong and has built-in actions to deal with a wide range of contingencies. The key success factor, however, is the full involvement/learning of the commanders on the ground in the development of the original plan (in other words, the business planning process). In this context, Simpson *et al* (2001) point out that the success of the franchise concept is based on the fact that virtually all the planning is done for the entrepreneur, a fact that is often overlooked when making the case for business planning.

THE STRUCTURE OF A BUSINESS PLAN

The physical output of the business planning process is a business plan, a document that typically summarises these points about a business:
- Where it has come from
- Where it is now
- Where it is going in the future
- How it intends to get there
- How much money it needs to fulfil its plans
- What makes it likely to succeed
- What threats or disadvantages must be overcome on the way.

Just as each business is unique, its business plan is also unique. However, bankers and investors have come to expect a broadly standard format that presents information in an easily-digested and logical sequence.

The traditional format is a document that comprises:
- **Executive Summary:** A single page that encourages further reading.
- **Introduction:** Basic information about the business and the purpose of the plan.
- **Promoter(s):** Who the entrepreneur (and their team) is and their qualifications for starting and running the business.
- **Project Overview:** A description of the business, its mission statement, trends in its industry, targets, employment (actual and potential) and the legal status of the business.

- **Marketing:** A summary of the marketing plan, backed up by a market overview, details of customers, competition, products/services, price, distribution and promotion strategies and a sales forecast.
- **Process & Resources:** The business' planned products/services in more detail, how they are made/delivered, how quality will be ensured, what staff are needed and how they will be organised.
- **Finance & Funding:** A summary of the business' financial projections, with the funding requirement (and the entrepreneur's personal contribution) highlighted.
- **Appendices:** Financial projections and any other relevant information.

The final piece of the jigsaw, often overlooked by entrepreneurs in their enthusiasm to get their new venture started, is evidence. Without evidence to underpin the assumptions and assertions within the business plan, it is virtually meaningless. As part of the process of business planning, the entrepreneur should collect evidence for every nugget of information in their business plan document – each assumption, figure and proposal must be grounded in reality.

Of particular importance to the success of the business plan is the Executive Summary. It is said that for each business plan arriving on the desk of a venture capitalist, an average of only 30 seconds is spent reading the plan initially (in other words, only the Executive Summary is read). If the attention of the venture capitalist is not captured in that time, then the plan gets binned. If they are interested in the idea, then they will read the plan more fully. The entrepreneur must excite the reader quickly and offer highlights that suggest that this business idea is worth pursuing for the reader. In America, this is called the "elevator pitch" (in other words, you meet a venture capitalist in an elevator and you have approximately 30 seconds to sell your idea to them).

A STARTING POINT

The Key Questions form the basic starting point for new venture creation. Without an awareness and understanding of these, it will be difficult to control the planning process. The next step is a frank assessment by the entrepreneur of themselves, their team (if any), their idea and their market. It is better to expose weaknesses in any of these now, before the real work of planning begins, rather than during the planning process when other factors may have begun to depend on the answers, or worse still when the business actually starts.

A useful tool is SPOTcheck (available at www.spotcheckonline.com), which uses 16 factors known to be critical to start-up success, and scores the business on the impact that these factors will have on its potential for success. SPOTcheck has three functions:

- To assess the potential for growth of an individual business
- To identify interventions needed to achieve that growth
- To benchmark performance for later measurement and comparison.

These functions assist the entrepreneur in developing their thinking through a series of key factors. The factors that SPOTcheck uses are:

- **Section 1: External factors** (outside control): Analysis of the macro-environment, the market, customers, direct competitors and suppliers.
- **Section 2: Promoters/Management team:** Quality of the promoters/management team.
- **Section 3: Internal factors (inside control):** Quality of overall corporate strategy, marketing approach, process, innovation, HRM, financial management, information systems and administration; analysis of sales achievement, product; and financial performance.

Each factor consists of a number of Line Items, which are rated on a numerical score, between 1 and 5. Scoring is based on the impact of the factor on the potential of the business for growth, as follows: Negative - 1; Negative to Neutral - 2; Neutral - 3; Neutral to Positive - 4; Positive – 5. **Figure 3.1** shows an example of a SPOTcheck factor and the questions it raises.

The output from SPOTcheck is:

- An overall score that assesses the overall start-up potential of the business, allowing for it to be benchmarked against other similar businesses
- Identification of areas (factors) for intervention/improvement (the score for each factor can also be benchmarked to assess the impact of subsequent intervention)
- A graph, which communicates the findings in an easy-to-read manner.

FIGURE 3.1 SPOTCHECK FACTOR

Anna Koloskova2, ARO
Remaining credits: 334

SPOTcheck

Personal Account
Buy more credits
New assessment
Log out

Assessment Questions

(No name)

Score each item within the Factor below for their impact on the growth potential of your business
1 - negative   2 - negative to neutral   3 - neutral   4 - neutral to positive   5 - positive

Section 2: Promoters/management team					
This factor is separated because of its importance					
Factor 6: Promoters / Management Team Quality of the promoters/management team					
Drive of promoters/management team	1	2	3	4	5
Relevant education and experience of promoters/management team	1	2	3	4	5
Network of promoters/management team	1	2	3	4	5
Personality of promoters/management team	1	2	3	4	5
Commitment of promoters/management team	1	2	3	4	5
Quality of management	1	2	3	4	5

Previous | Next | Process Data | Save and exit

Navigate Factors:

Terms and conditions | Contact us

CONCLUSION

A good business plan guarantees neither success in business nor in raising finance but it does improve the probability of both. Business plans are highly beneficial in clarifying the thinking of the potential entrepreneur, in helping them to analyse existing data and to determine what additional information might be required.

Each of the following chapters addresses part of the dynamic of the process of business planning. Each is complete but together they comprise a greater whole. Although this book is linear, in that one chapter follows another, in real life, business planning is a dynamic, iterative and non-linear activity.

QUESTIONS

1. What are the differences between the terms: business planning and business plan?
2. Describe the key elements in a business plan.
3. "Business planning is a continual process, even after the venture has been established." Discuss.

4. Download sample business plans for two different businesses from www.bplans.com and compare them.
5. Evaluate the role of a business plan in developing a business idea.
6. What makes a good business plan?

USEFUL WEBSITES

www.bplans.com
www.spotcheckonline.com
www.startingabusinessinireland.com

CHECKLIST FOR CHAPTER

After reading this chapter, check that you understand and appreciate:

- The reasons for, and benefits of, business planning in the context of new venture creation
- The difference between the process of business planning and the output, the business plan
- The steps involved in the process of business planning and how they inter-relate
- The structure of a typical business plan.

REFERENCES

Handy, C. (2001) - *The Elephant and the Flea* – Hutchinson, London.

Immink, R. and O'Kane, B. (2002) - *TENBizPlan: Dynamic Business Planning for Start-Ups,* 2nd edition, Oak Tree Press, Cork.

Pinson, L. (2001) - *Anatomy of a Business Plan* - 5th edition, Dearborn Trade Publishing, Chicago, IL.

Rich, S. R., and Gumpert, D. E. (1999) - How to Write a Winning Business Plan - *The Entrepreneurial Venture* (Edited by Sahlman, W.A.; Stevenson, H.H.; Roberts M.J., and Bhidé, A.), Harvard Business School Press, Boston, MA.

Sahlman, W.A. (1999,a) - How to Write a Great Business Plan - *Harvard Business Review on Entrepreneurship,* Harvard Business School Press, Boston, MA.

Sahlman, W.A. (1999,b) - Some Thoughts on Business Plans - *The Entrepreneurial Venture* (Sahlman, W.A.; Stevenson, H.H.; Roberts M.J. and Bhidé, A.), Harvard Business School Press, Boston, MA.

Sahlman, W.A.; Stevenson, H.H.; Roberts, M.J., and Bhidé, A. (Eds.) - *The Entrepreneurial Venture* - Harvard Business School Press, Boston, MA.

Simpson, V.P.; Fritz, W.P.; Fritz, L.J. and Courtenay, N.P. (1996) - *Business Planning Success* - Dynamic Pathways Company, Newport Beach, CA.

Stutely, R. (1999) - *The Definitive Business Plan* - Pearson Education, Harlow, Essex.

CHAPTER 4

MARKETING RESEARCH[1]

Declan Fleming[*]

LEARNING OBJECTIVES

- To define marketing research
- To understand the role that marketing research plays in decision-making
- To detail the types of research and the steps of a typical marketing research process
- To differentiate between primary and secondary data
- To describe widely used marketing research techniques
- To outline key issues in Internet-based marketing research.

INTRODUCTION

The key to successful marketing lies in a sound understanding of the market being entered. Marketing research is crucial in order to prevent entrepreneurs from making costly and often unnecessary mistakes, since decisions should be based on fact rather than intuition. While marketing research (or 'market research' – a popular synonym) sprung from liberal

---

[1] This chapter draws on material contained in *Marketing Research in Ireland: Theory and Practice*, by C Domegan and D Fleming, Gill and Macmillan, 1999, with permission.

[*] Declan Fleming is a lecturer in marketing at the Department of Marketing, National University of Ireland, Galway.

roots (social research), its theoretical approach and methodologies have been borrowed from probability statistics, descriptive economics, psychology, sociology, and cultural anthropology (Chisnall, 1992).

Marketing research is used to generate and interpret information to assist management with decision-making (Cowan, 1994). It is the principal method of answering questions such as: "Who are my customers? Where do they shop? What do they want? What price will they pay? Who are my competitors? What do my competitors offer?". It is used both for forecasting and for planning a firm's actions. Marketing research additionally enables the identification and anticipation of market demand, as well as measuring customer satisfaction with a product or service. Indeed, marketing research supports and implements the marketing concept of customer satisfaction. It is the process of listening to the voice of the market and conveying it back to management. Good decision-making relies upon a sound information base. As put by Roger Jupp, Lansdowne Marketing Research: "Good research is equivalent to the lights on a car – you can see where you are going". Thus, marketing research being interpreted as an information-gathering process to assist with decision-making is encapsulated in the many formal definitions of marketing research that exist in the literature.

DEFINITIONS OF MARKET RESEARCH

There are a wide variety of definitions of marketing research available in the literature, as each author has their own interpretation of what marketing research means. For the purposes of this book, the definitions used by practitioners have been considered most appropriate and so two are selected to give better understanding to the term:

"The formalised means of obtaining information to be used in making marketing decisions."
The Marketing Institute of Ireland

"The collection, analysis, interpretation and presentation of information obtained from individuals or groups of people in order to guide decisions on a wide range of matters, affecting consumers, either as buyers or as citizens."
The Marketing Research Society (UK)

Whatever definition of marketing research one chooses, there are several important characteristics inherent in the concept. Good marketing research must be *methodology-led*, *decision-driven*, and *information-orientated*.

Firstly, marketing research is a methodology-led process that systematically and objectively investigates a problem or opportunity. Marketing research denotes a process or sequence of steps to gather facts and figures in an objective and accurate manner. This means that marketing research is scientific in nature. Without this scientific orientation, marketing research would have little validity and it would degenerate into subjective assessments of market behaviour.

The second trait of marketing research is that it is decision-driven. The purpose of conducting research is to aid decisions. Specifically, marketing research is concerned with a particular decision – an opportunity or problem. In all of these cases, the decision is time-bound. As a result, marketing research has a definite beginning and a definite end.

Thirdly, marketing research is about information. The marketing research process can be applied to the huge variety of marketing problems that can arise, since there are a myriad of occasions that customers come into contact with the company and with the numerous activities that are undertaken to achieve customer satisfaction.

All three elements must be present for marketing research to contribute to informed decision-making.

WHY IS MARKETING RESEARCH ESSENTIAL?

Entrepreneurs are often deterred by the rigours of market research, or simply do not know how to carry it out inexpensively. They rely instead on their own subjective judgement and frequently develop an "iceberg syndrome", believing that the small number of customers they can see are a sure indicator of the mass of other customers. It is a fundamental mistake to believe that people are simply waiting to buy one's product or service and that competitors are not going to react. New businesses need a clear and detailed picture of their market well before they launch.

The purpose of marketing research for entrepreneurs investigating, or seeking to start, a new business is therefore twofold:

• To build credibility for the business idea the entrepreneur must prove, first to his or her own satisfaction, and later to that of outside financiers, a thorough understanding of the marketplace for the new product or service. This is vital, if resources are to be attracted to build the new venture.

- To develop a realistic market entry strategy for the new business, based on a clear understanding of genuine customer needs and ensuring that product quality, price, promotional methods and distribution chain are mutually supportive and clearly focused on target customers.

The information gathered will be used not only to develop the marketing plan but also to enhance the development of the other functional areas of the business plan. But note that marketing research is not just essential in starting a business – once the enterprise is launched, research must become an integral part in the on-going life of the firm. Customers and competitors are dynamic; products have life cycles; on-going marketing research is essential to understand both.

Some words of caution:

- Too much information can result in information overload, which is to say "paralysis by analysis"
- Information deprivation is equally dangerous – one can "drown in data, but lack information to make an informed decision"
- While marketing information can greatly enhance judgement, it never eliminates risk or uncertainty surrounding a decision.

Information is not a substitute for management judgement. The use of "gut feelings" does not exclude marketing research. Rather, it is necessary to appreciate the use of "instinct" and combine it with the formal scientific approach of marketing research to give a holistic and complete picture.

In understanding that marketing research must be carried out, a potential entrepreneur has two options on how it will be undertaken:

- Do the research themselves
- Hire someone else to do the research.

Doing It Oneself

Although amateur attempts can sometimes be misleading, there is no real reason why an entrepreneur cannot conduct the research themselves. However, performing research oneself is somewhat restrictive, insofar as it is limited by experience, time, and resources. Additionally, a lack of objectivity may distort the research findings.

Using an Agency

The second option is the use of an outside agency. However, while there are certain advantages to employing a research agency, using an agency incurs additional costs. Therefore, the entrepreneur needs to have confidence in the agency, based on its reputation, past performance, and experience. If the costs of employing a research agency are too high, a neglected source of inexpensive research is universities where business and marketing students are often required to undertake research as part of their course requirements. Contact should be made with the head of the appropriate departments within the universities.

Marketing research is essential for the potential entrepreneur, as it leads to better-informed decisions and reduces the risk being taken. It enables the entrepreneur to develop a more detailed business plan, with a clear rationale behind key decisions. It also allows the entrepreneur to validate the financial projections, based on the data generated by the research. Information gaps can be completed and outstanding questions answered. Marketing research is essential when making a presentation to a banker or investor, as it demonstrates attention to detail, thoroughness in planning, and an ability to offer reasoning for strategic decisions. Therefore, marketing research is not only essential in new venture creation, it is critical.

THE MARKETING RESEARCH PROCESS

The challenge of marketing research is to obtain and use accurate information upon which to base good decisions. This may appear to make a simple process of gathering information into a complicated and complex procedure. This is not so, as gathering information is not simple – not if you want that information to be accurate, objective, valid, and reliable. This section is devoted to an overview of the stages involved in research (the marketing research process). The stages outlined here are used as a structure for much of the remainder of the chapter.

The marketing research process refers to a set of stages that detail a number or sequence of tasks a researcher undertakes to gather and report valid and reliable information to assist with decision-making. Different authors categorise the various stages in marketing research differently. For the purpose of this chapter, the marketing research process is presented as a set of seven stages. While the stages of a marketing research study appear at face value to be mutually exclusive, they are highly dependent upon each other. They are depicted in **Figure 4.1**. Remember, many of the terms introduced here are explained in further detail in the latter half of the chapter.

FIGURE 4.1: THE MARKETING RESEARCH PROCESS

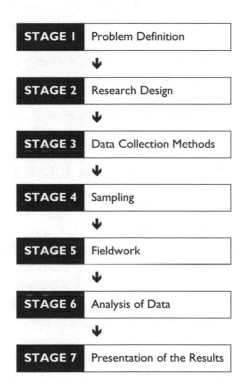

STAGE 1 – PROBLEM DEFINITION

As Albert Einstein said, "the formulation of a problem is often more essential than its solution"(Einstein and Infeld, 1942)). A research project is first concerned with correct and proper *problem definition*.

In this stage, the researcher decides what information is needed to solve the problem on hand. The researcher has to determine the purpose of the study and why it is being undertaken. Exploring the wrong issue or asking the wrong questions, no matter how efficiently, will result in useless information. Thus, the management decision has to be stated by the researcher as a question and/or an information-oriented statement.

Problem definition ends with, and results in, a list of objectives that essentially are broad statements of intent. A decision at Stage 1, problem definition, automatically and directly affects the remaining stages of research. At some point early on in the research process, budget and costing have to be considered in light of required information and proposed methods for collecting the data. A research proposal may also be necessary, especially if the research is being undertaken by a research agency on behalf of the entrepreneur.

In summary, finding the starting point for any marketing research project can be the most difficult part. Once the problem has been correctly identified and the information needs and objectives have been established, the research task gains momentum and starts to unfold.

STAGE 2 – CHOOSE A RESEARCH DESIGN

Choosing a research design is the second stage in marketing research. A research design is an overall blueprint, guideline, and plan of action or framework for the rest of the research process to facilitate later decisions that need to be made. One way to classify the nature of the required information, and hence research designs in marketing research, is according to the three terms: *exploratory*, *descriptive*, or *causal*, as shown in **Figure 4.2**.

FIGURE 4.2: RESEARCH DESIGNS

Exploratory research is research that aims to explore and to discover issues about the problem on hand, because very little is known about the situation by anyone. A research project is exploratory when there is uncertainty about the dimensions or characteristics of a problem or opportunity. The design is deliberately flexible. Exploratory research is often conducted before descriptive or causal work is undertaken.

On the other hand, the entrepreneur may already know a lot about the market and its behaviour, and instead may want to describe this market or facets of it in more detail. This kind of research is about quantifying some aspects of a market and so is referred to as descriptive research.

Causal research aims to establish a cause and effect relationship between two or more variables, for example, x causes y. The recognised data collection instrument for causal research is the experiment. Variations of product, packaging, advertising and price are some of the factors that could be subjected to experimentation. Experimental designs can range from the simple to the complex. **Table 4.1** offers more detail on each of these types of research designs.

TABLE 4.1: CHOOSING A RESEARCH DESIGN

	Exploratory Research	Descriptive Research	Causal Research
Data type	Qualitative	Qualitative or quantitative	Quantitative
Aims	To explore, chart, identify	To describe and quantify	To establish cause and effect
Nature of Variables	Unknown Undocumented	Known associations and documented	Known exactly Clearly supported
Degree of Formality	Relatively little	Some to extensive	High mathematical content
Data	Literature review Expert survey Focus groups In-depth interviews Projective techniques	Literature review Expert survey Surveys Observation Panels (Focus groups)	Literature review Expert survey Experiments (Surveys) (Observation)
Sample Size	Small	Small to large	Large
Question types	Probing Response-driven.	Some probing Interviewer-driven	No probing
Hypothesis	Generates Develops	Tests and/or Generates, Develops	Tests

Source: Domegan & Fleming (1999).

STAGE 3 – PLANNING THE DATA COLLECTION METHOD(S) & INSTRUMENT(S)

With problem definition and research design already decided upon, the researcher is now in a position to decide how, when and where the required information is to be gathered. This stage of the marketing research process incorporates choosing a data collection method and relevant data collection instrument, in light of the problem and the research design.

Data can be collected from *secondary* sources or from *primary* sources. Secondary data is information that has already been collected by someone else for another reason, other than the one on hand. Government published figures are an example of external secondary data. Primary data is defined as data or information collected first hand by the researcher to solve the specific problem/opportunity on hand. Here, one comes across an important rule of marketing research: Always exhaust secondary sources of data before planning to collect any primary data. In practice, this means that a researcher first plans what information is needed, and then checks that the required information is not already in a written report available in a library. If not, then one again plans what primary research to conduct before actually gathering data from respondents. **Table 4.2** presents the major distinctions between secondary and primary data.

TABLE 4.2: DISTINCTIONS BETWEEN SECONDARY AND PRIMARY DATA

	Secondary Data	Primary Data
Purpose	Collected for other reasons by others	Collected for specific problem in hand by researcher
Relevancy	Some to little	Complete
Objectivity	Unknown	High
Process	Easy to gather	Difficult to gather
Cost	Relatively cheap	Relatively expensive
Time Required	Relatively little	Relatively much

Source: Domegan & Fleming, 1999.

Secondary Data Sources

There is a myriad of secondary sources of information available to the researcher. These are generally readily available, easy to consult, and relatively inexpensive to gather. However, their data is not gathered specifically for marketing purposes and, to this end, will need to be adjusted. On many occasions, two or more sources will have to be combined to answer the query posed by the researcher.

Secondary sources of data available include:

A. Central Statistics Office (www.cso.ie)

The Central Statistics Office (CSO) collects, computes, analyses and disseminates statistical information relating to the economic and social life of Ireland. The CSO is located in both Dublin and Cork and publishes principal statistics in the following category areas:

- Agriculture
- Building and Construction
- Demography and Labour Force
- Distribution and Services
- External Trade
- Economy
- Industry
- Industrial Employment, Earnings and Hours Worked
- Prices
- Tourism and Transport
- Vital Statistics.

B. Government Departments

At present, there are 18 Government Departments, each charged with responsibility for policy in their respective areas. Information pertaining to each Department is available through their own Department libraries, local public libraries, university and college libraries and of course, over the Internet. Visit the Government of Ireland website (www.irlgov.ie) and follow the link to Government Departments.

C. State Agencies

The many Irish State-sponsored bodies are an important source of information for marketing researchers. The more relevant agencies for marketing/business purposes are listed below, though this list is by no means exhaustive. For a full listing again, go to the Irish Government website and follow the link to All State Organisations. Each agency has its own website. Examples of State agencies include: Bord Fáilte, Bord Bia, Enterprise Ireland, FÁS, Forfás, IDA, Shannon Development, Teagasc and Údarás na Gaeltachta.

D. Directories

Commercial directories provide profile data on companies, industries and organisations. Most are available through public and university/ college libraries.

The principal commercial directories include:

- Kompass Ireland
- Dun and Bradstreet
- Thoms Commercial Directory
- Kelly's Business Directory.

E. Trade Associations / Professional Bodies

Generally speaking, trade associations and professional bodies publish an annual report, a regular trade journal and *ad hoc* research reports. These include information on industry sales, growth patterns, and trade members. The number of trade associations in Ireland is sizeable. Listings are available in the Golden Pages. As an example, the following are the main trade associations relating to the tourism industry:

- Irish Hotel Federation
- Irish Hotel and Catering Industry
- Irish Country Holidays
- Hotel Sales and Marketing Association
- Restaurant Association.

One of the main professional bodies in Ireland is the Chamber of Commerce. Presently there are 55 affiliated members within the Chambers of Commerce of Ireland (www.chambersireland.ie). Links to local chambers are available within this website. One of the services provided by a Chamber of Commerce is the provision of information to individuals and groups through conferences and seminars, the European Business Centre and a trade reference library.

The Digital Age Of Secondary Data

The principal developments in this area have been the growing use of CD-ROMs, on-line databases, the Internet and the World Wide Web. Access to these resources is available in many public and college libraries. Some of the more widely used databases include: ABI Inform,

Anbar Abstracts, Dialog, Findex and FT Profile. A list of useful websites is contained at the end of this chapter.

However, in many cases, secondary sources of data are not sufficient to solve the problem. The marketing researcher then turns her/his attention to primary data collection methods.

Primary Data Collection

There are broadly two types of marketing research: quantitative and qualitative. Quantitative research answers questions that start with "How many … ?" or "How much … ?". Qualitative research addresses issues that deal with "Why … ?" or "How … ?".

In quantitative research, techniques, and sample sizes lead to the collection of data that can be statistically analysed and whose results can be expressed numerically. This data tends to come from large surveys, sales data, or market forecasts. Qualitative research deals with information that is too difficult or expensive to quantify – for example, subjective opinions and value judgements that are not amenable to statistical analysis and quantification, typically unearthed during depth interviews or discussion groups.

The choice of primary data collection method is closely tied to the type of research design that is being pursued. Generally speaking, *focus groups* and *in-depth interviews* are associated, though not exclusively, with exploratory research.

Focus Groups

A focus group consists of eight to 12 participants, who are led by a moderator in an in-depth discussion on a particular topic or concept. The main purpose of the focus group is to gain insights by listening to a group of people from the appropriate target market (Greenbaum, 1990). The group is generally selected so as to include people who have common backgrounds or experience regarding the topic at hand. The objective of focus group research is to learn and understand what people have to say and why.

Focus group sessions are used to explore and define the attributes and issues in customer terms (Gulledge, 1996). The emphasis is on getting people to talk at length and in detail about the topic in question and provide discussion and debate, and hence new ideas. Focus groups can be quite good if one has a specific topic, but for broad-brush issues focus groups are not great (Darling, 1998).

Focus groups can be used for three different types of purposes (Cadler, 1997):

- **Clinical** – to uncover feelings, attitudes, and beliefs
- **Exploratory** – to generate, develop, and screen ideas
- **Phenomenological** – to discover consumers' everyday life experiences such as thoughts and behaviour.

The physical setting for the focus group is also important. A relaxed informal atmosphere encourages spontaneous comments. Most Irish focus group settings consist of booking a conference room in a hotel, arranging seating, and installing a tape recorder and possibly a video camcorder. A circular seating arrangement enables all participants to see each other. Videotaping the session allows for the recording of facial expressions and body movements. Some researchers may choose to use a living-room setting as an alternative to conference-room setting, believing that the informality of the living room will make the participants more at ease, as in a typical home-like setting.

In-Depth Interviews

Also known as individual extended interviews, in-depth interviews are another way of obtaining qualitative data. Like focus groups, they are also an unstructured and direct way of obtaining information, and are used primarily for exploratory research. But unlike focus groups, in-depth interviews are conducted on a one-on-one basis.

In-depth interviews permit the discovery of emotional "hot buttons" that provide psychological insights (Sokolow, 1985). The technique uses extensive probing in the context of a personal interview to get a single respondent to reveal motivations, beliefs, attitudes, and feelings on a topic (Knox, 1986). The purpose of the technique is to descend beneath the superficial answers that are often provided by respondents and to discover the more fundamental reasons underlying the respondent's attitudes and behaviour (Kahan, 1990). In-depth interviews may last for half an hour, an hour or up to two hours. Normally, the interviewer will take brief notes during the session, and it is advisable (with the permission of the interviewee) to tape-record the discussion. The main weakness with in-depth interviews is that, because sample sizes are small, statistical extrapolation of research findings becomes a problem.

Descriptive Research

There are two basic methods of obtaining information from individuals – either ask them or observe them. Collectively, they are known as descriptive research.

The first of these alternatives, an approach that is sometimes mistakenly equated with market research itself, is survey research. It is probably fair to say that surveys are the most widely used method of data collection in marketing research (Seymour, 1996). Survey research relies on a questionnaire (or measuring instrument of some sort) to record responses. It should be stressed that the use of questionnaires is not intrinsic to surveys. One can have surveys based on observation where no questions are asked of any respondents.

Survey research can be classified based on the modes of communication and administration. There are four major survey methods:

- Personal interviews
- Telephone interviews
- Postal interviews
- Internet.

The Personal Interview

Personal interviews are direct, face-to-face communications between the interviewer and a respondent (Tull and Hawkins, 1990). Personal interviews may take place in a variety of different locations, including the home of the respondent, a street corner, or a shopping centre. They are sometimes referred to as face-to-face interviews.

The personal interview begins with the interviewer approaching the respondent. The first concern is to ensure the full co-operation of the interviewee. This is followed by a brief explanation of the study and how the respondent can help. Because there is greater interaction between interviewer and respondent, the personal interview has great flexibility.

The personal interview tends to have less non-response error than other survey methods. Refusal rates tend to range from about 10% to 30% on average. Interviewers rely primarily on their sales ability to convince individuals to co-operate. Personal interviews are often impractical to conduct over wide geographical regions for reasons related to time and cost.

Increasingly, personal interviews are being conducted in large, high-traffic areas such as shopping centres (Bash and Parasuraman, 1985). The advantage of the shopping mall interview is that it is more efficient for the respondent to come to the interviewer than *vice versa*, and thus many interviews can be conducted quickly (Proctor, 1997).

The Telephone Interview

Telephone interviews involve phoning a sample (unless it is a census) of respondents and asking them a series of questions. Telephone interviews are becoming increasingly popular and are probably one of the most efficient methods for collecting data quickly (Tyebjee, 1979).

While the telephone interview has many characteristics similar to that of the personal interview (for example, respondent co-operation must be sought, questions can be clarified, respondents can be probed, etc.), it does not lend itself as easily to the collection of lengthy and detailed information. Telephone interviews are more suited to concise and straightforward data collection.

Telephone interviewing depends on a representative sampling frame – a list of population units with their telephone numbers. The telephone directory is the normal sampling frame used (Czaja, 1982).

The Postal Interview

The postal survey is a self-administered questionnaire sent to respondents through the post. It is very much a paper-and-pen method of collecting data. There is no interviewer available to:

- Ask the question
- Probe for more information
- Induce co-operation
- Record answers
- Clarify questions for the respondent
- Guide the interview.

The questionnaire is administered to the respondent by the respondent, and the respondent completes and returns the questionnaire. As there is no interviewer present to clarify issues or to encourage the respondent's co-operation, the construction of the questionnaire and related materials is crucial to the success of this survey method. Thus the researcher must make critical decisions about the various elements of the postal interview package, which composes:

- Out-going envelope
- Cover letter
- Questionnaire itself

- Return envelope
- Incentives used.

Unless the curiosity and co-operation of the respondent are quickly aroused, it is likely that the respondent will "shelve" the questionnaire. The cover letter that accompanies the questionnaire is an important means of inducing the reader to complete and return the questionnaire. Mail surveys are usually plagued by low rates of return and often drag over many weeks.

The response rate for postal questionnaires depends on the length of the questionnaire, content, group surveyed, incentive employed and other factors (Berdie, 1989). Techniques for improving postal response rates, ranging from including a small cash incentive, to the colour of the envelope, have been the subject of many experiments (Faria and Dickinson, 1992).

Postal surveys are particularly versatile in reaching all types of people (consumer or business), in all geographic areas, rural and urban areas, and at the same low cost. The postal survey method generally will have a cost advantage over other survey methods, though it is not cheap. The respondent has more time to formulate and record his or her answers. The questionnaire can be filled in at a time and place convenient to the respondent. However, the researcher often has little control over the postal questionnaire sample. Even with a good mailing list, it is often hard to control who at the mailing address fills out the questionnaire (Jobber, 1989). There is also the danger that the questionnaires received are either poorly filled out or incomplete, further adding to analysis problems (Becker, 1995).

Internet Surveys and Group Research

Many researchers are turning to the Internet to gain individuals' participation in surveys. The main advantage of using the Internet, instead of traditional methods, is that the information is available very quickly. Additionally, researchers can survey a greater number of people with fewer costs compared to written and mailed surveys, and data can be analysed as it is collected.

There are four main types of online surveys (Cross, 2000):
- **Pop-Up Surveys:** When an Internet surfer leaves a web site, another window containing a questionnaire pops up on the screen. Internet users have the option of either completing the survey or closing the

browser window. The response rate for this type of survey ranges from 15% to 45%

- **E-Mail or Web Surveys:** Via e-mail, a company can invite someone to participate in an online questionnaire. The response rates for these surveys range from 25% to 50% and are usually completed by the user in two to three days
- **Online Groups:** A research company can organise what is essentially a focus group discussion on the Internet. These discussions are held in chat rooms on the Internet
- **Moderated E-Mail Groups:** Researchers can carry on long discussions with individuals by communicating through e-mail. Online bulletin boards are an example of this type of research.

The choice of survey method depends on a number of factors, such as budget, geographical spread, and information required. Each method has strengths and weaknesses (detailed below in **Table 4.3**) that should be considered in advance of a decision being taken. While each method will generate information, the quality of that information pertinent to the research question will be influenced by the choice of method.

TABLE 4.3: STRENGTHS AND WEAKNESSES OF PRINCIPAL SURVEY METHODS

	Mail	Telephone	Personal	Internet
1. Flexibility	Poor	Good	Excellent	Fair
2. Quantity of data that can be collected	Good	Fair	Excellent	Good
3. Control of interviewer effects	Excellent	Fair	Poor	Excellent
4. Control of sample	Fair	Excellent	Fair	Fair
5. Speed of data collection	Poor	Excellent	Good	Excellent
6. Response rate	Poor	Good	Good	Poor
7. Cost	Good	Fair	Poor	Excellent
8. Sample frame	Good	Excellent	Fair	Poor

Source: *Principles of Marketing*, Chapter 8, p. 328, European edition, 1999, Philip Kotler *et al.*

Observation Methods

This chapter has already looked at surveys as a methodology for conducting descriptive research. Observation research is the second way to conduct descriptive research.

The term observation is usually used to refer to methods of generating data that involve the researcher immersing him/herself in a research setting and systematically observing dimensions of that setting, interactions, relationships, actions, events, and so forth. Observation involves systematically recording the behavioural patterns of people, objects, and occurrences without questioning or communicating with them. Information may be recorded as events occur or completed from records of past events.

It is rare for a research design to rely entirely on observational research. In practice, observational research is used alongside other data collection methods. The same scientific approach should be used when carrying out observational research as is applied to other types of research.

Questionnaires and Design

The data collection instrument normally associated with surveys and observation is the *questionnaire*. By definition, a questionnaire is a structured list of questions asked of the respondent (Hart and Stapleton, 1981). Other instruments, such as an interviewer checklist, can also be used.

In developing the questionnaire, attention must be paid first to:

- Defining your research objectives – What exactly is it that you need to know?
- Who are the customers to sample for this information?
- How are you going to undertake the research (for example, face-to-face on the street)?

Having confirmed the above, one is now ready to design the questionnaire, which usually consists of three sections:

- A request for cooperation
- The main body of questions
- Classification questions.

Some tips for questionnaire design include:

1. **Qualification:** Make sure that you have a screening question at the beginning, to eliminate unsuitable respondents (for example, those who never use the product/service).

2. **Length:** Keep the number of questions to a minimum. Don't ask unnecessary questions.
3. **Simplicity:** Keep the questions simple. Answers should be either Yes/No/Don't Know or offer multiple-choice alternatives.
4. **Relevancy:** Does the question relate to the topic? Each question, and each word in each question, should be viewed by the researcher and respondent as relevant.
5. **Brevity:** Questions should be 20 words or less, excluding answer categories.
6. **Objectivity:** Questions should not suggest a particular answer by leading the respondent.
7. **Non-ambiguity:** Is the question expressed clearly? Avoid unfamiliar words and words with unfamiliar meanings, as well as words such as near, much, most, few, often and occasionally. Also avoid should, could and might.
8. **Specificity:** Can potential participants answer the question? Does the question demand knowledge and information that the respondent does not have? Respondents sometimes provide answers to questions regardless of knowledge so that they do not appear ignorant.
9. **Vocabulary:** Can potential participants understand the question? Select words that the least educated respondent can understand. Use natural and familiar language.
10. **Question type:** Should the information be gathered using an open or closed question?

The design of the questionnaire is critical to obtaining the type of information that is being sought. Asking leading questions may provide the desired answer but it may not be the right answer. Leading questions may generate information that is incorrect, thus causing decisions to be taken that are not based on reality. The purpose of research is to generate good information, not information that one wishes to hear.

STAGE 4 – SAMPLING

The fourth stage of a marketing research project centres on deciding whom to talk to or observe (identifying who or what has the required information). The technical name given to this stage is *sampling* – choosing a small number of people or objects to represent the larger population or universe from which they are drawn. Many researchers like to consider this question before selecting a data collection method, as the respondent with whom one is talking can influence the form of the primary research selected.

The total group of people that the researcher wants to study is called the population. For an election opinion poll, the population would be all eligible voters. For research about a new cosmetics line, it might be all women in a certain age bracket. The sample is a representative group from this population. Researchers rarely gather information from a study's total population. If they do, the results are known as a census. Unless the total population is small, the costs of a census are very high and generally only the government can afford to conduct a census.

Once the population is defined, the next step is to search for a sampling frame, that is a list of the chosen population from which a sample can be selected. An example of a sampling frame is the register of electors, or the Kompass directory of companies. Sampling frames should be carefully checked for their adequacy, completeness, lack of duplicated entries and suitability for specific research projects (Chisnall, 1992).

Samples can be classified as either probability samples or non-probability samples. A probability sample is one that gives every member of the population a known chance of being selected. Probability samples conform to the laws of large numbers – the bases of probability theory and modern statistics. Accordingly, theoretically, it is the only type that researchers should use for statistical influence (Groebner and Shannon, 1985). Types of probability samples include simple random samples, stratified samples, and cluster samples. In a simple random sample, every member of the relevant population has an equal opportunity of selection. In a stratified sample, randomly selected sub-samples of different groups are represented in the total sample. In a cluster sample, researchers select areas (or clusters) from which they draw respondents.

In contrast, a non-probability sample is an arbitrary grouping that does not permit the use of standard statistical tests. Types of non-probability samples are convenience samples and quota samples. A convenience sample is a non-probability sample selected from among readily available respondents. Broadcasters' "on-the-street" interviews are a good example. A quota sample is a non-probability sample that is divided to maintain representation for different segments or groups. It differs from a stratified sample, in which researchers select sub-samples by some random process; in a quota sample, they hand-pick participants.

As part of sampling, the *sample size* has also to be decided upon (how many people does one talk to or observe?). Sample sizes can vary from one to many thousands and really depend on how confident the researcher wants to be about the information collected. "The more, the better" is not true of sample size. Quality is more important than size. The goal of sampling is to obtain responses from representatives of the entire population of interest. Consult a marketing research text for more information on sampling designs.

The only way to know whether your data collection instrument is ready to use is to have several people try it. This is known as pre-testing. A pre-test of the data collection instrument should be carried out on people who are as similar as possible to the research population with respect to age, education, knowledge of the market and other relevant factors.

STAGE 5 – FIELDWORK, GATHERING THE REQUIRED INFORMATION

Knowing who, what, where, how, and why, about the required information, the researcher can now begin to collect the primary data. This is often referred to as *fieldwork*.

It is in obtaining and conducting the interview that field research projects encounter most difficulties. Poor field research is usually attributable to lack of experience in interviewing and/or insufficient preparation. In conducting an interview, interpersonal techniques are very important. A cold question and answer dialogue must be avoided – instead, the interviewer should create a relationship where the interviewee actually wants to pass on information. The interviewer must be well-briefed and understand the subject fully.

STAGE 6 – ANALYSIS OF THE DATA

Once all the fieldwork is completed, the data has to be translated into information to satisfy the objectives of the study. The *analysis* stage of marketing research is about the processing or translation of data into information.

Prior to any detailed analysis, the data collection instruments and procedures must be checked for completeness and accuracy. This is data preparation and includes the functions of *editing* and *coding* the data. The data can then be entered into a computer for analysis or analysed by hand. A computer package such as Minitab, SPSS or SAS may be used. This is often referred to as *data reduction*.

Simple analysis, cross tabulations, and frequency distributions are the basic form of *data analysis* in marketing research. Measures of central tendency or location (for example, mean, mode, median) and measures of dispersion (for example, range and standard deviation) are also used to summarise the data in basic data analysis.

Data analysis should not end with summary information. It should also include some cross-tabulation of the responses. Cross-tabulation consists of analysing the responses to one question separately for each category of another question. For example, do responses of frequency of purchase vary between men and women, or between younger and older respondents? These cross-tabulations can provide valuable insights into the subject of interest.

STAGE 7 – PRESENTATION OF THE RESULTS AND FINDINGS

The final and remaining stage in any marketing research process is to communicate the findings and information to solve the problem/opportunity. This involves the researcher preparing and presenting a written report.

To write such a report, the researcher must first understand the audience for the report. If the *raison d'être* of research is to assist with decision-making through the provision of information, then the marketing research report reflects this by primarily discussing and explaining the findings and results. A brief explanation of the methodology followed should be sufficient. Limitations of the study would also be acknowledged at this point.

Table 4.4 gives a brief overview of the key points to be taken from each stage of the marketing research process. It highlights the key questions that need to be addressed and the sequence in which they should occur.

As previously stated, an expertise in this area is not necessary to undertake marketing research but understanding the process, the techniques, and the potential pitfalls aids the entrepreneur in ascertaining good information that will enable them to make better-informed decisions, thereby increasing the possibility of establishing a successful new venture.

TABLE 4.4: SUMMARY OF THE MARKETING RESEARCH PROCESS

Marketing Research Stage	Typical Concerns
Problem definition	What decision has to be made? What are the problems facing management?
Research design	What type of information is needed? How much is already known? Are we looking for insights or facts and figures? What is the aim of the study?
Data collection	What information exists within the firm? What information exists outside the firm? Do we need to gather the data ourselves? How? Where/when?
Sampling	Who has the necessary information? Where can we talk with them? How many people do we talk with?
Fieldwork	What time do we visit people? How many researchers are needed? How much are they paid? Who will supervise them?
Analysis of data	How do we translate the raw data into a meaningful picture? What computer package will we use?

CONCLUSION

Marketing research is, and will continue to be, a valuable tool in the evaluation of alternative courses of action. Information will always be required to reduce the uncertainty and risk that is inherent in all business planning. While marketing research cannot make decisions, it does significantly help with problem-solving. It is not technically very difficult but it is hard work. Consult a good marketing research text and/or bring in a consultant for advice and then just dig in and do it.

QUESTIONS

1. Describe the principal methods of gathering primary data.
2. Evaluate the different survey methods.
3. Analyse the principal differences between exploratory, descriptive, and causal research.
4. Undertake a group discussion on how to engender entrepreneurship more effectively in Irish third-level colleges.
5. "Anyone can do marketing research". Discuss.
6. Design a questionnaire to assess the attitudes of students towards facilities in your college.

USEFUL WEBSITES

www.acnielsen.com
www.ama.org
www.chambersireland.ie
www.cso.ie
www.dejanews.com
www.dnb.com
www.esomar.nl
www.gallup.com
www.google.com
www.marketresearch.org.uk
www.mintel.co.uk
www.mra-net.org
www.nua.ie
www.qrca.org
www.spss.com
www.surveysite.com
www.surveys-online.com
www.worldopinion.com

CHECKLIST FOR CHAPTER

After reading this chapter, check that you understand and appreciate:
- What is marketing research
- The role that marketing research plays in decision-making

- The types of research and the steps of a typical marketing research process
- The differences between primary and secondary data
- Marketing research techniques
- The key issues in Internet-based marketing research.

REFERENCES

Bash, A and Parasuraman, A. (1985) - Mall Intercept versus Telephone Interviewing Environment - *Journal of Advertising Research*, April – May.

Becker, E. (1995) - Automated Interviewing has Advantages - *Marketing News*, January.

Berdie, D. (1989) - Reassessing the Value of High Response Rates to Mail Surveys - *Marketing Research*, September.

Cadler, B. (1997) - Focus Groups and the Nature of Qualitative Marketing Research - *Journal of Marketing Research*, August, pp. 353-64.

Chisnall, P. (1992) - *Marketing Research* - 4th edition, McGraw-Hill, Maidenhead.

Cowan, D. (1994) - Good Information - *Journal of Market Research Society*, 36(2), pp. 105-14.

Cross, R. (1990) - Real-Time and Online Research is Paying Off - *Direct Marketing*, May.

Czaja, R. (1982) - Respondent Selection In Telephone Survey: A Comparison Of Three Techniques - *Journal of Marketing Research*, August.

Darling, E. (1998) - Banking Leaves Nothing to Chance - *Business Plus*, April.

Einstein, A and Infeld, L. (1942) - *The Evolution of Physics* - Simon and Schuster, New York, p. 95.

Faria, A.J. and Dickinson, John R. (1992) - Mail Survey Response, Speed and Cost - *Industrial Marketing Management*, February.

Greenbaum, T. (1990) - Focus Group Spurt Predicted for the 1990s - Marketing News, January.

Groebner, D. and Shannon, P. (1985) - *Business Statistics – A Decision Making Approach* - Merrill Publishing Company.

Gulledge, L. (1996) - Satisfaction Measures, *Marketing News*, October.

Hart, N. and Stapleton, J. (1981) - *Glossary of Marketing Terms* - Butterworth-Heinemann, Oxford.

Jobber, D. (1989) - An Examination of the Effects of Questionnaire Factors on Response to an Industrial Mail Survey - *International Journal of Research in Marketing*, 6(2).

Kahan, H. (1990) - One-to-Ones Should Sparkle Like The Gems They Are - *Marketing News*, September.

Knox, M. (1986) - Indepth Interviews can Reveal What's in a Name - *Marketing News*, January.

Proctor, A. (1997) - *Essentials of Marketing Research* - Pitman Publishing.

Seymour, H. (1996) - Conducting and Using Customer Surveys - *Marketing News*, September.

Sokolow, H. (1985) – In-depth Interviews Increasing in Importance - *Marketing News*, September.

Tull, D. and Hawkins, D. (1990) - *Marketing Research* – Macmillan, New York.

Tyebjee, T. (1979) - Telephone Survey Methods: The State of the Art - *Journal of Marketing Research*, Summer.

FURTHER READING

Domegan, C. and Fleming, D. (1999) - *Marketing Research in Ireland: Theory and Practice* – Dublin: Gill and MacMillan. (Second edition forthcoming 2003.)

Malhotra, N. (2002) - *Basic Marketing Research: Applications to Contemporary Issues* - Prentice-Hall.

Proctor, A. (2002) - *Essentials of Marketing Research* - 2nd edition, Prentice-Hall.

Webb, J. (2002) - *Understanding and Designing Marketing Research* - 2nd edition, Thompson Publishing.

Zikmund, W. (2002) - *Exploring Marketing Research* - 8th edition, Thomson Publishing.

CHAPTER 5

INTELLECTUAL PROPERTY

Niall Rooney, Cathal Lane** and Sinead Dunne****

LEARNING OBJECTIVES

- To define intellectual property
- To understand what is meant by patents, trade marks, copyright, and registered designs
- To analyse the different methods of achieving legal protection
- To examine the legal process involved for each method.

INTRODUCTION

Intellectual property can be described generally as anything arising from the exercise of human creativity or ingenuity. Legally, however, it means the property rights that arise as a result of certain forms of intellectual creation and which are exercisable against third parties. These rights include patents, trade marks, copyright, and registered designs, which will be discussed in detail in this chapter. But first, it is best to understand what is meant by each of these terms so that it will be easier for the reader to appreciate how each method relates to the others. The standard interpretations for these terms are:

---

*   Niall Rooney is a Solicitor and European Trade Mark Attorney with Tomkins & Co.
**   Cathal Lane is a European, Irish and UK Patent Attorney with Tomkins & Co.
*** Sinéad Dunne is a Patent Specialist and Trade Mark Attorney with Tomkins & Co.

- **Intellectual Property:** A group of legal personal property rights arising from intellectual creation – for example patents, copyrights, trade marks or registered designs
- **Patent:** A property right, limited for a specific term of years, that grants the owner certain exclusive rights against third parties in relation to using, or doing other restricted acts in relation to, the subject matter of an invention
- **Registered Trade Mark:** A property right, renewable for potentially indefinite terms of years, that grants the owner certain exclusive rights against third parties in relation to using the registered trade mark (or confusingly similar marks) in relation to particular goods and/or services
- **Copyright:** A property right under which the author of certain works has the right to authorise or prevent copying of the work, making the work available to the public, or making an adaptation of the work
- **Registered Design:** A property right, renewable for a finite period, that grants the owner the exclusive right to use, and to authorise others to use, particular design features of an article
- **Passing Off:** A common law economic tort, namely a misrepresentation resulting in damage, or likely damage, to another party's reputation or goodwill.

This chapter will offer fuller details on each of these terms but, as in the case of any abridged commentary, the text below is merely an overview and readers with particular queries should seek professional advice.

PATENTS

The main objective of a patent is to protect an invention. Each country has its own statutory provisions for the granting of patents. In Ireland the current main legislation is the Patents Act, 1992. Ireland is also a member of the European Patent Convention, whereby a European patent can be granted covering Ireland (and over 20 other European countries).

Unlike some other intellectual property rights, there is no form of protection that automatically protects an invention. While one can keep information secret, it is not legally protected if it makes its way into the public domain legitimately. If secret information is disclosed by breach of confidence, legal proceedings might be taken on this ground. However, the protection of secrecy might be irrevocably lost as a result.

Reasons for obtaining patent protection include:

- Creation of an exclusive right in a (niche) area of technology
- Strong legal protection of valuable information (otherwise the high investment costs incurred in the innovation may be wasted because of the negligible or low cost of copying/imitation)
- Generation of revenue (for example, creating investment incentive or through direct income under patent royalties)
- Creation of an asset, namely a legal property right
- Creation of a favourable tax regime (in Ireland, tax relief may apply to income generated by a patented invention)
- Monopoly right for a fixed term (the term of a patent is generally 20 years).

Patent rights are granted to those who seek them. Most countries operate systems that grant patent rights to the person who is first to file a patent application for an invention.

Most countries are members of a system that enables an application to be filed in one country, with later applications in other countries within 12 months based on the initial application (claiming "priority"). National patents or regional patents (such as the European patent) can also be obtained. An International (PCT) application exists (for over 100 countries), which has some advantages, but there is no system whereby a single patent provides international coverage.

To be patentable, an invention must be novel (new) and inventive (at the date of filing the patent application), among other things. The terms novel and inventive usually have no geographical restriction and, for most countries, every disclosure (including one's own) counts. If one were to disclose an invention in a non-confidential manner one day and file an application for it the next day, the application may be invalid due to the prior disclosure. Confidentiality prior to patenting is essential.

A patent is usually directed to an inventive product or a process, with a technical function or character. Examples include processes, chemical compositions and drugs, biological materials such as genes, electronic equipment, and computer programs.

A patent is a registered right. One must file a patent application in, or for, the countries of interest. An application includes an official form, a patent specification, and an official fee. A search may be conducted against the invention to determine if it is patentable and an Examiner may be appointed to carry out an objective examination process.

The patent specification is the key document. It:

- Describes the invention in relation to its technical field
- Describes in detail at least one way the invention may be carried out
- Most importantly, includes one or more "claims", which are one sentence statements defining the scope and protection for the invention.

The claim wording must define the invention sufficiently generically so as to cover the "heart" of the invention so that minor adaptations will not escape infringement — but not so broadly that it encompasses known technology. Once written, usually the specification cannot be amended to add anything new, so it is important to think through the inventive concept thoroughly.

If, and when granted, the patent is enforceable. Relevant products can then be marked with the granted patent number. While a patent application is pending, the words "patent pending" can be used.

A patent is normally subject to the payment of renewal fees (in most countries, on an annual basis) to keep it in force.

An application for revocation can be taken by a third party after the patent has been granted. Usually this is done on the basis that the patent is invalid (the wording of the claims encompasses technology known before the application filing date – in other words,, the claims are not novel and/or inventive).

Patent law provides that the right to the grant of a patent resides with the inventor(s). Any other person/entity wishing to own the patent must show derivation of rights from the inventor(s). Accordingly, there are implications for employer/employee relationships and co-operating parties. Prior written agreement as to the ownership of rights developed under any project is advisable.

A granted patent gives the owner exclusive rights that prevent third parties from:
- Making, offering, putting on the market or using a product that is the subject matter of the patent
- Importing or stocking the product for those purposes;
- Using a process that is the subject matter of the patent.

The product of a process, in which the process is the subject of a granted patent, is also usually similarly protected. Where infringement is found, an injunction can be granted, damages awarded, profits calculated and awarded, and/or delivery up/destruction of infringing goods ordered.

Normally, patent owners will exploit the technology themselves, sell (partially or outright) the patent to an interested party, or licence it to such a party. Many modern companies try to create value in their companies by protecting as much as possible with patents and other intellectual property. This is a useful enticement to attract investors.

Searching patent databases is a rich source of technological and commercial information. Through patent searching, one can:

- Identify technology being pursued by a competitor
- Identify technology which is not protected in a country of interest (patents are territorial in nature) and thus potentially exploit it in that country
- Evaluate one's own technology (is it out of date?) against that of others
- Rank competitors in terms of patenting activity, technology, etc.

The searches may highlight potential problems and it is advisable to conduct a patent "clearance" search before commercialisation of an invention. A granted patent is not a shield that provides immunity from infringement of another's rights. It only gives a right to take an action against a party infringing the rights granted by the patent.

Because of the legal technicalities involved in patenting, it is essential for an entrepreneur to seek professional advice from a patent attorney on obtaining a patent for their idea.

TRADE MARKS

A trade mark distinguishes the goods or services of one trader from those of others. A trade mark is usually a word (or words), a symbol or a logo, or a combination of these. The word may be a name, dictionary word, or combination of letters. A label, product "get up", packaging or even the distinctive shape of a product may be a trade mark.

There are two ways of gaining protection in Ireland in a trade mark, such as a name or a brand. The first arises under the common law through use of the name or brand. The second arises under statute, namely registration as a registered trade mark.

Common law rights can be enforced by way of an action for "passing off". This provides protection for names or signs that have been used in the marketplace, and which have acquired a reputation and goodwill. The classic case of passing off is where one trader misrepresents his goods or services as those of another and this causes damage to the second trader's reputation or goodwill. To succeed in an action for passing off, the plaintiff must be able to show (a) a reputation or goodwill in the name or sign, (b) a misrepresentation made by the defendant, and (c) damage or likelihood of damage to the plaintiff's goodwill or reputation. However, the passing off remedy is dependent on substantial trade use and the building up of a reputation and goodwill, which can take years to accrue. Proving a case for passing off can be difficult and expensive as it is based on common law principles rather than statute law or a registration.

The second way of protecting a name or sign is to register it as a registered trade mark. In Ireland, the relevant law is contained mainly in the Trade Marks Act, 1996. It is very important for a business to register its names and brands as registered trade marks, since it can take years of use to build up common law passing off rights, and these rights can be difficult to prove and enforce. In addition, the mere registration of a company name, domain name, or registered business name will not grant any exclusive property rights in a name. Accordingly, the best way to protect a name or brand is by trade mark registration.

The principal reasons to register trade marks include:
- The only way to adequately protect a start-up trading or product name
- Grants a legal property right;
- Grants exclusivity in your name or brand in your product field
- Renewable potentially forever (every 10 years on payment of renewal fees)
- Can be licensed, transferred or mortgaged
- A return on the financial investment in creating the brand
- Could become your most valuable asset.

The mark to be registered must have some distinctiveness and must not be directly descriptive of the goods or services in relation to which it is used or intended to be used. Generic words in the particular trade cannot be registered. An invented word (or words) is an ideal trade mark. A dictionary word that has no meaning in the context of the goods or services is also a good trade mark. A slightly, or covertly, descriptive word or words may also be registerable. A symbol (on its own, or with a word or words) may also be a good trade mark. Some of the best known trade marks are surnames or geographical names, but these are not ideal for new businesses as it can take years of substantial use to build up distinctiveness in these names so that they can be registered.

A trade mark must be registered for a specific list of goods and/or services, which are classified into one or more of 45 classes according to an international system. Applications are filed (usually by, and with the advice of, a Trade Mark Attorney) with the Patents Office or the relevant official body in other countries.

Taking an Irish trade mark application as an example, after filing, a Patents Office Examiner reviews the trade mark for distinctiveness and checks for any earlier trade mark rights on the register (earlier trade mark applications or registrations covering the same or similar mark and the same or similar goods or services). The Examiner may raise objections at this stage. If all is in order, the application proceeds to publication in the Patents Office Journal and a three-month opposition period follows, during which any person claiming earlier rights (including earlier trade mark rights on the register and earlier user rights) may file opposition to the registration during that period. If no opposition arises, the application proceeds to registration. The trade mark is deemed registered as of the filing date. Registered trade marks may be renewed every 10 years thereafter on payment of official fees.

When registered, the symbol "®" or words like "Registered Trade Mark" may be used to indicate that the mark is registered, but this is not mandatory. However, while the mark is unregistered or a pending application, it is an offence to use such indicators, although the symbol "™" or the mere words "Trade Mark" may be used without penalty.

A registered trade mark grants the owner exclusive rights in the registered mark as of the filing date, namely the right to prevent use or registration of a later mark that is:

• Identical to the registered trade mark, and is used or to be registered for identical or similar goods/services
• Confusingly similar to the registered trade mark, and is used or to be registered for identical or similar goods/services

The consequences of registered trade mark infringement can be severe. Remedies granted by the Court can include an injunction, payment of money damages, delivery and destruction of materials, and account of profits. Not knowing that a conflicting registration exists is not a defence.

Ideally, a trade mark should be registered in the separate countries where it is intended to be used. If the European Union is the territory of interest, it is possible to file a single Community Trade Mark application covering the whole of the European Union. This can be quite cost-effective. Under an international convention, it is possible to file an Irish or Community Trade Mark application first and, up to six months later, apply to register the same trade mark in other foreign countries claiming the filing date of the first application. Another option is to file an International Registration under the Madrid Protocol. Under this system, Irish entities can apply to register their mark in multiple countries (over 50 countries) in one procedure.

Trade mark searches in the countries of interest are important before using or applying to register a new trade mark. It is also advisable to do "in use" searches of the marketplace as there could be earlier user rights that might conflict. Internet searches (web or domain names) are no substitute for proper trade mark searching of trade marks registers and the marketplace.

COPYRIGHT

Copyright is the right of the creator of a work to stop others copying the work. There is no registration procedure for copyright under Irish law – the copyright arises by operation of law upon creation of the work. The current law is contained mainly in the Copyright and Related Rights Act, 2000. Copyright arises in respect of:

- Original literary, dramatic, musical or artistic works
- Sound recordings, films, broadcasts or cable programmes
- The typographical arrangement of published editions
- Original databases.

Copyright arises most commonly in relation to original literary, dramatic, musical or artistic works. The term "original" work does not mean unique or new, but simply that the creator of the work produced it independently by the exercise of his own skill and effort. The term "literary work" does not imply literary quality or merit in the ordinary sense of the word. Examples of literary works include printed documents, a computer program, a set of rules, timetables, or directories.

The copyright is owned by the "author" of the work. This is usually the creator of the work, for example, the writer of a printed work, or the artist in the case of a drawing. In other cases, the "author" is defined by the Act. For example, the "author" of a sound recording is deemed to be the "producer". An important exception arises where a work is created by an employee in the course of employment. Here, the employer is the owner of the copyright, subject to any agreement to the contrary.

As copyright arises by operation of law and not by registration, it can be difficult to prove the existence and ownership of copyright in a particular work. It is important to document properly all relevant materials and facts to ensure that the existence and ownership of the copyright can be proven if required. Copyright protection is for a finite term of years depending on the type of work. These terms are substantial, meaning that copyright can be a powerful and enduring right. Examples of copyright terms include:

- A literary, dramatic, musical or artistic work – Term expires 70 years after the death of the author
- An original database – Term expires 70 years after the death of the author
- A sound recording – Term expires 50 years after the sound recording is made, or 50 years after the date it was first lawfully made available to the public.

It is an infringement of copyright in a particular work to do any of the following without authorisation:

- Copy the work
- Make the work available to the public
- Make an adaptation of the work.

The term copying is defined broadly and includes, for example, storing the work in any medium. The concept of making the work available is also broadly defined and includes, for example, making the work available for copying by on-demand wire or wireless means including on the Internet.

There are also other secondary acts that can constitute an infringement of copyright. Examples include knowingly dealing in the copyright-protected work (for example, selling, renting, lending, offering, importing other than for private use, possessing in the course of business), or knowingly providing means for making infringing copies of the work. Such secondary acts may also attract criminal penalties.

There may be a limited "fair dealing" defence to infringement available, but this only applies in restricted circumstances – for example copying for private research or study, or for the purposes of criticism or review. It is not an infringement of copyright for a lawful user of a computer program to make a back-up copy of the program for lawful use. Other lawful copying includes copying for the purposes of achieving interoperability of another independently-created program, copying for the purposes of error correction, and copying for the purposes of testing or observing the functioning of a program (provided certain conditions are met).

The author of a copyright-protected work may exercise two "moral" rights. These are the right to be identified as the author (the "paternity" right) and the right to object to derogatory treatment of a work that would prejudice his/her reputation (the "integrity" right). These moral rights last as long as the copyright term in the work lasts.

REGISTERED DESIGNS

A registered design is a form of protection granted for novel features of the appearance of a product. In Ireland, the current law is contained mainly in the Industrial Designs Act, 2001.

A design may be registered for the appearance of the whole or part of a product resulting from the features – in particular, the lines, contours, colours, shape, texture or materials – of the product itself or its ornamentation. Products for which registration may be sought include any industrial or handicraft item, packaging or graphic symbols. Features of appearance of a product that are solely dictated by technical function are not registerable as designs.

The design must be new and have individual character. A design is considered to be new, if no identical design was made available to the public anywhere before the date of the application for registration. A design will be considered identical to another design, if their features differ only in immaterial details that are commonly used in the trade. In order to have individual character, a design must create an overall impression on the informed user that is different from the overall impression produced on such a user by any design that was publicly available before the date of filing the application.

Within the EU, a "grace period" applies, whereby a valid application for registration of a design can be filed within 12 months of non-confidential disclosure of the design by the designer or someone legitimately authorised to do so; outside the EU, the grace period may not be available.

Applications to register a design are filed usually through a Patent or Trade Mark Attorney. Any person claiming to be the proprietor of a design may apply to register the design but the author, namely the creator of the design, is usually the proprietor of the design unless the right to the registered design is transferred (for example, from employee to employer). Some jurisdictions allow registration of two or more designs in a single application, a so-called "multiple design application".

The design application may be examined for registerability (new/individual character/conflict with any earlier application or registration). If the application is in order, the design proceeds to registration. The procedure is usually completed quite quickly (typically within a few months). In most countries, the term of protection is five years from the date of registration, and is renewable at five-year intervals up to a total term of protection of 25 years. The design is deemed to be registered as of the filing date. Once registered, the owner should label the product "Registered Design No. xxx" to indicate that the design is registered.

A registered design is a monopoly right conferred on the proprietor. The legal property right conferred by the registered design can be licensed, transferred, or mortgaged, similar to other property. Registered designs may be valuable assets, particularly to a business that is primarily involved in making products whose appearance is a major selling point.

Typically, a registered design confers on its owner the exclusive right to use the design and to authorise others to use it, including the right to make, offer, put on the market, import or use a product in which the design is incorporated or to which it is applied, or to stock such a product for those purposes. The rights conferred are granted on registration and are backdated to the filing date of the application. A registered design gives the proprietor the exclusive right to prevent third parties not having his consent from applying the same design or a design not substantially different from the registered design to a product. Hence, a registered design gives the proprietor the exclusive right to the design as such rather than solely to the design when applied to the product for which it was registered. Remedies that may be granted by the Court can include an injunction, seizure of infringing products or articles, delivery up, damages or an account of profits.

A design can be registered in the individual countries where it is intended to be made or used. The procedure is similar to that in Ireland, although advice should be sought from a Patent or Trade Mark Attorney in the relevant country. Under an international convention, it is possible to file an Irish design application and, up to six months later, apply to register the same design in other foreign countries claiming the filing date of the Irish application.

A new system for European design protection has recently been introduced. European Union (EU) Council Regulation No. 6/2002 entered into force on 6 March 2002. It introduces two forms of protection:

- A Registered European Design Right
- An Unregistered European Design Right.

The European Registered Design offers a single unitary right covering all EU member countries. This is quite a cost-effective method of obtaining protection in several EU countries.

The European Unregistered Design Right runs for a three-year period, which comes into existence automatically by making the products incorporating the designs available to the public on or after 6 March 2002. The proprietor of an unregistered design right must prove copying to benefit from any remedies.

CONCLUSION

The protection of intellectual property may offer an entrepreneur a competitive advantage that may be profitable and sustainable for many years. Where an entrepreneur has an idea that they believe is unique, then they should take expert advice immediately. It is important to note that an invention cannot be patented once it has entered the public domain (where it has been made known to someone other than the inventor/innovator/creator/entrepreneur). Confidentiality agreements can be signed that will offer protection, but again it is best to seek professional advice before drafting or signing such agreements.

In an attempt to bootstrap operations, many entrepreneurs will take financial short-cuts. However, protecting your idea, invention, design, or trade mark legally is not an area in which to take chances, since the money saved in the short-term may result in a loss later. Remember, as regards patent and registered design protection, once the invention or design is made public, it is usually too late to claim legal protection. On the other hand, a trade mark can be registered whether it has been disclosed or not, and copyright protection arises on creation and, while not required to be registered, should be properly documented.

QUESTIONS

1. Explain what is meant by the terms: Patents, trade marks, copyright, and registered designs.
2. Visit the website www.patentsoffice.ie and detail the opportunity offered there for an Irish entrepreneur to protect a new product idea legally.
3. Discuss the protection of material written by a songwriter through copyrighting.
4. Describe how the registration of a trade mark benefits an organisation.

USEFUL WEBSITES

www.epo.org
www.ipr-helpdesk.org
www.oami.eu.int
www.patent.gov.uk
www.patentsoffice.ie
www.uspto.gov
www.wipo.int

CHECKLIST FOR CHAPTER

After reading this chapter, check that you understand and appreciate:
• The term intellectual property
• What is meant by patents, trade marks, copyright, and registered designs
• The different methods of achieving legal protection
• The legal process involved for each method.

REFERENCES

Clark, R. and Smyth, S. (1997) - *Irish Intellectual Property Law* – Butterworths, Dublin.

Phillips, J and Firth, A. (1999) - *An Introduction to Intellectual Property Law* – Butterworths, Dublin.

McMahon, B. and Binchy, W. (2000) - *Irish Law of Torts* – Butterworths, Dublin.

Byrne, R. and McCutcheon, P. (2001) - *The Irish Legal System* – Butterworths, Dublin.

CHAPTER 6

LEGAL ISSUES

*Michael Purtill**

LEARNING OBJECTIVES

- To understand the advantages and disadvantages of the different legal structures available to a start-up enterprise
- To examine the broad requirements of employment law
- To understand the legal implications of health and safety
- To introduce the concept of contract law.

INTRODUCTION

An enterprise cannot be created and sustained without a wide range of laws and regulations impacting upon its operations. Once the venture has been created, some legal status must be decided, even in the simple situation of being a sole trader. But the entrepreneur must also be familiar with employment law should they employ any personnel, with health and safety for employees, customers, and other stakeholders, and with contract law for agreements into which they might enter. It is advisable that an entrepreneur secures the services of a good legal representative, as legal protection is of critical importance to the enterprise and the personal assets of the entrepreneur. This chapter introduces the broader legal issues of which the entrepreneur should have an understanding.

---

* Michael Purtill is a barrister-at-law.

LEGAL TRADING STRUCTURES

There are essentially four types of legal trading structure an enterprise can take:

- Sole trader
- Partnership
- Company
- Co-operative[2].

Every business has a legal trading structure. Even if an entrepreneur never fills out any forms or takes any steps to assume a legal trading structure, once they commence trading, they automatically become a sole trader. The vast majority of businesses operate as either a private limited company or as a sole trader.

Sole Trader

What is a sole trader? A sole trader can be defined as a person who sets up and owns a business with a view to making a profit while assuming personal responsibility for all the debts of the business. The word "sole" refers to the fact that there is one owner of the business and not to the number of employees. A sole trader can have any number of employees working in the business.

As stated above, the entrepreneur automatically adopts the status of sole trader once they commence trading. However, to ensure compliance with all legal requirements, it is advisable to be more proactive than this in becoming a sole trader. Sometimes licences must be obtained before it is legal to commence trading – for example, a licence must be obtained to run a public house, or to set up an employment agency.

Other possible requirements include registering a business name. A sole trader need only apply for this where the name of the proposed business is different to their own surname. Where there is an add-on to the sole trader's name, then the business name must be registered. For example, if a sole trader decided to trade under their own name of "John O'Brien", then there would be no need to register a business name. However, if they decided to call the business, "Electrical Appliances' or "John O'Brien Electrical Appliances", then they would have to register this business name.

---

[2] Co-operatives are rarely used as a means of setting up a business.

A business name can be registered at the Companies Registration Office in Parnell Square in Dublin, using the RNB1 form. This is relatively inexpensive and must be done for the following reasons:

- It is a legal requirement. Failure to register a business name does not preclude somebody from being a sole trader but non-registration is a minor criminal offence
- Lending institutions can look for a certificate of business name registration
- In order to obtain a ".ie" presence on the Internet, it will be necessary for a sole trader whose business name is different to his own surname to provide the certificate of business name registration.

In choosing a business name, caution should be exercised, as it may be unlawful to use a name already in use. Consequently, it is prudent to check whether the proposed name is already in use. This may be checked by inspecting the Register of Business Names and the Register of Companies[3]. The Trade Marks Register should also be checked.

The sole trader will also have to register for tax and, possibly, Value Added Tax (VAT). Registration for tax can be done after commencement of trading, but fines and penalties can be imposed in the event of excessive delay in registering.

While insurance is not a legal necessity for most businesses, there are some exceptions to this general rule. One example is childminding, where pursuant to the Childcare Act 1991 childminders must have insurance.

Advantages
The advantages of being a sole trader are:
- A sole trader is answerable to him/herself alone
- They are the sole recipient of all profits
- They need only show their accounts to the Revenue and to nobody else
- There are fewer formalities to be complied with in setting up and running the business of sole trader than in any other legal trading structure.

Disadvantages
The disadvantages of being a sole trader are:
- They are personally liable for all losses of the business

---

[3]   These may be checked, free of charge, using the search facility at www.cro.ie.

- Their personal assets, including family home and non-business assets, may have to be sold to discharge business debts
- The business does not have a separate legal entity and, if involved in litigation, it is the sole trader themselves as opposed to the business that is sued.

While this is the simplest form of legal entity, being a sole trader carries the greatest danger of personal liability risk and therefore is considered undesirable by many entrepreneurs. It offers little protection against their personal assets (for example, their home) being taken and is frequently deemed to be an unwarranted risk.

Partnerships

A partnership can be defined as a "relationship that subsists between persons carrying on a business in common with a view to profit". At least two partners are required and, generally, the maximum is set at 20 partners. A private limited company can be a partner in a partnership.

A partnership can be set up by means of a written partnership agreement signed by all partners. Alternatively, a partnership can arise through the conduct of two or more people in their business practices – even where the partners never actually agreed to enter into a partnership. A partnership may be deemed to exist if there is a pooling of assets and a sharing of profits. If there is no written agreement or if the written agreement is not comprehensive, then the Partnership Act 1890[4] will provide the legal framework to govern the relationship between the partners and also the relationships between the partnership and those with whom it trades. If the business name of a partnership is anything other than the true names of the partners, then it must be registered at the Companies Registration Office, using the RBN1A.

Advantages

The advantages of a partnership are:
- A partnership that has been established on foot of a well-thought-out and comprehensive partnership agreement allows for people to pool resources and carry on a business in a structured way
- Privacy may be well served in that only the Revenue Commissioners are entitled to inspect the accounts of the partnership.

---

[4] The Partnership Act 1890 can be obtained from the Government Publications Office.

Disadvantages

The disadvantages of a partnership are:

- Personal liability: Partners are liable for all debts of the business once the debts were incurred while they were partners. This is significant because a partner may be responsible for the debts incurred by all of his partners provided they were incurred on behalf of the business. Careful selection of business partners is therefore essential.
- If there is no written agreement or there is an incomprehensive agreement, then it may be extremely difficult to prove its terms in the event of a dispute between partners.

Partnerships are most commonly found in areas of professional services such as solicitors, doctors, accountants, and dentists.

Private Limited Company

A private limited company[5] limited by share is a legal mechanism of creating a separate and artificial legal entity that permits a businessperson who is trading to avail of limited liability towards potential and actual creditors in the event of the business being wound up. "Limited liability" means that, at worst, the owners of the company (the shareholders) will only have to pay a limited sum of money (determined at the time of formation of the company) to the creditors. Limited liability may be lost where there has been non-compliance with the Companies Acts.

The following are required before a company can be set up:

- **Shareholders:** A minimum of one and a maximum of 50 is set out in the Companies Acts
- **Directors:** A minimum of two directors is required. In certain circumstances, directors may be made personally liable for the debts of the company. These circumstances include fraud, reckless trading, and failure to keep proper books of account where such failure led to the company's demise
- **Secretary:** One secretary is required.[6]

---

[5] There are other types of companies including a public limited company and a private limited company limited by guarantee. However, the private limited company limited by share is the type of company most favoured and most suited to those setting up a business.

[6] There is a useful booklet available from the Companies Registration Office on the Secretary's duties.

In terms of personnel, at least two people are required in the setting up of a private limited company. One person can fill the role of shareholder, director, and secretary. A second person will be required to be a director. The existence of a company can never come about unintentionally. Positive and specific steps must be taken before a company can be created: Two documents – the Articles of Association and the Memorandum of Association – must be compiled. In addition, a form called the A1 form must be completed and returned to the Companies Office. A fee must also be paid. A company can be set up by complying with the above requirements oneself or by using the services of an agent who specialises in setting up companies for others.

Prior to trading, the certificate of incorporation must be obtained from the Companies Registration Office and the first directors' meeting must be held. A company seal must also be obtained. Once the company has been set up, then the business is said to be incorporated.

There are certain on-going requirements that must be complied with by all companies. These include the holding of annual general meetings, keeping of proper accounts, and compiling and keeping registers of directors and shareholders.

The name of a company is automatically afforded a certain amount of protection, provided it is not identical, or overly similar, to the name of another business. The best way to protect any business name is to register a trade mark at the Patents Office (see **Chapter 5**).

A company is a separate legal entity and will exist until it is formally brought to an end. This can be done by liquidation. Alternatively, if the company has no assets and no liabilities, then a letter to the Companies Registration Office may suffice.

Advantages

The main advantages of incorporation are:

- There is limited liability. However, if a personal guarantee is given by a shareholder, then the guarantor, if called upon by the lending institution, will have to discharge this debt out of their own personal assets. Limited liability does not absolve the guarantor of discharging this debt
- There may be tax advantages. Advice should be sought from the appropriate advisors before incorporation
- Incorporation imposes a discipline in that all monies spent must be carefully accounted for and recorded.

TABLE 6.1: CONTRASTING THE DIFFERENT LEGAL STRUCTURES FOR BUSINESS

	Sole Trader	Partnership	Private Limited Company
Owners/ Members	1	2 — 20 (50)	1 — 50
Liability	Personal liability	Personal liability	Limited liability, subject to personal guarantees, fraudulent and reckless trading and serious non-compliance with Companies Acts 1963-2001
Set-up formalities	Sole trader status is automatic May need to register a business name May need a licence Must register for tax	Can arise by implication — better to have a written agreement Partnership Act of 1890 may apply in the event of "gaps"	Never automatic A1 form, Memorandum and Articles of Association and cheque required Two directors, one secretary required Seal, certificate of incorporation and first directors' meeting
On-going formalities	Tax and possibly the renewal of any licence	Depends on agreement	Registers / Meetings / Minutes / Annual returns / Directors' duties / Secretary's duties / Accounts Compliance with Memorandum and Articles Compliance with Companies Acts 1963-2001
Number of employees	Any number	Any number	Any number
Tax rate	Personal tax rates	Personal tax rates	Corporation tax rates, with some special rates and reliefs
Decision-making	Sole trader decides	Partners decide	Directors decide on day-to-day running of business Shareholders wield some power at Annual General Meetings
Termination	Need only close the door	As provided by agreement or on death of partner or by court order	Letter to Companies Registration Office in certain circumstances Liquidation

Disadvantages

The main disadvantages of incorporation are:

- There must be compliance with many formalities
- Members of the public are entitled to view some of the company's accounts
- There may be some tax disadvantages – again, appropriate professional advice should be taken.

Establishing a limited company requires more by way of legal compliance but it does offer greater protection against liability, thereby reducing the risk to the personal assets of the entrepreneur.

The choice of legal structure will be influenced by the type of business that is being entered into, the level of risk that the entrepreneur is willing to take concerning the protection of their personal assets, and the level of work that they are prepared to undertake regarding legal compliance. It is a decision whose importance is frequently underestimated, yet it can have a significant impact on the business and the entrepreneur in later years.

EMPLOYMENT LAW

There is an ever-increasing volume of legislation, mainly EU-driven, aimed at protecting the employee. Employees' awareness of their rights, coupled with employers' uncertainty as to their own obligations, ensures that employers are often exposed to various claims and litigation costs.

Part-time employees have essentially the same statutory protection as full-time employees. Employees and prospective employees have a number of avenues open to them in seeking redress. These include the Rights Commissioners, the Labour Court, the Employment Appeals Tribunal, and the ordinary courts in this jurisdiction.

There are a large number of legal issues that an entrepreneur should be aware of when considering employing a person, including:

- **Discrimination:** The Employment Equality Act 1998 prohibits discrimination by employers on nine specific grounds: Marital status, family status, sexual orientation, religion, age, disability, race, and membership of the Traveller community. An employer may not discriminate against any of his own employees or against any prospective employees. It is unlawful to advertise for "young dynamic people" (on the "age" ground), or for a "cleaning lady" (on the gender ground). Even if the interviewee or the job applicant who has been discriminated against never had any realistic chance of getting the job on the basis of inexperience or insufficient qualifications, then they may still make a claim for discrimination.

- **Job specification:** The job specification must not tend to discriminate on any of the above grounds. Essentially, the job specification sets out the various duties and responsibilities associated with the job. It may also set out the traits and characteristics that a job applicant will need to possess to perform the job properly. This is the foundation of safe and proper recruitment and should be fully attended to before entertaining job applications and interviews. In order for the recruitment process to be seen as transparent, there should be some form of scoring system whereby the candidate whose traits best mirror the traits set out in this job specification should get the highest score and be offered the job.

- **Application forms:** An application form is generally preferred to a curriculum vita as a means of initially obtaining appropriate information from job applicants. It allows the employer to ask a defined set of questions of all applicants. It also enables the employer to sift through the applications in a more administratively-friendly manner.

- **Shortlisting:** Employers must be able to justify the elimination of candidates at this stage. The use of a scoring system is recommended in this regard.

- **Interviews:** Interviewers should be trained and, where possible, should adhere to a pre-selected list of questions for all candidates. Notes of all interviews should be kept for a minimum of one year. Questions that infringe upon the nine grounds of discrimination ought not to be asked, except where they are necessary, can be justified, and where they are asked of all candidates. Interviewers should highlight the duties and responsibilities associated with the job and ascertain whether the candidates are ready willing and able to undertake and perform these. The interview notes should record the reasons for the selection and non-selection of candidates.

- **References:** Employers are generally not legally obliged to furnish references. Employers should however try to obtain references from a prospective employee's previous employer(s) before employing staff.

- **Job offer:** This should be made only after a medical report and references have been obtained and evaluated carefully.

- **Written contract:** While a full and comprehensive written contract is not a legal requirement, the Terms of Employment (Information) Act 1994 sets out certain terms of the contract that must be available to the employee in writing. These include the full names of the employer and the employee, the place of work, details of rest breaks, and the date on which employment commenced. An employer must furnish these terms within two months of the employee commencing employment.
- **Probationary period:** This is the period during which an employee is being assessed to determine their suitability for employment, and are provided for in many contracts of employment. If an employee is dismissed during such a period, then they will usually not be able to bring a case under the unfair dismissals legislation.
- **Disciplinary procedures:** An employer should have a disciplinary procedure in place that sets out the standards of conduct and behaviour required of employees and the sanctions that may be imposed for non-compliance with these standards. The imposition of any sanctions must be in strict compliance with fair procedures, including the employee's right to respond to any complaint against them, and their right to be represented at a fair hearing. The purpose of a disciplinary procedure should be to improve the employee's performance rather than to dismiss or punish the employee. However, if the employee's performance does not improve after the disciplinary procedure has been complied with, or if the employee is guilty of gross misconduct, then the ultimate sanction of dismissal may be necessary. A code of practice on disciplinary procedures is contained in Statutory Instrument 146 of 2000.[7]
- **Annual leave:** The Organisation of Working Time Act 1997 sets out employees' minimum annual leave entitlement. An employee who has worked a minimum of 1,365 hours will be entitled to four weeks annual leave. Part-time employees are entitled to annual leave on a *pro rata* basis. Employees are entitled to be paid while on annual leave. Essentially, it is the employer who decides on the timing of the annual leave.
- **Parental leave:** The Parental Leave Act 1998 provides that employees with one year's service are entitled to take parental leave. This is unpaid leave, which either parent can take where they have a child

---

[7]   This is available from the Government Publications Office.

under the age of five years. The maximum leave allowable is 14 weeks. It can be taken in one block or, with the employer's consent, in separate periods. The employer must receive notice of the employee's intention to take this leave.

- **Force majeure leave:** The Parental Leave Act 1998 introduced "force majeure" leave. This leave entitles an employee to paid leave where, for urgent family reasons, the presence of the employee is indispensable owing to an illness or injury to a close family member. This leave is subject to a maximum of three days over a 12-month period and subject to a maximum of five days over a 36-month period.
- **Rest periods:** The Organisation of Working Time Act 1997 provides that employees are entitled to certain rest periods. Generally, an employee is entitled to a minimum break of 15 minutes in a four-and-a-half hour work-period and a break of 30 minutes in a six-hour work-period.
- **Minimum wage:** The National Minimum Wage Act 2000 provides that employees are guaranteed a minimum wage. From October 2002, the rate is €6.35. Some employees are not entitled to the minimum wage, such as those under 18 and those who are undergoing certain training.
- **Payslip:** An employee is entitled to receive a pay slip under the Payment of Wages Act 1991.
- **Sick pay:** There is no statutory right to sick pay. However, the contract of employment may provide for sick pay entitlements.
- **Dismissal:** Employers must be very careful in dismissing their employees. If an employee has been improperly dismissed, they may be able to seek redress *inter alia* by bringing an unfair dismissals action in the Employment Appeals Tribunal under unfair dismissal legislation. Alternatively, the employee may sue the employer in the courts for wrongful dismissal.
- **Notice:** Unless an employee is being dismissed pursuant to their contract of employment for gross misconduct, then they will be entitled to notice. The length of notice to which they will be entitled will depend on the contract of employment, which cannot provide for less notice than the employee would be entitled to under the Minimum Notice and Terms of Employment Acts. This legislation provides that the employer must give one week's notice to the employee who has been employed for between 13 weeks and two years, and up to eight weeks for those who have been employed for

15 years or more. Unless otherwise agreed, the employee must give one week's notice to the employer, irrespective of length of service.

Although not comprehensive in either its breadth or depth, the list of issues above offers a good overview of the issues that an entrepreneur will face when deciding to recruit staff. Good legal advice and attention to detail can ensure that such issues never become problematic.

HEALTH AND SAFETY

The obligations and duties imposed on employers *vis-à-vis* health and safety emanate from legislation and the common law.

The main legislation is the Safety, Health and Welfare at Work Act 1989 and the Safety, Health and Welfare at Work (General Application) Regulations 1993. The former established the National Authority for Occupational Safety and Health (*the Health and Safety Authority*) and has extensive enforcement powers. The legislation deals with such areas as safety statements, use of work equipment, manual handling of goods, visual display units, electricity, first aid, notification of accidents and dangerous occurrences, and personal protective equipment. If an employer breaches this legislation, they may be exposed to prosecution or they may, in the event of an employee being injured, be confronted by a claim for personal injuries.

The common law requires an employer to provide a safe place of work, a safe system of work, competent co-workers, safe access and egress, proper and safe equipment, and safety equipment.

Duties owed to employees can differ, as an employer owes a separate duty to each employee. For example, the duty of care owed to a young and inexperienced employee would be greater than the duty owed to an experienced employee.

An employer is liable for the acts and omissions of his employees once these acts or omissions occurred in the course of the employee's employment. This is called "vicarious liability".

The principal duties and liabilities of an employer regarding health and safety include:

- **Providing a Safety Statement:** A safety statement is a document that details all the hazards in a place of work, together with the precautions that must be taken to reduce or eliminate these hazards. In preparing the safety statement, employees should be consulted.

Once it has been prepared, all employees should have access to it. The safety statement should be up-dated at regular intervals. All self-employed people need a safety statement, even if they have no employees.

- **Providing a grievance procedure:** A grievance procedure is a channel through which an employee can inform his employer of any work-related problem or concern that he/she has. This procedure has advantages for both the employee and the employer: The employee is empowered in dealing with the problem and it assists the employer in providing a safe place of work for the employee (and other employees). Increasingly, the presence of a proper grievance procedure is becoming a factor in determining whether an employer is liable for claims for personal injuries arising out of work-related stress, bullying and harassment. Once a grievance procedure is in place, it is imperative that employees are genuinely invited to air any grievances they may have and that the employer takes such reasonable steps as may be necessary to deal with these grievances.
- **Providing training:** The employer should assess the training needs of each of the employees and provide such training as is necessary. Records of this training should be kept. Training may have to be updated to allow for changing work practices and for refreshing the employees' work skills.
- **Insurance:** There is no general legal requirement on employers to have insurance (other than motor insurance, where vehicles are operated by employees). However, on a practical level, it is unwise not to have insurance. Once an employer is notified of a claim against them, they should immediately inform their insurance company. Usually, the insurance company reserves the right to settle the claim at any stage. The employer, in seeking insurance, should disclose all material facts to the insurance company. A material fact is one that may alter the risk to be insured – for example, if there were any fires on the premises previously.
- **Employers' duty of care:** The employer is legally bound to take reasonable care for the employee's safety in all the circumstances of the case. An employer is not legally responsible for all workplace accidents – instead, an employee must prove on the balance of probabilities that they sustained personal injuries as a result of the negligence and/or breach of statutory duty on the part of the employer. Negligence encompasses acts and omissions on the part of the employer. Cases in which the employer was found to have been

liable include the provision of defective and unsafe scaffolding, the inhalation of chemical fumes, lifting excessive weights combined with inadequate training in lifting techniques, failing to provide safety guards to slicing machines, providing unsafe pathways to the workplace, failing to provide helmets, giving an excessive workload to an employee thereby causing undue stress, and exposing an employee to excessive dust. Stress-related claims are now becoming more common and can arise from bullying and harassment. Ideally, employers should have policies on bullying and harassment in place, defining bullying and harassment and providing a mechanism for investigating and dealing with such complaints.

- **Employees' duties:** The employee is under a duty to take reasonable care of themselves at work and should also report any defects to equipment to the employer.
- **E-mail and Internet usage:** While e-mail and the Internet are used by most businesses, they can lead to legal exposure for the employer unless there are proper procedures in place. For example, untrue statements written about somebody, which would damage that person's reputation, may lead to a claim in defamation; an employee might inadvertently enter into a contract over the Internet that would be legally binding on the employer; or a claim for sexual harassment might be brought on foot of an employee receiving e-mails of a pornographic nature. Furthermore, time ill-spent on the Internet leads to loss of productivity. Employers ought to have a policy on e-mail and Internet usage, setting out what usage is permissible and what sanctions may be imposed in the event of non-compliance with this policy.

As employees become ever more knowledgeable about their rights, the area of health and safety becomes increasingly critical. While there are legal obligations to be fulfilled in protecting an employee, there are also moral and ethical obligations to be satisfied.

CONTRACT LAW

A contract is an agreement between two or more parties that is binding in law. Generally, a contract need not be in writing to be enforceable legally. One exception to this rule is a contract for the sale of land, which must be evidenced in writing.

A contract comprises both express and implied terms. An express term is one that has been specifically agreed between the parties – for example, the price at which the goods are to be sold. An implied term is one that, although not specifically agreed, is nevertheless an actual term of the contract. Terms can be implied into the contract by the courts, by statute, or by custom and practice in a particular industry. An example of a term implied by statute is that an employee will have implied into their contract of employment an entitlement to annual leave.

The key elements of a legally enforceable contract are:

- **Agreement:** An agreement comes about when an offer that is made by the *offeror* is accepted by the *offeree*. The terms of the offer must be unequivocally accepted. This acceptance must be communicated to the offeror.
- **Intention to be bound legally:** Parties to a contract must intend to be bound legally. Social arrangements, such as promising to meet up for lunch, are generally not legally enforceable. On the other hand, businesspeople entering into trading agreements are presumed to have the requisite intention to be bound legally.
- **Consideration:** The contract must be for consideration – in other words, there must be some reciprocal exchange of benefits, or the promise of benefit exchange, between the parties. The benefit given by one party need not reflect adequately the value of the benefit received by them – for example, a person can agree to pay €300 to buy a fountain pen that they know is only worth €100 and this contract will be enforceable legally, provided that they are not coerced or wrongfully pressurised into buying it.
- **Legality of contract:** An illegal contract will not be enforceable legally – for example, a contract that has tax evasion as its objective is illegal.
- **Contractual capacity:** While the general principle is that everybody has full contractual capacity to enter into contracts, contracts entered into by minors, drunkards, and lunatics are not legally binding.
- **Sale of Goods legislation:** The Sale of Goods and Supply of Services Act 1980 regulates the relationship between consumers and traders that arises out of the purchase of goods or services. Obligations imposed on vendors of goods are that the goods sold must be of merchantable quality and they must be reasonably fit for their intended purpose. Obligations imposed on service providers are that the service provider must have the necessary skill to provide the service and the service must be provided with due skill and diligence.

- **Consumer information:** The main purpose of the Consumer Information Act 1978 is the prevention of false or misleading indications about goods and services and prices given in the course of a business trade or profession.
- **Consumer credit:** The Consumer Credit Act 1995 contains wide ranging provisions for the protection of consumers in such areas as credit sale agreements, hire purchase agreements, housing loans, and money-lending agreements.
- **Unfair terms:** The Consumer Communities (Unfair Terms in Consumer Contracts) Regulations 1995 (Statutory Instrument 27 of 1995) outlaws certain standard terms in consumer contracts that have not been individually negotiated and which are unfair. A term may be unfair, if it leads to an imbalance in the parties' rights to the consumer's detriment.
- **Product liability:** The Liability for Defective Products Act 1991 provides that a producer may be liable for damage caused wholly or partly by a defect in his product, irrespective of whether or not he was negligent.
- **Exclusion clauses:** An exclusion clause is a term of a contract that limits or excludes one party's liability to the other for damage sustained as a result of a breach of contract. These clauses can be difficult, and sometimes impossible, to enforce in consumer contracts due to the protection afforded by the Sale of Goods legislation. However, in business-to-business contracts, the courts are more willing to accept these clauses. Exclusion clauses must have been agreed to by the parties before the contract was concluded. Furthermore, the person seeking to rely on this clause to limit their liability must show that the clause covered the loss or damage suffered. Exclusion clauses are also known as "exemption clauses".
- **Electronic commerce:** The Electronic Commerce Act 2000 attempts to regulate the legal aspects of electronic commerce. A contract will not generally be denied legal effect, validity, or enforceability solely because it is an electronic contract. An electronic contract is a contract that was concluded wholly or partly by means of an electronic communication. The Act provides that, in the formation of a contract, an offer, or its acceptance, may be made by electronic communication. The Act also allows for electronic signatures.
- **Trading over the Internet:** The European Communities (Protection of Consumers in Respect of Contracts Made by Means of Distance Communication) Regulations 2001, while affording protection to the

consumer who makes purchases over the Internet, give some cause for concern to internet retailers ("e-tailers") in relation to the vast majority of contracts between consumers and businesses. Business-to-business contracts generally tend not to be covered by this legislation. These Regulations compel e-tailers to do four things:

1. *Provide pre-contract information:* This information can be set out on the website and includes *inter alia* the identity of the retailer; a detailed description, and price, of the goods or services offered; cost of delivery of goods; and the duration for which the offer remains valid.
2. *Confirm the transaction:* This confirmation must be given in writing or some other durable medium.
3. *Give the consumer the right to withdraw:* The consumer must have seven days to completely extricate themselves from the agreement.
4. *Complete the contract:* Performance of the contract must be completed within a maximum period of 30 days from contract formation.

- **Discrimination:** Where businesses provide goods or services to the public, the Equal Status Act 2000 applies in that it prohibits discrimination in the provision of these goods or services on nine separate grounds: Gender, marital status, family status, sexual orientation, religion, age, disability, race or membership of the Traveller community. Where a complaint is to be made, it should be made directly to the person against whom the claim is being made, within two months. If no response, or an unsatisfactory response, is received, the complaint should be referred to the Office of the Director of Equality Investigations within six months of the incident.

Contract law is complex and, again, having good legal advice is highly beneficial to the entrepreneur. There is a clear need for the entrepreneur to make themselves familiar with the key legal issues involved in contract law as it may prevent a damaging claim arising at a future date. Representative organisations, such as the Small Firms Association (SFA), can assist owner-managers in these matters also.

CONCLUSION

This chapter has touched only the surface of the legal issues involved in starting and running an enterprise. However, it does offer a good overview of the key issues and should lead the entrepreneur to learn more about business law for themselves and to engage a good legal practitioner as an advisor.

With an increasingly litigious culture developing within Ireland, preventative processes through knowledge and action can save a great deal of difficulty and expense. Employees and customers are well aware of their rights, so it is imperative that the entrepreneur is aware of their own responsibilities.

QUESTIONS

1. Explain the advantages and disadvantages of the different legal trading structures.
2. Describe the key legal issues involved in employment law.
3. Define what is meant by "discrimination" in terms of employment law.
4. Discuss the role of Health and Safety law in protecting employees within the workplace.
5. Compare contract law for traditional businesses with electronic commerce.

USEFUL WEBSITES

www.comhairle.ie
www.cro.ie
www.entemp.ie
www.has.ie
www.irlgov.ie
www.lawsociety.ie
www.legal-island.com
www.lrc.ie
www.odca.ie
www.sfa.ie

CHECKLIST FOR CHAPTER

After reading this chapter, check that you understand and appreciate:
- The advantages and disadvantages of the different legal structures an enterprise can take
- The broad requirements of employment law
- The legal implications of health and safety
- The essentials of contract law.

REFERENCES

Comhairle (2000) - *Employment Rights Explained* – Dublin.

Keenan, A. (2001) - *Essentials of Irish Business Law* - 3rd edition, Gill & Macmillan, Dublin.

MacMahon, B. and Binchy, W. (2000) - *The Law of Torts* - 3rd edition, Butterworths, Dublin.

Meenan, F. (1997) - *Working within the Law* - 2nd edition, Oak Tree Press, Cork.

Doolan, B. (1999) - *Principles of Irish Law* - 5th edition, Gill & Macmillan, Dublin.

Department of Enterprise, Trade and Employment (2001) - *Guide to Labour Law* - Dublin.

Garavan, T. (2002) - *The Irish Health and Safety Handbook* - 2nd edition, Oak Tree Press, Cork.

O'Kane, B. (2000) - *How to Form a Limited Company* - 4th edition, Oak Tree Press, Cork.

CHAPTER 7

MANAGING THE NEW VENTURE

Naomi Birdthistle* and Briga Hynes**

LEARNING OBJECTIVES

- To understand the concepts of contemporary management practices as they apply to the new and growing venture
- To comprehend the various definitions of management
- To examine the issues that impact on and influence management practices in the new venture
- To appreciate how traditional management functions are applied to the new venture.

INTRODUCTION

New and emerging technologies, fast-changing market conditions, and global competition are among the primary factors revolutionising the way business is conducted. Business now needs to be more flexible to respond quickly to the impact of these changes to maintain a competitive advantage. Therefore, the role and task of the manager is less structured

*   Naomi Birdthistle is a junior lecturer in entrepreneurship and management at the University of Limerick.
** Briga Hynes is a lecturer in entrepreneurship and management at the University of Limerick.

and requires a flexible multi-skilled individual who is receptive and open to managing constant change. In this changing business environment, it is difficult to define "management" in one specific definition, relevant to all business scenarios.

Management as a subject has been researched and developed over the years, initially with an emphasis on the traditional "them and us" approach, which was characterised by managers having command and control over employees. In this traditional approach, management was viewed as a profession, associated with a set of skills and knowledge that could be applied to manage specific situations, which were predictable and determined by a set of boundaries. However, these boundaries are now less predictable and the business context for managers has changed to a more volatile and unpredictable set of circumstances that lead to the need for managers to have a broad set of skills and abilities, which can be modified to effectively manage the characteristics of the specific situation in hand. This leads to the more contemporary viewpoint of management that researches the dynamics of management from a specific firm context, content and process perspective. This "contingency" viewpoint emphasises the need for the manager to have an understanding of both internal firm and external environmental factors that impact directly or indirectly on management decisions, which, in turn, influence management behaviour and styles. These changes in the nature and complexity of the work of the manager are reflected in the more contemporary definitions of management by authors such as Tiernan, Morley and Foley (1996) and Deakins (1999).

The definitions put forward by these authors have a common philosophy that views management, not as discrete individual tasks, but rather as a process of interlinked activities to achieve new venture goals and objectives. The definitions are effectively summarised by Tiernan *et al* (1996) who purports that most definitions have the following three common characteristics:

- Management is viewed as a process or series of continuing and related activities
- Management is viewed as involving the achievement of organisational goals
- Management reaches organisational goals by working with and through people (page 1).

Benedian, as quoted in Tiernan *et al* (1996, page 1), defines management as:

The process of achieving desired results through effective
utilisation of human and material resources.

Management is not only about outputs, but equally emphasises the process or means to achieve these outputs.

Many of the writings on management practices predominately focus on, and are more readily applicable to, the general characteristics of the large firm. Therefore, when discussing the role of management in the small firm context, it is necessary to customise the more generic literature to the specific characteristics of the newly established and growing venture.

MANAGEMENT IN THE SMALL FIRM CONTEXT

The majority of small firms are established and managed by a sole entrepreneur. However, this is now changing and more new ventures, especially in the high technology sector, are established by more than one person in teams. Entrepreneurship training programmes and initiatives offered by many State agencies and universities encourage and facilitate the use of teams in the new venture creation process.

Few individuals have both the technical and commercial skills and the knowledge necessary to establish a new venture. Even the sole entrepreneur, who starts the business with the intention of going it alone, will find it necessary at certain stages of business growth and expansion to assemble a team to compensate for personal skills and knowledge shortcomings in areas such as marketing, finance, and production. This is particularly evident in the high technology sector, where only a few of the technical entrepreneurs have the associated and necessary business knowledge and skills to commercialise their technical business idea.

Vyakarnam *et al* (1996) identified the "top team" as the driving force behind growth firms. Family firms also commonly comprise of entrepreneurial teams, where family members are encouraged to participate in the management functions of the business. These family members are frequently appointed to these roles, simply because they are members of the family and not because they have been selected objectively based on experience or competencies. This practice of business nepotism occurs due to a resistance in family firms to hiring an "outsider", because the owners fear relinquishing control and thus not maintaining the family in the business. The consequences are inefficiencies and an inward subjective approach to management practices and behaviour.

The key to the success of an entrepreneurial team is to ensure that the right decisions are made initially on the composition of the team, and then on the composition of management, and later on monitoring of the team's performance and contribution to the specific new venture goals and objectives. The composition of the team involves decisions on:

- How many people are needed for the team
- Where to source potential team members
- What factors should be considered both on a professional and personal manner when finally choosing team members
- The roles and duties of each team member
- Their level of participation in the operational activities of the business
- Exit mechanisms and procedures for team members.

The ongoing management and monitoring of the team can be time-consuming and is reliant on having clear and agreed guidelines that give direction to behaviour and ensure each team member is capable of undertaking the activities defined for them. It is important that any form of agreement devised by the team on ownership is covered by legally binding contracts and that all conditions are clear from the outset.

Kamn and Aaron (1993) suggested that that the following issues are critical for managers to consider to ensure the successful operation and longevity of the team, which will be reflected in the growth of the venture:

- Ownership distribution
- Team mission and goals
- Interpersonal relationships/conflict management
- Team management.

Ownership Distribution

An important issue (and cost) in assembling and maintaining an effective entrepreneurial team is the distribution of ownership amongst its members. Ownership can be divided equally or unequally amongst the members, while sleeping partners may also exist. The basis upon which ownership is divided can vary, according to the financial input or level of expertise of the members. It may be more difficult to decide on levels of ownership based on expertise as this is intangible and it may be difficult to quantify the market value of certain areas of expertise (for example, technical members may not perceive the value of marketing expertise to the firm or *vice versa*).

Team Mission and Goals

The team must be clear on what the overall venture goals are and how their own personal goals are aligned and consistent with these broader business goals. The challenge facing teams is to ensure that, as the firm grows, the original team's vision adapts accordingly, and that future growth is a personal aim for each of the founders. Any changes in personal goals, which will impact on the firm's goals, need to be quickly and clearly communicated to other team members.

Interpersonal Relationships/Conflict Management

As the team will work closely together, it is important that there exists a good and complementary balance, not only of skills, but also of personalities. The mix of interpersonal skills should encourage open and honest debate and, at the same time, should ensure no latent conflict exists that may hamper the growth of the venture. Disagreement and a certain level of conflict is inevitable in any team, due to the diverse backgrounds and skills of its members, to differences in ages or over the amount of equity to offer as an inducement to prospective members. It is important that some process/procedures are in place to manage this conflict before it hinders the progression of the firm. The common goal of the team is often used as a criterion upon which conflict is resolved, combined with the help of discussions amongst members.

The additional team members who join with the founding member not only bring professional expertise with them, but also provide valuable personal and psychological back-up and support to the founder through encouragement, more objective advice, finance, and access to a broader set of networks. They also reduce the isolation that is often attributed to starting a business as a sole entrepreneur.

Team Management

The team founders are often called upon to play a variety of roles and to provide a range of services to the team, underlining the importance of complementary skills in the team. Team boundaries and membership protocols need to be set. This is a maintenance issue that teams should address and, in doing so, will permit all members some degree of participation in recruitment, termination and reward decisions.

At the outset, the founders should agree on who is going to lead the firm and on how responsibilities will be allocated. The appointment of the *managing director* will vary in teams, sometimes being the technical entrepreneur, particularly if the business is based on their idea or expertise. This founder contributes to the leadership function of problem-solving, setting quality standards, and continually improving and setting goals.

Teams can achieve growth most effectively by establishing a structure and systems that allow for the smooth running of the business. To achieve this, shared assumptions about the team structure and mutual acceptance of the structure as it exists must be obtained. In doing so, it provides for the establishment of a management team, clarity of roles within the team, and leadership. In the operational and strategic management of the new venture, team members work closely together, resulting in shared peer learning, where team members learn new knowledge, skills and competencies from each other that will prepare them to be flexible and multi-skilled managers, more component in undertaking a number of different roles in the growing venture.

Once the new venture is established, owner/manager(s) need to decide on their objectives for the venture – specifically, the level and type of growth they want to achieve and within what time frame. It is important not to assume that all new ventures want to grow and expand. McCormack (2000) identified that some small businesses are really "lifestyle" businesses, managed to keep their owners in a certain lifestyle and not to maximise profits. McCormick (2001) postulated that, as the venture becomes established, the inevitable opportunities for real growth and development can be ignored by its founder, who may prefer to keep the business small and directly manageable as a lifestyle company. However, irrespective of the objectives decided upon by the owner/manager(s), a number of issues will determine how the venture is managed. These issues are considered in the next section.

NEW VENTURE GROWTH – THE MANAGEMENT ISSUES

Management in the small firm has a wide and varying job, managing a wide variety of often-unrelated tasks, which, in a larger firm, would be represented by different hierarchical levels. This places extra pressure on the owner/manager(s), who often is not from a business background and is/are operating under time and financial resource restrictions. This results in the owner/manger constantly fire fighting, reacting to immediate problems, with the perceived need to "jump to it" whenever a customer snaps their fingers, resulting in too much concentration on the present and lack of planning for the future requirements of the venture.

The management style and behaviour evident in the venture cannot be separated from the personality set, experience and training of the owner/manager(s). In the new venture, the management process is characterised by the highly personalised preferences, prejudices and attitudes of the owner-manager(s). The owner/manager(s) is close to the operating personnel and activities being undertaken, thus influencing these personnel and activities directly. However, relationships are often informal, with no precise definition of hierarchies, duties or responsibilities. Appointments and promotions are often made on the basis of family or personal friendship rather than on the objective basis of ability, education, experience and/or technical qualifications.

At the early stages of venture development, the owner/manager(s) manage all aspects of the venture in an integrated way. On the establishment of the venture, management focuses on obtaining the resources the firm requires such as money, people, capital, equipment, customers and knowledge. This requires management skills in a broad sense and requires the manager to be flexible and outward-looking in terms of the best and most efficient methods of securing these resources.

In the next stages of venture development, management duties focus on maintaining and building on these resources to ensure stability and growth of the venture. In growing the venture, the owner/manager(s) need to have the ability to move from just acquiring resources to creating and maintaining structures that facilitate and encourage the desired growth and development. Managing the small venture now involves managing change, exploiting opportunities and giving direction to the new venture. These challenges require the owner/manager(s) to have not only an internal firm focus but also to have an understanding of the influences in the business environment that determine and influence management practices in the new venture. This understanding of the business environment requires knowledge of global business trends; economic, demographic and social factors; technological; and legal and physical environmental factors – as illustrated by **Figure 7.1**. These factors can directly or indirectly impact on the performance of the venture and their impact will vary as the venture grows or as changes occur in general competitive and market conditions. Effective analysis of the impact of these factors requires the owner/manager(s) to have a constant external business focus at both industry and business-specific sector level.

FIGURE 7.1: BUSINESS ENVIRONMENT

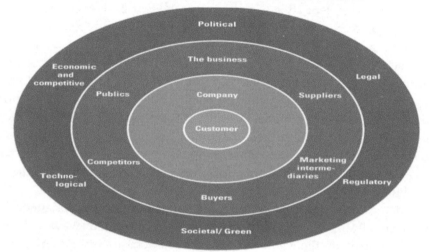

Source: Dibb *et al* (2000).

As the venture becomes more established with the introduction of new products and a broader market and competitor base, the owner/manager(s) may not have the competencies, skills or time to manage effectively or efficiently all aspects of the growing venture and will need to relinquish some of the tasks to other individuals. The owner/manager(s) may underestimate the value of this need to source external management expertise for particular functions (for example, marketing, human resources, accounting) and the need to dedicate resources to these functions as the venture grows and develops. Where the owner/manager(s) find it difficult to delegate responsibility and authority at this stage, potential growth opportunities for the venture may be lost. Owner/manager(s) should not view relinquishing responsibilities and duties in a negative sense as losing control – instead, they should view it as a means to develop and use further their key competencies and skills that will add value to the venture.

As the venture expands, formerly successful management practices may become less effective. Furthermore, the qualities of the entrepreneur that are most needed during the start-up stage may have a less effective impact on the business during its growth phase. Therefore, it is essential for the owner/manager(s) to recognise at an early stage that sometimes radical changes in the manner in which the venture operates will be required if the venture is to survive in the long-term.

BALANCING ENTREPRENEURIAL AND PROFESSIONAL MANAGEMENT

Owner/manager(s) need to recognise that the manner in which they engage themselves and apply their skills and competencies to the growing firm differs to what was required in the infant stages of venture start-up. Watson (1994, page 42) questions the distinction that is made between entrepreneurial and professional management. His key argument is that all companies need a mix of entrepreneurial and professional management. Therefore, the key issue for the growing firm is not how to evolve from entrepreneurial to professional management but rather it is:

> ... *an issue of moving from a situation where the mix of entrepreneurial and other managerial skills are carried out by one or two people with a limited or non-existent division of labour to one where they are carried out by a team of people with a significant division of labour.*

This is where the owner manager should relinquish control for emerging functional areas to specifically qualified personnel in marketing, finance, etc. Indeed, this philosophy of a mix of entrepreneurial and professional management is encouraged in today's larger firm, where there is a need for more enterprising and flexible managers. The challenge facing owner/manager(s) is how to achieve the best balance between entrepreneurial and professional management practices as required by the different stages of venture development.

Managing growth in the small firm requires integrated management, which is ideally a blend of entrepreneurial and professional management practices to create both a personal and business advantage for the owner/manager(s). Traditional management practices, if implemented in a traditional way, will only have limited impact on small firm development; however, if implemented entrepreneurially in the context of the then needs of the small firm, they will be more effective and successful. Owner/manager(s) sometimes find it difficult to let go of the entrepreneurial approach they have developed and become accustomed to; they do not find the role of traditional manager a comfortable one. Managing in the small firm does not mean abandoning traditional management practices; it is about knowing when and where to apply these practices to complement existing entrepreneurial management practices. However, the gap between entrepreneurial and professional management is seen most often in the growing stages of the small firm, as the nature and essence of professional management and its application to the small firm is confused and overcomplicated by theory and terminology, not relevant to the small firm's needs.

The owner/manager(s) needs to realise that this gap exists and identify where, how and when the necessary managerial competencies and skills should be acquired. The ideal solution is to build these capabilities internally. This requires participation in training and development initiatives geared not only at management but also at employee level in the small firm. Internal capability building allows a more flexible and customised approach to ensuring the necessary skills and competencies are acquired by the owner/manager(s). Any initiative undertaken to build capabilities must take into consideration the time and resource constraints of the owner/manager(s).

Mentoring

One method used to build competencies in the small firm is mentoring, which is not only effective from the owner/manager(s) perspective but also from the employee development perspective.

The www.mentoringgroup.com website gives a simple and concise definition of mentoring:

> ... *the process in which successful individuals go out of their way to help others establish goals and develop skills to reach them.*

It continues by stating that mentoring helps increase confidence, widen the perspective and enhances the life and career of the mentee (the person receiving the assistance).

www.e-mentoring.com states that, by definition, the mentoring relationship contains a certain inequality but also a necessary equality.

Both parties bring different perspectives to the relationship but both parties gain and are equally accountable for the success of the relationship.

Shea (1994) identified three types of mentoring:

- Situational
- Informal
- Formal.

Situational mentoring tends to be short and in isolated episodes, on an *ad hoc* basis, often dealing with discrete problems and issues, when a mentor provides the relevant information or ideas at the right time. Neither party may see the activity as mentoring – nonetheless, the activity results in adding value and facilitating owner/manager(s) decision-making at that specific time.

Informal mentoring is possibly the most common type of mentoring and may last from a few weeks to a lifetime. Informal mentoring may lead to friendship with occasional mentoring experiences as well. These mentoring acts can be flexible, loosely structured, informal relationships, where the mentor voluntarily shares expertise or special insights. Informal mentoring is particularly suitable for owner/manager(s), as it accommodates their resource and time constraints and enables learning and competence building that incorporates professional management practices not held previously by the owner/manager(s).

With **formal** mentoring, the goals of mentoring tend to be focused narrowly, which makes the programmes suitable for extensive planning, measurement and evaluation. The programmes are usually systemic and structured and are generally characterised as being focused on achieving organisational or sub-unit goals. This type of mentoring is often aligned with formal management development programmes such as the Business Development Programme (Limerick City Enterprise Board) and the Plato programme.

Mentoring is a flexible, customised and adaptable process, which takes cognisance of the changing needs of the growing venture. Whichever form of mentoring the owner/manager(s) uses (situational, informal or formal) will depend on his/her goals and objectives. According to Doyle & O Neill (2001), the benefits gained by a mentee from a mentoring assignment may vary from business to business. Given the right attitude, mentoring can be a very beneficial learning experience for the owner/manager(s).

Due to the effectiveness of both informal and formal mentoring as a means of owner/management development, many State agencies and the City and County Enterprise Boards offer programmes that provide mentors to entrepreneurs in a variety of fields – for example, the Business Guidance Programme (www.limceb.ie/bsf.htm).

Capability and competency building for the owner/manager(s) provides them with a broader set of skills and knowledge, which will allow them to be more effective in balancing the required mix of entrepreneurial and professional management practices and in gaining the synergies of both. This should result in more effective execution of the business functions necessary to grow the business.

MANAGEMENT FUNCTIONS APPLIED TO THE NEW VENTURE

Management literature suggests a range of functions that are necessary to undertake effectively the management of the business, irrespective of its size. These traditional functions are planning, organising, leading and controlling. The literature tends to focus the application of these functions to the large business set-up and their relevance and application to the new and growing venture varies.

This section will address how these functions apply to the new venture. Tiernan, Morley and Foley (1996), and Kreitner (1995), stated that, to manage any venture effectively, the owner/manger(s) needs to plan business activities and set objectives for the firm (planning); to organise a structure around people and activities to facilitate the achievement of these business objectives (organising); to recruit, motivate and retain high calibre staff to achieve these objectives (leading); and, finally, to monitor and evaluate all activities and personnel in the venture to ensure objectives are achieved in an effective and efficient manner (controlling). **Figure 7.2** illustrates these management functions.

Planning

Planning is concerned with deciding a future direction for the venture and defining the courses of action and projects needed to move the venture in that direction (Wickham, 1999). Plans, and the objectives on which they are based, give purpose and direction to the organisation for short-term (plans of less than one year); medium-term (plans for one to five years); and long-term (plans for five to 15 years) (Tiernan *et al*, 1996).

Planning in the small firm is frequently *ad hoc* and unstructured, with a focus on short-term operational issues in the early stages of venture development. At this stage, planning revolves around the formulation of business plans, which are devised for specific purposes such as funding and are geared towards a specific external audience. These plans are operationally focused and need to be modified as the venture grows (www.startingabusinessinireland.com). It is important that business plans have a practical and realistic focus and application to guide the direction of the venture in its early stages of growth. They should also act as a useful mechanism for evaluating venture performance and achievement. Critical to any planning activity is the ability of the owner/manager(s) to make decisions on a speedy and definite basis.

FIGURE 7.2: MANAGEMENT FUNCTIONS

Organising

The organising function relates to decisions on the most effective and efficient structure for the new venture (Wickham, 1999). Developing an appropriate structure involves decisions on the roles, activities and tasks to be undertaken by all staff. It then requires organising the physical environment of the venture to facilitate the effective and efficient achievement of venture objectives. It also involves identifying the chain of command, division of labour, and the assignment of responsibility for all within the organisation.

Organisation structures, in so far as they exist in the new venture, are likely to develop around the interests and abilities of the owner/manager(s) and are likely to be organic and loosely-structured rather than mechanistic and highly-formalised. According to Curran (1988), the typical structure of owner-managed firms is that of a spider's web with the owner/manager(s) in the centre controlling and directing the venture alone. As the venture grows in terms of employee numbers, products, markets and sales, this centralised structure will need to change to accommodate growth. This need to change the organisation structure has been highlighted by authors such as O'Farrell and Hitchens (1988) and Curran (1988).

However, introducing structural changes in the small venture can be a complex process, which requires a managerial skill that is often lacking. Such a change, if managed ineffectively, can have negative consequences for the growth of the venture. Levie and Hay (1997) point out that professional managers are often recruited from larger organisations who are trained with large organisation systems in mind. Imposition of "large company" systems and structures may actually impede growth in small firms, where strength lies in a rapid and focused combination of cross-functional skills (www.entrepreneurs.about.com /cs/planning/). The new venture structure needs to be flexible to facilitate growth and to allow it to respond speedily to the market and to the competitive demands of the business environment.

Leading

Organisations are only as good as the people in them. Leadership involves facilitation, co-ordination and integration of people and activities to achieve desired objectives. This is achieved by establishing direction, aligning people, motivating, inspiring and empowering staff and management, either on an individual basis or through the use of teams. Good employees are a key resource for the small firm and thus the challenge facing owner/manager(s) in today's competitive employee market environment is how to attract, retain and motivate employees to stay with a small and often insecure venture. The owner/manager has to build trust and credibility with their staff by creating a positive culture in the firm. An important aspect of management today is motivating individuals to pursue collective objectives by satisfying both personal and professional needs and meeting expectations with meaningful work and valued rewards (Krietner, 1995). There are many ways in which the owner/manager(s) may motivate their staff, for example, by sharing responsibility for tasks, by recognising staff achievements by having a "Staff Member of the Month" competition and by providing incentives and rewards. Managers become inspiring leaders by serving as role models and adapting their management style to the demands of the situation (Krietner, 1995).

Successful management of employees is becoming more time-consuming and complex for owner/manager(s), due to the increasing volume of employment legalisation and regulations, which increases the cost of employing staff and reduces flexibility. Small firms find it difficult to compete with the attractive salary rates offered by larger firms resulting in higher staff turnover and staff shortages.

The owner/manager(s), in a leadership capacity, has to assume a number of sub-roles such as coach, mentor and problem-solver. He/she must be able to reward achievements and encourage a certain level of risk. In achieving this, the ability to delegate effectively is critically important to achieve the desired results. Churchill (1997) identified that, in order for delegation to be effective, four basic objectives must be set and achieved:

1. Delegate responsibility
2. Agree upon the objectives to be attained
3. Grant others the authority to take the actions needed to achieve the objectives
4. Collect and monitor information on how activities are progressing.

However, Churchill (1997) identified that owner/manager(s) have difficulties with the delegation of authority, as they are so close to the venture they find it difficult not to interfere when they observe an employee doing something wrong and/or wasting limited resources. To be an effective leader and to delegate efficiently, it is important that the owner/manager(s) understands the importance of communications and their role as a communicator and manager of critical information.

Internally, within the venture, the owner/manager(s) need to communicate constantly with employees, to hear their views, to gain feedback from sales people and to encourage ideas and suggestions from employees on how improvements can be implemented for the development of the firm. Recognising that communication is a two-way process, the owner/manager(s) should be responsive to feedback and upward communication. The owner/manager(s) can organise regular formal and informal meetings with their staff to listen to their views and to communicate any new developments in the venture (www.entrepreneurs.about.com).

Externally, the owner/manager(s) is the figurehead and the image associated with the venture. Therefore, they need to communicate their firm's activities and achievements to relevant stakeholders – such as financial institutions, customers, competitors, etc. – in a positive manner. The potential benefits of the role of external communicator are often underestimated by the owner/manager(s).

Controlling

Controlling is the function that is concerned with ensuring that the right resources are in place, that they are used effectively and that their use is properly accounted for (Wickham, 1999). Control is the process of identifying whether desired objectives are achieved and if not, why not, and then deciding on the interventions needed to improve performance at company and/or individual level. Deviations from past plans should be considered when formulating new plans (Krietner 1995). This process needs to be underpinned by the establishment of realistic objectives and needs to be undertaken in an objective manner.

The owner/manager(s) tends to be poor at monitoring the firm's activities, due to time and resource constraints. However, if, from the conception of the business, the owner/manager(s) devises a business plan, it can be used as a control mechanism and a benchmark for the future objectives and operations of the venture.

The measurement and evaluation of individual and firm performance is critical to ensure that all other management functions are completed in an effective and efficient manner. The owner/manager(s) has to be flexible and have the ability to understand the importance of each of these functions to the development of their venture, even if their objectives are merely to maintain the *status quo* for the firm and maintain it as a lifestyle business.

To undertake the above functions, the owner/manager(s) requires a number of different skills and expertise, which may be sourced externally from development agencies and commercial institutions (see the **Appendix** to this chapter).

CONCLUSION

Management in the small firm is a wide and varied job, managing a variety of unrelated tasks, which in the larger firm would be represented by different hierarchical structures. Managing growth in the small firm requires integrated management, which is a blend of entrepreneurial and professional management practices to create both personal and business advantage for the owner/manager(s). This requires the owner/manager(s) to have the skills and competencies to adapt the traditional management functions of planning, controlling, organising and leading, within an ever-changing business environment.

Small firms are a critical resource for sustainable economic and social development in the Irish economy. Therefore, a key challenge facing policy makers, development agencies, and institutions facilitating small firms is how to increase the quality and sustainability of such firms. This can be achieved through the design and delivery of relevant hard and soft support programmes geared at owner/manager(s) and their employees.

QUESTIONS

1. What differences exist between managing a firm with five employees and one with 250 employees?
2. Describe the benefits of a firm founded by an entrepreneurial team.
3. Discuss the main functions of an owner/manager in a new venture.
4. Explain and contrast entrepreneurial and professional management.
5. Evaluate the advantages and disadvantages of mentoring for an owner-manager.

CHECKLIST FOR CHAPTER

After reading this chapter, check that you understand and appreciate:
- The concepts of contemporary management practices as they apply to the new and growing venture
- The various definitions of management
- The issues that impact on and influence management practices in the new venture
- How traditional management functions are applied to the new venture.

USEFUL WEBSITES

www.entrepreneurs.about.com
www.entrepreneurs.about.com/cs/planning/
www.e-mentoring.com
www.limceb.ie/bsf.htm
www.mentoringgroup.com
www.startingabusinessinireland.com

REFERENCES

Churchill, N. (1997) - Breaking Down the Wall, Scaling the Ladder – *Mastering Enterprise* (Edited by Birley, S. and Muzyka D.F.), Financial Times Pitman Publishing, UK.

Clutterbuck, A. (2001) – *Mentoring* - www.clutterbuckassociates.co.uk/

Curran, J. (1988) - *Management, Motivation in the Small Firm* - Epping, Gower Press.

Deakins, D. (1999) - *Entrepreneurship and Small Firms* – 2nd Edition, McGraw Hill, UK.

Dibb, S., Simkin, L., Pride, W.M. and Farrell, O.C. (2000) - *Marketing: Concepts and Strategies* - Houghton Mifflin.

Doyle, B. and O Neill, N.V. (2001) - *Mentoring Entrepreneurs: Shared Wisdom from Experience* – Cork, Oak Tree Press.

Kamn, R and Aaron, P. (1993) - The Stages of Team Formation: A Decision Making Model - *Entrepreneurship Theory and Practice*, Vol.17, No.2.

Kreitner, R. (1995) - *Management* - 6th Edition, Houghton Mifflin Company, USA.

Levie, J. and Hay, M. (1997) - Life Beyond the Kitchen - *Financial Times*, January 20th

McCormack, T. (2000) - *Profit Maximisation for the Small Firm*, www.imi.ie/iminew/membership/persapplicfr.html

McCormick, S. (2001) - *Strategic Planning for the Growing Companies* - www.imi.ie/iminew/membership/persapplicfr.html

O'Farrell, P.N. and Hitchens, D. (1988) - Alternative Theories of Small Firm Growth: A Critical Review - *Environment and Planning Journal*, Vol.20

Shea, G.F. (1994) - *Mentoring: Helping Employees Reach their Full Potential* - AMA Publications, New York.

Tiernan S., Morley, M. and Foley, E. (1996) - *Modern Management: Theory and Practice for Irish Students* - Gill & Macmillan, Dublin.

Vyakarnam, S., Jacobs, R. and Handelberg, J. (1996) - *Building and Managing Relationships: The Core Competence of Rapid Growth Business* - paper presented to the 19th National Small Firms Policy and Research Conference, Birmingham, November.

Watson, T. J. (1994) - *In Search of Management* - Routledge, London.

Wickham, P.A. (1999) - *Management Consulting* - Financial Times, Pitman Publishing.

www.entrepreneurs.about.com/cs/planning/
www.e-mentoring.com
www.limceb.ie/bsf.htm
www.mentoringgroup.com

APPENDIX

TABLE 7.1 - GOVERNMENT AGENCIES, PROFESSIONAL ASSOCIATIONS, UNIVERSITIES AND INSTITUTES OF TECHNOLOGY

	Contact Details
Association of Chartered Certified Accountants	www.acca.ie
Athlone Institute of Technology	www.ait.ie
Bord Fáilte	www.bftrade.travel.ie
Central Statistics Office	www.cso.ie
Chambers of Commerce	www.chambersireland.ie
City Enterprise Boards	See specific location for address
Cork Institute of Technology	www.cit.ie
Department of Enterprise Trade and Employment	www.entemp.ie
Dublin City University	www.dcu.ie
Dublin Institute of Technology	www.dit.ie
Dublin Institute of Technology	www.dit.ie
Dublin University	www.dcu.ie
Dún Laoghaire Institute of Art, Design and Technology	www.iadt-dl.ie
Dundalk Institute of Technology	www.dkit.ie
Enterprise Ireland	www.enterprise-ireland.com
FÁS	www.fas.ie
First Tuesday Club	www.firsttuesday.ie
Galway-Mayo Institute of Technology	www.gmit.ie
IBEC	www.ibec.ie
Institute of Carlow	www.itcarlow.ie
Institute of Certified Public Accountants in Ireland	www.cpaireland.ie
Institute of Chartered Accountants in Ireland	www.icai.ie
Institute of Directors in Ireland	www.iodireland.ie
Institute of Industrial Engineers	www.iie.ie
Institute of Project Management	www.projectmanagement.ie
Institute of Public Administration	www.ipa.ie
Institute of Technology, Blanchardstown	www.itb.ie

	Contact Details
Institute of Technology, Letterkenny	www.lyit.ie
Institute of Technology, Sligo	www.itsligo.ie
Institute of Technology, Tralee	www.ittralee.ie
Institution of Engineers of Ireland	www.iei.ie
InterTradeIreland	www.intertradeireland.com
Irish Hotels Federation	www.ihf.ie
Irish Institute of Purchasing and Materials Management	www.iipmm.ie
Irish Internet Association	www.iia.ie
Irish Management Institute	www.imi.ie
Irish Marketing Institute	www.mii.ie
Irish Travel Agents Association	www.itaa.ie
Leader+	www.leaderii.ie
Limerick Institute of Technology	www.lit.ie
Limerick Institute of Technology	www.lit.ie
National University of Galway	www.nuigalway.ie
National University of Ireland, Galway	www.ucg.ie
Network Ireland	www.networkireland.ie
Revenue Commissioners	www.revenue.ie
Shannon Development	www.shannon.dev.ie
Small Firms Association	www.sfa.ie
Tallaght, Institute of Technology	www.it-tallaght.ie
Trinity College Dublin	www.tcd.ie
Údarás na Gaeltachta	www.udaras.ie
University College Cork	www.ucc.ie
University College Dublin	www.ucd.ie
University College Dublin	www.ucd.ie
University of Limerick	www.ul.ie
University of Limerick	www.ul.ie
Waterford Institute of Technology	www.wit.ie

CHAPTER 8

MARKETING IN THE ENTREPRENEURIAL NEW VENTURE

*Pauric McGowan**

LEARNING OBJECTIVES

- To create a greater awareness of the overlap that exists at the marketing/entrepreneurship interface
- To provide insights into the marketing advantages of small new ventures
- To provide insights into the practice of marketing in such enterprises
- To consider the elements of a marketing planning process for the entrepreneurial new venture
- To examine the nature of marketing planning processes in such a context
- To explore the important aspect of implementing the marketing plan
- To examine the importance of networked relationship management and the Internet in effective marketing practice in new venture creation.

---

* Pauric McGowan is a lecturer in entrepreneurship and marketing at the University of Ulster.

INTRODUCTION

Marketing matters to the entrepreneurial new venture (ENV). However, how it is practised in such enterprises may not reflect the marketing prescribed in conventional theoretical models and techniques as set out in major textbooks. It is essential to recognise at the outset that the practice of marketing in the ENV is different from that which is practised in larger, more mature companies – simply because ENVs are different. The context for many of the established theories and models presented in the conventional marketing texts has, for the most part, been the larger, more mature companies in the economy. Each ENV, however, describes a very different type of business context. It reflects the earliest stages of the life cycle of a new enterprise, a period of often rapid, radical and unexpected change. Consequently, it is difficult to be overly prescriptive, in a generic sense, or indeed dogmatic, about how the lead entrepreneur should do business, particularly from a marketing point of view. The focus of this chapter is to provide some insights on how new venture entrepreneurs "do marketing" and also to provide an agenda for students for further research.

THE MARKETING/ENTREPRENEURSHIP INTERFACE

The relationship between marketing and entrepreneurship has been the focus of the efforts of numerous researchers in recent times (Carson *et al*, 1995). Common themes that define the nature of this relationship and that are at the heart of the entrepreneurial process are innovation and change (Cunningham and Lischeron, 1991; Drucker, 1985).

The entrepreneurial process describes a dynamic in which the central entrepreneurial individual is dedicated persistently to seeking new opportunities with potential for growth in the marketplace, and to marshalling the resources needed to exploit them. The management of change and the maintenance of a good fit between these two core constituents of the process constitute a strategic imperative facing the new entrepreneur seeking to establish a new venture that is itself entrepreneurial. Innovative activity is at the heart of any understanding of this process. It is also essential for gaining any appreciation of the nature of the interface between marketing and entrepreneurship.

Gardner (1991) defines marketing and entrepreneurial behaviour as "that area where innovation is brought to market" (p.3), which defines any enterprise's competitive advantage (Vraking, 1990). A core task for the marketing-oriented entrepreneur in any new venture, therefore, is to remain persistently innovative and opportunity-focused. Such innovative activity will largely focus on either the development of new products or new ways of doing business, which help the entrepreneurial new venture obtain and maintain a competitive advantage in meeting the needs of its customers. The ENV defines an enterprise where marketing and entrepreneurship take on complimentary, even similar roles.

THE MARKETING ADVANTAGES OF AN ENTREPRENEURIAL NEW VENTURE

In the light of the relatively unique characteristics and circumstances that describe the ENV discussed in earlier chapters, it is hard to believe that such an enterprise actually has any marketing advantages at all. Yet it does. Understanding the peculiar character and circumstances of the ENV gives insights into how marketing is practised in such enterprises and an appreciation of how it is different from marketing practice in more established companies.

The lead entrepreneur in such enterprises is one who, because of their background, their personality and their behaviour, has an obsessive focus on market opportunities, a commitment to continuous innovative activity, and a high tolerance of change and attendant risk. As a consequence they will adopt, adapt, and improve, in an intuitive and subconscious way, conventional marketing concepts, and techniques to suit their relatively unique circumstances.

Such ventures have a number of marketing advantages that help them do this, and which can give the ENV an edge, even over larger competition (Neilson 1995). In an environment such as the current one, where consumer markets, in particular, are becoming increasingly fragmented, the potential for increased product and market differentiation is high. Direct marketing and the Internet have greatly contributed to this fragmentation, enhancing the opportunities for entrepreneurs and new venture founders, encouraging them to challenge even the most established companies.

Other marketing advantages of the ENV include the flexibility to offer very specialised and customised goods and services to those with whom they do business. In addition, the owners of such ventures can bring to their customers a "personal touch", in order to build those essential relationships that encourage loyalty. These firms will have a strong local image and presence and one consequence of this will be their scope to respond, in a speedy and flexible way, to the specific needs and wants of individual customers. Finally, those customers can have direct access to the key decision-maker, the venture founder, if and when required. The new venture founder has to recognise these important marketing advantages and to use them to his or her benefit when seeking to develop an approach to marketing planning within the new firm.

DEVELOPING A MARKETING PLAN FOR AN ENV

Research into the relationship between marketing planning and organisational effectiveness has been extensive (Greenley and Bayus, 1993; McDonald, 1989), and there remains a core belief that it is a valuable, even essential practice for continuous enterprise development. McDonald (1992) considered marketing planning to be, in essence, an approach to doing business that improved the chances of even the smallest company to survive. He recognised however, that it should never be seen as a panacea to the difficulties facing owner/managers in developing their enterprises. It involved an intelligent analysis of the business environment both outside and within the enterprise and equal proportions of perspiration and inspiration to make it come alive and bear fruit.

For any new venture, a commitment to even the most informal planning activity offers benefits. The very act of writing down some basic objectives is an essential discipline in itself that challenges the entrepreneur to think sensibly about the future development of the enterprise. In addition, the completion, in even the broadest terms, of the most rudimentary marketing strategies for accomplishing those business objectives provides the new venture founder with an opportunity to examine alternatives critically. Writing down these basic plans also provides the venture founder with scope to engage members of his/her network for validation of his/her thinking. The challenge is not to become bogged down in the detail of the planning activity but to maintain a broad perspective. In this way, the element of flexibility and commitment to change, which is so characteristic of the way that new venture entrepreneurs do business, can be maintained. By engaging in a planning process and writing down a basic plan, the entrepreneurial founder can engage supporters both within and outside the enterprise more effectively to contribute to, and help refine, his/her thinking on how the ENV might meet the needs of its targeted customers better, and how best to make that sale over and over again.

MARKETING PLANNING IN THE ENV

Conventional understanding of the planning process suggests that it involves a logical and systematic determination of where a business manager wants to go, the identification of the means of getting there and a focusing of the operational activities of the business on the necessary tasks. Planning then is a process, the outcome of which will be a plan.

There are many examples of this process, perhaps the best known being Leppard and McDonald's (1991) cascading model of strategic marketing planning. The plan is usually a document that captures the combined thinking of the primary decision-makers of the enterprise and lays out objectives, an appropriate rationale, and a detailed and timetabled programme for action, with those responsible for executing the plan clearly identified. However, in the light of what has been written to date about the entrepreneurial new venture, the application of such systematic thinking is likely to be limited. From a marketing perspective, what is needed are new approaches that are meaningful in the specific context of the entrepreneurial new venture. There are core issues that we know really must form a part of any entrepreneur's thinking but there is really no one right sequence of steps to be taken. In addition, there is the need to adhere to the broadest possible timetable for action. So this is not the context for straight-line thinking. Key constituents of a planning process that might be considered by the lead decision-maker in the ENV are listed in **Table 8.1**.

TABLE 8.1: THE MARKETING PLANNING PROCESS

Constituent 1: Business aims and objectives - identification of appropriate benchmarks, achievable, measurable, and timetabled.

Constituent 2: Marketing aims and objectives - identification of appropriate benchmarks, achievable, measurable and timetabled.

Constituent 3: Research and analysis of ENV's base potential for marketing-led success:
a. Identification and evaluation of market opportunities
b. Identification and evaluation of core competitive advantages
c. Identification and evaluation of key resources available and access to them.

Constituent 4: Planning:
a. Developing details of marketing operations => for the manipulation of the marketing mix elements
b. Marshalling the required resources.

Constituent 5: Implementation:
a. Making the sale
b. Maintaining a competitive advantage.

Constituent 6: Constant review of progress against benchmarks.

Business Aims and Objectives

The marketing planning process in the context of the ENV will reflect the nature and character of the type of enterprise and the lifecycle stage it has reached. **Table 8.1** above outlines some of the key constituents of this process. These are not wholly sequential, as in the case of a step model. One constituent may require to be addressed simultaneously with another or before later constituents, depending on the nature of the challenges facing the new venture as it seeks to establish itself in the marketplace.

A starting point is the definition of business aims and objectives. The new venture founder may have numerous business aims. Examples of these might be:

- To develop an enterprise that will be successful
- To develop an enterprise that is enduring
- To develop an enterprise that is ethical and conscious of its responsibilities to society
- To develop the most successful enterprise in a particular industry sector within a given time period.

Business aims are likely to be quite broad and limited in detail, outlining in a general way how the new venture founder sees the enterprise developing over time.

Business objectives, on the other hand, begin to outline in more detail how these business aims might be achieved. The primary business objective, closest to the heart of most new venture founders, will be profit. They will need to have some idea, based on research (an issue addressed later) of what it is possible to achieve in terms of profit. The decision as to how much profit might be sought will depend on what is reasonable, once a thorough analysis of the many issues that will determine its level has been carried out. It will need to be expressed in quantifiable terms and be set against a timetable within which this level of profit can reasonably be expected to be achieved. These are the benchmarks for the new venture, against which the ongoing progress of the new venture can be measured. The successful achievement of these business objectives will contribute to the fulfilment of the business aims.

Marketing Aims and Objectives

To achieve the business aims and objectives of the new venture, the founder entrepreneur must obtain and maintain a strategic fit between an opportunity identified in the firm's marketplace and the resources needed to exploit it. The market opportunity and access to key resources are the key constituents of this entrepreneurial process. Appropriate marketing aims and objectives need to be identified which, if obtained, will contribute to the achievement of those business aims and objectives.

Again, marketing aims may be light in terms of details, reflecting the determination of the founder entrepreneur to provide existing customers within the firm's market with more of its products, and to develop even more innovative offerings for sale, as well as to seek access to additional new markets with those existing and innovative products.

Marketing objectives on the other hand, as with business objectives, need to be expressed in much more quantifiable ways, and should be set against reasonable timetables. By establishing appropriate benchmarks, the performance of the marketing activity of the new venture in contributing to the achievement of the business aims and objectives of the new enterprise can be measured. This can be done at different points of the planning period to confirm that real progress is being made against planned progress. In this way, the likelihood of success or failure in their achievement can be ascertained and the need for and nature of any remedial action, if required, can be identified. Marketing objectives primarily address issues to do with products and markets but also focus on matters to do with price, promotion and place – elements of the marketing mix. This issue will be dealt with in more detail shortly. First, we need consider the important matter of gathering the essential marketing intelligence needed to ensure that good decisions are made.

Research and Analysis

To establish the base potential of the ENV for marketing-led success, the entrepreneurial founder needs to undertake a considerable amount of research and analysis of key factors that will be key determinants of that potential success.

One dimension, often overlooked, is an examination of the new venture's internal market. Any analysis here will need to consider issues from personal competencies of people within the enterprise, including the new venture founder, to the availability of resources. The lead entrepreneur needs to undertake an audit of the new venture's strengths and weaknesses with respect to these types of internal factors to establish the potential of the new venture to meet the inherent challenges of addressing the demands of the external market and to identify what shortcomings there may be within the new venture in seeking to make that response.

From an external marketing point of view, the key factors will include the needs and wants of the new venture's potential customers, and the likely challenges of the competitors in the new venture's chosen market. Additional issues will include the need for insights to aspects of the wider marketing environment that can have an impact on the potential of any new venture for continued growth and development, including social issues, technological changes, economic developments, and political influences. The founding entrepreneur needs to analyse the potential opportunities and threats inherent in these important factors.

In seeking to establish the base potential of the new venture for successful performance in the marketplace and, hopefully, continued growth, the lead entrepreneur needs detailed insights into what intelligence is available to make a decision, what gaps exist in that knowledge, and how might those gaps be filled. The wider the gaps in the market intelligence available to the founder entrepreneur, the riskier the decision-making activity. Entrepreneurs are calculating risk-takers, not speculators. They need current, quality, and comprehensive market intelligence in order to be able to make decisions in which they can have confidence.

There are a number of points with respect to market research that need to highlighted. First, that data gathering is to a large extent a relatively indiscriminate activity, in that it seeks to gather up lots of information about a market in broad, essentially unrefined terms. Second, that market intelligence is information which has been distilled and refined in a way that allows specific decisions to be considered and made. The founder entrepreneur needs to know their potential customers' needs and wants and what issues influence their purchase decisions. They need to know how best to get their product to their customers, how best to communicate with them and to build relationships with them. They need to know what will give their new venture a competitive edge. They need to have intelligence about the nature of any competitive threat that they may face in seeking entry to a particular market. Gathering such data, and distilling intelligence from that data to help make informed marketing decisions, may be done formally through primary research or through accessing secondary research sources. These approaches can be time-consuming and expensive and, more often than not, will be largely beyond the resources of the new venture. The nature of the ENV demands an approach to information management that is innovative, flexible, and quick, and dependable in terms of results. The ability of the founder entrepreneur to build and manage a network of contacts is an essential resource in this activity of gathering information and confirming the value of that information so essential for effective marketing decision-making in an entrepreneurial context.

Planning

Operationalising marketing strategies designed to obtain and maintain a fit between a marketing opportunity and available resources requires action by the founder entrepreneur in a number of key areas. The marketing mix provides an elementary framework for understanding those key areas and how they might be manipulated in order to obtain the marketing, and ultimately the business, aims and objectives of the new venture.

The product is the primary element in the mix. As a consequence of market research undertaken, the founder entrepreneur will have formed valuable insights to what the customers' needs and wants are in terms of a particular product, whether it is a good or service. The challenge for the new venture is to meet those needs and wants in a way that is significantly better than competing companies. At a basic level the product must do what it is supposed to do – it must work – and do so in a way that meets the expectations of customers. Any product is essentially a solution to a problem or challenge faced by the end-user. For example, a car meets the needs of people for transport and travel, a CD player meets people's need for entertainment, or the Internet meets people's need for greater access to information and communication opportunities. The founder entrepreneur needs to be clear why the customers that they are targeting make the purchase decisions that they do. Understanding these motivations will provide the founder entrepreneur with insights into how they might differentiate their product offering from their nearest competitors. By providing greater added value in their products, which provide particular benefits to customers that they value, the new venture can go a long way to defining a unique competitive advantage. In any highly competitive market, of course, the challenge will be one of sustaining that competitive advantage. Consequently, the founder entrepreneur is constantly under pressure to identify new product and new market opportunities. As discussed above, this commitment to innovation is at the very heart of marketing and entrepreneurship.

Once the founder entrepreneur is satisfied that the product on offer performs at a level that meets the expectations of customers, the challenge then becomes one of making them aware that they can acquire it from the new venture, and to persuade them to do so. In addition, the founder entrepreneur must be able to deliver the product to the customer when and where the customer wants it and at a price that represents value as the customer understands it. With respect to promoting the new venture, the founder entrepreneur needs to be clear about who is being targeted and why, what is being said and how, and whether timing is important in the delivery of the message.

The importance of the founder entrepreneur undertaking constant research activity, in order to understand the needs and wants of customers, is critical to success. This research may give the founder entrepreneur insights into ways of segmenting the market into different niche groups, each with differing needs and wants. Such analysis will go some way to answering the questions above.

The founder entrepreneur will be challenged in any promotional campaign to build awareness initially in the mind of the targeted customers of the existence of the new venture and subsequently to inform them of what the new venture has to offer. The next stage will be to persuade those customers that the new venture is the one with which they should do business, as opposed to any others that they might consider. The final promotional challenge is to reinforce that message and thus to encourage repeat business and the possibility of developing deeper customer relationships.

There are several ways by which the founder entrepreneur might promote the new venture. Advertising offers a non-personal approach that may allow access to a wider or mass market. Personal selling, on the other hand, offers scope to interact with customers directly and to build important customer relationships. Direct marketing and, in particular, the Internet play a role here too and have enhanced the opportunities for effective promotional activity by the entrepreneurial new venture. Other methods for promoting the new venture are the use of publicity, particularly on occasions of a product launch, and sales promotion activity, when special incentives are used for a limited period of time to encourage sales.

The founder entrepreneur then will need to develop a promotional campaign that highlights the relative benefits of the product. A part of that message will focus on how the product on offer is real value for money. Setting the price of a product is a difficult challenge for any new venture. Getting it right requires a detailed consideration and research of the new venture's costs in producing its product or products and making them available to the marketplace, the new venture's customers, both actual and potential and the new venture's competition. No one issue can be overlooked by the founder entrepreneur or be given exclusive attention. To focus on one and to ignore the others would be both short-sighted and risky. The challenge for the founder entrepreneur in setting price is to strike that balance between what research suggests the market will bear and the crucial need to cover costs. Given the greater likelihood of the new venture targeting niche groups with high added value, quality products, the scope for market-skimming must be high and the prospects for setting relatively higher prices is greatly increased. A price penetration policy, on the other hand, would only be appropriate in circumstances, for example, where the focus is on gaining access to a much wider market, suggesting much lower prices, an arena where the new venture entrepreneur is unlikely to be at the outset.

Ultimately, the founder entrepreneur must ensure that the customer can get access to the product as and when it is wanted. "Place" in the marketing mix focuses on the delivery of the good or service in a way that is consistent with expectations of the customer. It addresses the logistical arrangements necessary to ensure that the new venture can do just that. It may involve the sourcing of raw materials through to distributing the product to the marketplace where it can be bought by the customer. The key challenge is to ensure that the customer is not inconvenienced by any failure on the part of the new venture to ensure that the product is available to that customer in the way that they want it, when they want it and where they want it. Any deviation from what the customer expects in this regard is to increase the sense of "hassle" that that customer experiences and risks their seeking an alternative, more sympathetic supplier.

The founder entrepreneur needs to consider how the new venture's products will be delivered to market. There are a number of marketing channels available to be considered, in order to increase the prospects of satisfying the needs of customers who want to buy their product. These include agents, who may represent the founder entrepreneur's new venture in certain markets, wholesalers and, where appropriate, retailers. Negotiating the roles and responsibilities of those involved in the distribution channels is a critical marketing responsibility of the founder entrepreneur that requires sensitivity and foresight.

Thus, ensuring product choice, that product supply is timely, that the product can be managed by the customer, are all "delivery" issues that the founder entrepreneur needs to consider.

Equally, there is a need to consider the resource implications for the new venture of producing or making a particular product available for sale. Here the emphasis will be on issues such as the sourcing of raw material at competitive prices and the management of quality control, including the minimisation of waste and package design.

Implementation

The marketing mix provides an elementary framework for gaining insights to the decision areas that will exercise the mind of the founder entrepreneur seeking to establish a new venture. What is clear is that any decisions on the product(s) to be sold, prices to be charged, promotion policies to be pursued and the distribution or delivery of the final product offering, cannot be taken in isolation from each other or of the environment outside and inside the new venture itself. However loosely it is practised, what is required is a planned, integrated marketing management approach that recognises the impact on the new venture of the dynamics of both the internal and external environment. What is also required is a commitment by the founder entrepreneur to implementing any marketing plan in a way that ensures the maintenance of a sustainable competitive advantage that defines meaningful differences between the new venture and its competition and enhances the prospects of making that sale again and again.

Review of Progress

The final point in **Table 8.1** focuses on the crucial issue of control within the planning process. It is an area where new venture entrepreneurs need greater clarity and conciseness. The importance of setting clear, quantifiable, and timetabled objectives was discussed above. What is also needed is a clear definition of appropriate performance measures for each aspect of the business. Sales, for example, might be analysed according to product group, sales territory, retails outlets, or customer groups. The founder must then identify a means of establishing where the venture is making and where it is losing money. Any analysis of the venture's products, for example, should identify those that are contributing to the profitability of the new venture and those that are not, over a particular time period. Where performance starts to deviate from objectives set down, there may be a need for some remedial action to be taken. This can take many forms and will depend on the nature of the problem, the availability of resources, and the characteristics of the danger actually posed by the deviation.

What is essential to recognise here is the need for an optimum degree of flexibility in implementing such a planning process within any ENV. To be effective in implementing such a process within such a context, what is needed are approaches that take account of the inherent characteristics of the entrepreneur and of the firm such a person is trying to create. Furthermore, there is a need to recognise the inherent marketing competencies and competency deficiencies that exist in those establishing such enterprises at this early point of its life cycle. Such "new" approaches will focus then on the individual entrepreneur's personal competencies and his/her use of networked relationships. There is now a need to turn to consider briefly the marketing challenges inherent in the need by the new venture founder to maintain the entrepreneurial effort of his or her firm into the future.

MAINTAINING THE ENV'S
ENTREPRENEURIAL EFFORT

The establishment of any new venture is only the beginning. Whether such an enterprise will remain entrepreneurial will be determined by the individual or group of individuals leading it and, as discussed above, whether they can nurture a strong marketing orientation within their firm. Such an orientation challenges the lead entrepreneur to remain constantly innovative, continuously opportunity-focused, and ultimately comfortable with change. The small firms they direct and manage will be committed to growth and business development as a fundamental strategic aim. However, maintaining the entrepreneurial effort needed to drive the process of growth and development forward, in a proactive way, presents the lead entrepreneur with different challenges.

The pursuit of growth, as a strategic aim, will impact on the simplicity of the pioneering firm, where there is "limited marketing", forcing it to develop more of a "comprehensive marketing" approach. It must do this in order to meet the changing needs of an increasingly complex environment, characterised by an increasingly sophisticated customer base, expanding markets, new collaborators (for example, suppliers, intermediaries and distributors) as well as competitors (McKee *et al*, 1990).

The emerging complexities of the new external environment, in which the entrepreneurial firm finds itself deeper with each success, will have implications for the way that those in the firm do business. The emerging new complexities that come to characterise the growing firm threaten to open gaps in the competency portfolio of the lead entrepreneur or members of the entrepreneurial team. The pressure for a greater formulism in the practice of marketing will challenge the need to maintain the entrepreneurial effort of the firm, focused on persistent innovation and change (Carson *et al*, 1995). To be effective, however, there is a need for people in the firm to acquire the competencies necessary to meet the emerging new challenges facing the growing firm.

CONCLUSION

The practice of marketing in the ENV, therefore, must reflect its relatively unique character and circumstance. The approach to marketing decision-making in such a context will be largely unstructured, highly informal, reflecting a great deal of short-term, haphazard thinking. The emphasis will be very much on identifying and evaluating marketing opportunities and finding the resources needed to exploit them. The approach will be essentially opportunistic and sub-conscious, based on a great deal of poorly-developed intuitive guess-work as the new venture founder confronts all sorts of information gaps and inconsistencies about the firm's markets. Contrary to conventional models, planning practice in the ENV, insofar as it can be identified, will be non-linear in character. Instead, it will be largely chaotic, highly centralised and unsophisticated, focusing on product and price issues and how best to get that next sale.

Entrepreneurial individuals have a preference for face-to-face communications. This is particularly important for gathering data before making decisions about issues that may determine the future potential of their infant enterprises. In a bid to enhance the potential for better marketing decision-making within the ENV, what is important is how effectively the founding entrepreneur can develop and manage personal contacts or networked relationships. The networked relationships of the founders of new ventures emerge as a key resource in identifying new market opportunities, in accessing essential resources, in confirming the rights and wrongs of marketing and business development decisions, in researching the potential of a market opportunity and in determining how best to approach it for real success. In determining that approach, the new venture founder will seek information and guidance from appropriate network members as to the nature of the product sought by customers, the value that they place upon it, the best way to make that product available to them, and how best to ensure that they know that it is available. Through networked relationships, they can nurture customer loyalty and define significant competitive advantages.

An innovative aspect of this commitment to relationship marketing is the influence of technology, either as a means of increasing channel efficiencies by lowering costs or as a means of increasing effectiveness by facilitating more meaningful relationships between channel parties. This focus on technology points up the potential importance of the Internet as a key marketing resource. The Internet, it is argued, constitutes a veritable revolution in the way key marketing relationships can be managed (McGowan and Durkin, 2002). The interactivity it offers enables one-to-one marketing. As markets continue to fragment, this new technology presents the entrepreneur with both marketing opportunities and threats. A crucial challenge that faces the founder entrepreneur therefore is to develop competencies in these areas of marketing activity. If the new venture remains entrepreneurial and develops and grows into the future, the founder entrepreneur and his or her team will face increasing complexities and different challenges that will expose weaknesses in their portfolio of skills and knowledge. As the need for ever-increasing sophistication in the practice of marketing makes its impact, the need for equally sophisticated marketing competencies will make itself felt. An openness to such professional growth will be crucial if that entrepreneurial effort is to be maintained.

QUESTIONS

1. Discuss the nature of the interface between marketing and entrepreneurship, examining the areas of overlap and differences that exist between them.
2. Examine the marketing advantages of the entrepreneurial new venture seeking entry to a competitive market
3. How might the founder entrepreneur of a new venture approach marketing planning in a way that is different to that adopted by more established companies?
4. What are the constituents of marketing planning for an entrepreneurial new venture?
5. Examine the implications for growth of the practice of marketing in the entrepreneurial new venture.

USEFUL WEBSITES

www.cim.co.uk
www.mii.ie

CHECKLIST FOR CHAPTER

After reading this chapter, check that you understand and appreciate:
- The overlap that exists at the marketing/entrepreneurship interface;
- The marketing advantages of small new ventures
- The practice of marketing in such enterprises
- The elements of a marketing planning process for the entrepreneurial new venture
- The nature of marketing planning processes in such a context
- The important aspect of implementing the marketing plan
- The importance of networked relationship management and the Internet in effective marketing practice in new venture creation.

REFERENCES

Carson, D., Cromie, S., McGowan, P. and Hill, J. (1995) - *Marketing and Entrepreneurship: An Innovative Approach for SMEs* - Prentice Hall International, London.

Cunningham, B.J. and Lischeron, J. (1991) - Defining Entrepreneurship - *Journal of Small Business Management*, Vol.29, No.1, pp 45-61.

Drucker, P. (1985) - *Innovation and Entrepreneurship* - Pan Business Books.

Gardner, D.M. (1991) - Exploring the Marketing/Entrepreneurship Interface - *Research at the Marketing/Entrepreneurship Interface* (Edited by Hills, G. and LaForge, R.W.), UIC/AMA Publication, pp 3-21.

Greenly, G.E. and Bayus, B.L. (1993) - Marketing Planning Decision-Making in UK and US Companies: An Empirical Comparative Study - *Journal of Marketing Management*, Vol.9, pp 155-172.

Leppard, J. and McDonald, M.H.B. (1991) - Marketing Planning and Corporate Culture: A Conceptual Framework Which Examines Management Attitudes in the Context of Marketing Planning - *Journal of Marketing Management*, Vol.7, No.3, pp 213-236.

McDonald, M. (1992) - Strategic Marketing Planning: A State of the Art Review - *Marketing Intelligence and Planning*, Vol.10, No.4, pp 4-22.

McGowan, P. and Durkin, M. (2002) – "Toward an understanding of Internet adoption at the Marketing/Entrepreneurship Interface" – *Journal of Marketing Management*, Vol.18, pp 361-377.

McKee, D.O., Varadarajan, P.R. and Vasser, J. (1990) - A Taxonomy of Marketing Planning Styles - *Journal of the Academy of Marketing Science*, Vol.18, No.2, pp 134-141.

Vraking, W.J. (1990) - The Innovative Organisation - *Long Range Planning*, Vol.23, No.2, pp 94-102.

CHAPTER 9

OPERATIONS – DESIGNING THE PROCESS

Bill O'Gorman[*]

LEARNING OBJECTIVES

- To understand the "process of making"
- To examine the supply chain and the transformation process
- To gain a general understanding of process and process types
- To analyse design for manufacturing (DFM), service, and delivery
- To assess the impact of customer requirements on the design of a process
- To evaluate the impact of product/process design on the design of process and delivery
- To understand the importance of considering location.

INTRODUCTION

In theory, at least, the "factory" should not be designed, let alone built, until the entire "process of making" – all the way to the final customer – is understood (Drucker, 1990). It is essential that the entrepreneur/new

---

[*] Bill O'Gorman is a lecturer in entrepreneurship, operations and management at University College Cork.

business venture owner understands fully what the customer requires, what it is that they are offering to the customer, and what is the optimum way to provide this product or service to the customer. It is the understanding of the entire process of making that is essential to providing excellent customer service, and managing a successful, profitable, sustainable business.

This chapter will trace the process of making from inception to delivery. First, it will define the notion of supply chain and identify the meaning of the "process of making". It will explore the generic meaning of process, and examine some common process types. The criteria for location will be explored, as well as the importance of technology and systems. Finally, the importance of, and connection between, process/ service design and the design of the transformation process will be assessed. The chapter will also explore the issues involved in deciding what a new business venture requires in order to design and set-up its facility to meet the goals, objectives, and aspirations of the company while at the same time "delighting the customer" (Ho, 1999).

OPERATIONS DESIGN IN CONTEXT

Fundamentally, the notion of operations, operations design, and operations management as core elements of providing products and services has its roots in the 18th century during the Industrial Revolution (Schroeder, 1993; Russell and Taylor, 2000; Chase, Aquilano, and Jacobs, 2001). Smith (1776) describes the move from craftsmanship and an individual completing an entire job as the division of labour. It is this division of labour that enabled mass production, automation, and productivity, which ultimately leads to the success of business and the wealth of nations. This core concept of the division of labour is still applicable today in the 21st century and, even though the nature of work has changed with the introduction of high-speed computers, the World Wide Web, and intelligent machines, it is still necessary to consider the *new* division of labour when designing and setting up a process to deliver a product or service to customers.

The role of managing operations became more prominent in the aftermath of the World War II. Much of the research at that time was focused on manufacturing. However, many researchers (Schroeder, 1993; Slack, Chambers and Johnston, 2001; Naylor, 2002; and Chase, Aquilano, and Jacobs, 2001) today see little difference between the provision of services and the provision of products. As Schroeder (1993) states:

> *On the surface, it may appear that service operations have very little in common with manufacturing operations. However, a unifying feature of these operations is that both can be viewed as transformational processes.*

The role of operations is to create value (Russell and Taylor, 2000). Skinner (1985) saw manufacturing as the ultimate competitive weapon and Dilworth (2000) saw operations as having a vital role in achieving the company's goals and strategic plan. This central role of operations is another good reason why organisations and entrepreneurs who are starting their own business need to pay considerable attention to the design and development of their operations and the delivery of their products/services to their customers. Without a well-coordinated, efficient and effective transformation process, the company, after the initial euphoria of start-up, will struggle and find it difficult to continue being competitive. As Drucker (1992) maintained, organisations must be organised for constant change and flexibility.

Another point to consider is that there is no "one and only one right way" to set up a new process. This chapter proposes a set of guidelines that ought to be used when considering starting a new business and setting up and developing a new transformation process. As Loch (2000) concluded in his research about new product development:

> *It is not sufficient to determine project positioning and new product development process by "implementing best practice"; they must be tailored to strategic position and existing process structures.*

So too in developing a new transformation process, this process must be tailored to the strategic intent of the organisation. Managing the operation is managing the transformation process and, as Naylor (2002) suggested "operations lie at the heart of all organisations".

DEFINING THE PROCESS OF MAKING

Many entrepreneurs and/or new business venture owners have a tendency to take a short-term view of the product/service they are providing. Often the reason for this short-term view is a question of *survival*. They have a business idea and are afraid that, if they delay any longer, somebody else will develop the same idea and put them out of business before they start. In other cases, entrepreneurs can be so excited by their own creation and ideas that they just want to get into action as soon as possible.

This short-term urgency can work well in the initial stages of start-up, in that the owner-manager knows what he/she wants to provide to customers. Maybe he/she is able to provide the product/service entirely through their own efforts, and the number of customers and products/services are few. But as the business begins to grow in volume of output and number of customers, this "one person operation" will not be able to cope with the expansion and required levels of additional customer service. Therefore, it is vital that the "process of making" is fully understood as early as possible in the delivery cycle, so that the process is developed with a view to providing as comprehensive a service as possible to multiple customers (Drucker, 1990).

The process of making means assessing everything that is involved in providing products/services to customers. It is not just what is happening within the office or manufacturing facility, it includes inputs from suppliers, employees, legislation, etc. This is supply chain management. All of the items depicted in **Figure 9.1** below need to be taken into consideration when deciding how a product or service is to be provided to customers. It is the understanding and managing of the entire supply chain that makes the process of making efficient, effective, profitable, and sustainable.

TRANSFORMATION PROCESS

The transformation process is key to the provision of products and services to customers. It is the central activity of any business venture (Naylor, 2002). Within the transformation process, change is implemented to an item in order to alter it from one state to another. A simplified version of the transformation process is shown in **Figure 9.2**.

FIGURE 9.1: SUPPLY CHAIN MANAGEMENT

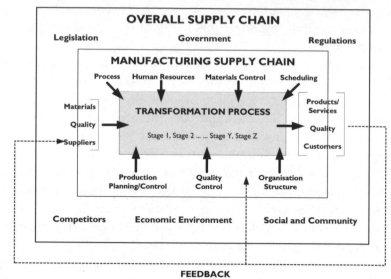

© O'Gorman, B., 2000

FIGURE 9.2: THE TRANSFORMATION PROCESS

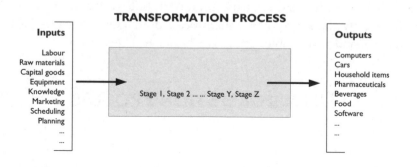

The transformation process is that part of the overall manufacturing system that adds value to the inputs. Value can be added to an item in a number of different ways. Five of the major ways of adding value are:

- **Alter:** Something can be changed structurally. This is one of the most common methods of adding value in a manufacturing system. For example, in light engineering, a sheet of metal may be transformed into a box or metal frame. In the service sector, the alteration may happen to an individual. If a person goes to a beautician, there is (or should be) an alteration in the appearance of the individual

- **Transport:** Within the transformation process, there is movement of material from one stage of the process to the next. This can be either automated or manual. When the product is complete, unless it is transported to the consumer, it is a liability to the manufacturing company. Here, transportation adds value to the product
- **Store:** Storage can add value to certain products. In the making of wine, whiskey and brandy, storage is an essential part of the transformation process. In the production of brandy, once the liquid is produced from the fermentation of the grapes, it is not worth much in monetary terms until it has been stored in an oak cask for at least six years
- **Inspect:** This is mainly associated with adding value in relation to service industries. However, it can also apply to manufacturing industries in relation to customer service and warranty. For example, in the building business, a high-rise office block cannot be populated until the authorities have inspected the building and passed it for use
- **Adding or Assembling:** This is the most used method of adding value in a manufacturing system, especially in electronic, mechanical and electro-mechanical manufacturing operations. The value-adding is in the form of assembling raw material into a particular pattern to give the combination of the raw material in the finished product a far greater value than the sum of the individual parts. This, combined with all the other elements of the transformation process, is what gives the total value that the consumer is willing to pay for the product.

Thus, the first step in designing the manufacturing and delivery process is for the entrepreneur/new business owner to decide which transformation process is best suited to their business. Once this fit has been identified, then the next step of designing the process itself can be embarked upon.

PROCESS

The basic factors affecting the design of a process are:
- The volume of the product, and the level of service required to be performed or delivered to customers
- The degree of involvement of the customer
- The design and nature of the product and service itself.

Volume and Level of Service

The volume and size of product to be produced has a major implication on the type of process that is designed and used. For example, if the business is the manufacture of aircraft, large boats, houses, or bridges, then the type of process used will be a *fixed location*. Fixed location is where all or most of the resources are brought to the location where the product is made and, when the product is completed, the resources move to another location.

If business requires products or services in small batches, then it will use a *jobbing shop* or *batch type* process. Most small engineering works are jobbing shops, in that they manufacture small batches for several customers. Other forms of jobbing or batch process include hairdressers or beauticians, in that customers can avail of specific services or a range of services. The number of customers to be processed will have an input on the size and layout of the jobbing or batch facility. Larger volumes are catered for in larger facilities and the process is more streamlined. Compare, for example, a corner shop to a supermarket. In the corner shop, the facility is small and personable, and the customer can spend time over their shopping. In the supermarket, the facility and volumes are large and the focus is on processing as many customers as quickly as possible. The process is generally anonymous and impersonal.

From a manufacturing point of view, large volumes will be processed in a *continuous line flow* process, whereby the making of products is divided into small steps and the product progresses through these steps with additional value being added at each step. An example of this type of process is the manufacture of computers and other large volume consumer products.

The last major process design to consider is that of *processing*. For low volumes, this may take the form of a laboratory or microbrewery-type of set-up. For large volumes, it may require major capital investment and would resemble major chemical, pharmaceutical, or brewing-type industries.

Degree of Involvement of Customers

This is a very important consideration when defining the design of the process, facility and delivery system. Operations are not influenced only by volume and the nature and design of the product and service but also by the degree of involvement of the customer (Naylor, 1999). The degree of involvement can be categorised into two main features:

- **Manufacturing and isolated services:** Where the customer is distant and often isolated from the process of making, and the main concern is with the way goods flow through the production process
- **Personal service:** Where the customer enters the facility area and is part of the process of making. In this scenario, the attention switches to questions such as queues, convenience, comfort and the way the work environment contributes to sales.

Therefore, an entrepreneur and new business venture owner has to decide on the degree of involvement customers have with their process of making. This degree of involvement is also volume-dependant. If the product or service is one that has mass appeal and therefore needs to be provided in large volumes, then standardisation will be required so that all customers receive the same or similar quality. For example, when manufacturing personal computers or other electronic consumer goods, volumes are large, and organisations such as Dell, Intel and Glen Dimplex have standardised manufacturing processes that happen away from the customer. Thus, the link between customer and the process of making is narrow and defined by the "gate-keepers" – sales and marketing and customer services. However, if the volumes are low because the company has decided to provide a customised service, like that of top-of-the-range Rolls Royce or Morgan cars, then the facilities will be small and even though there will be some isolation between customers and the process of making, there will be a greater deal of interaction between them.

If the product or service being provided is such that the customer is an integral part of the process of making, then the process and facility needs to be laid out accordingly. For example, if the entrepreneur or new business venture owner is setting up a health and sports facility, then everything about the facility, from the moment customers arrive at reception all the way through the whole facility, has to proclaim health and fitness.

Design and Nature of the Product and Service

To many people, these are the most important aspects of designing the process and facility. No matter how well capacity is planned to handle volumes, and even when the facility is designed to cater for the degree of customer involvement, nothing will work smoothly if the product or service is not manufacturable or deliverable. There has to be synergy between the product/service and the manufacturing/delivery process.

Basic rules to keep in mind when designing this synergy include:

- Keep the functional and physical characteristics as simple as possible – the more features that are designed into a product, the more complex the product, and therefore the more difficult it is to manufacture. Obviously, if the customer wants the features, then they need to be designed in, but these must be taken into consideration when designing the process. For example, if a product and process is designed with features that use electronic IC (integrated circuit) devices of 0.25mm pitch, then there is no point in agreeing additional features with customers that would demand the use of 0.10mm pitch devices, if the manufacturing facility does not have the equipment to place these devices on the printed circuit boards
- Design for the most economical production/delivery method and minimum number of process steps – design the product/service in such a way that there are as few steps as possible in the process. The more steps there are in the process, the greater the chance of making mistakes. This results in a greater potential for error and scrap and reduced customer satisfaction.

Also, the more steps in the process, the greater the cost of producing, which in turn means a higher cost to the consumer. This point is demonstrated by comparing Ryanair, a low cost airline, to "traditional" airlines. Traditionally, airlines offered a comprehensive service to consumers. They had different types of aircraft for different routes, catering services and cabin crew to match, and tickets were booked through agents. Ryanair simplified this process by:

- Having only one type of aircraft, making maintenance easier and more cost-effective
- Not providing complimentary meals and drinks, so the number of cabin crew required and the time required to ready planes between flights is reduced
- Using technology of the day to enable customers to do online booking directly, through a very user-friendly e-commerce system.

Such changes allow for a more economic production/delivery of flights to consumers.

When designing the process, it is essential to understand customer requirements. There is not much point in supplying products and services that customers do not require. However, what is very important is to provide customers with products and services that not alone meet their requirements but exceed them (Ho, 1999). But exceeding requirements should not be at a cost to the operation; rather, it should be an integral part of the cost of provision and delivery of products and services. Ho offers examples from Japanese industry:

> There is a trend in modern day competition between Japanese companies to give you rather more in order to "delight" you. So when you buy a lamp bulb that has a "mean time between failure" of 1,000 hours, the Japanese manufacturer will try their best to ensure that you get at least 20% more. Likewise, when you buy a Japanese brand video-tape specifying 180 minutes, it can normally record up to 190 minutes. When you buy a "mink" coat from a department store in Japan, they will invite you to store the fur coat in their temperature-control room during the summer season free-of-charge. They call these extra little things "extra-ordinary customer satisfaction" or "delighting the customers".

These "little extras" are provided at little additional cost to the company, but they are valued by customers, and so have the knock-on effect of greater customer satisfaction and increased market share.

LOCATION

After a company has defined *what* will be provided and *how many*, it must address the question of *how* those goods and services are to be provided (Dilworth, 2000). Thus location is another important factor to take into consideration when designing the "process of manufacture" and delivery. Location is also dependant on volume and the nature of the product and service that is being provided. For example, if the product or service is linked to the sea-fishing industry, it makes sense that the facility is located near its source (the sea). If the business is a processing industry such as chemical, pharmaceutical, or brewing, the facility will need to be close to a clean water source. If the business is a high-tech design industry, it makes sense to be located near a technical institute or university. If the business is high-volume and labour-intensive, the facility needs to be located near an area of high population.

The new business venture also needs to consider customer requirements, and importance of location of customers. Some major, large-volume, multinational companies like to have their suppliers located near them. That is one of the reasons why Ireland has done so well as regards inward investment of high-tech companies during the 1990s. Some customers like to have the comfort of having their suppliers close at hand; it gives them a feeling of security, flexibility, and greater responsiveness from suppliers. However, with today's technology and physical infrastructures, there is probably less of a need to be located so close to customers. By the same token, it is necessary to work with customers in such a fashion, and to communicate with them (even visit) on such a regular basis that the physical distance between the new organisation and the customer is not visible. Selection of good facility locations enables a company to provide convenient, dependable service to its customers (Dilworth, 2000).

Technology and Systems

Technology is the hardware (for example, plant and equipment) that transforms materials and information into products and services, which become the added-value items that are sold, and the systems and "software" that energises, controls and makes effective the hardware (Samson, 1991). Without up-to-date technology, the business venture will have difficulty surviving. This does not mean that the new venture needs to reinvest in modern technology every few months, but it does mean that management should monitor the competitor environment and assess, on a regular basis, the needs of upgrading technology.

For example, in electronic manufacturing, there is still a niche for hand assembly, but this will not be competitive in medium- to high-volume manufacturing for two reasons. First, hand assembly is very costly *versus* machine insertion. Second, it is extremely difficult to successfully hand-place advanced technology components such as 0.10mm pitch IC devices.

IT systems such as MRPII, ERP, CRM, and financial packages are essential to the effective and efficient operating of integrated businesses. The new business venture does not need to invest to the same degree as larger businesses, but it still needs to invest in some systems to enable the sustainability of their venture.

New business ventures also need to have quality systems in place. It is not necessary that the new business venture has the equivalent of ISO, but it does need to have a good, repeatable quality system in place that is used and adhered to by all employees from receptionist to managing director. It is essential that customers can trace their products and services through the quality system and, most importantly, that there is a good corrective action process in place so that customers have confidence that, if anything does go wrong, it can be fixed quickly and the problem will not be repeated.

Design for Manufacturing and Design for Service

Meredith and Shafer (1999) made the point that, too often, the traditional firm whips up an engineering design as quickly as it can (since it has had to start from scratch) and then passes the design on to manufacturing without giving a thought to how it can be made (sometimes it cannot be made). Not alone do the engineers not give a thought for the manufacturing process, they equally do not give a thought to how the product or service is to be delivered to customers. Such a scenario is costly, both from a manufacturing point and a potential for loss of market share. If a product is not manufacturable, additional costs will be incurred in the process to include modifications to the design, the use of additional (often unplanned) resources, and the cost of additional material to compensate for the fallout of product during the manufacturing process. Equally, if the product or service is not designed for ease of delivery to customers, additional costs will be incurred in managing non-standard deliveries. There is also a high risk of loss of revenue (and market share) due to product returns and customer dissatisfaction.

It has been estimated that 70% or more of a manufactured product's cost is fixed by its design, because this establishes the number of parts that must be made or purchased, the types of material and equipment that will be used, and the amount of labour that will be needed (Dilworth, 2000). Thus, it is essential that the entrepreneur/new business owner considers in great detail the design of their products, services, manufacturing and delivery processes.

The literature generally outlines that there are three simple, basic rules to design for manufacturability:

- **Standardisation:** This involves having fewer choices of components and products to be produced. It means standardising the designs so that most components are reusable in new designs, or that many components are used in many different products
- **Simplification:** This involves having as few components as possible in the product. It also involves having as few steps as possible in the manufacturing process. The fewer components to be used and the fewer steps in the process lessen the probability of making mistakes
- **Modularisation:** This makes it possible to have relatively high product variety and low component variety at the same time. The idea is to develop a series of basic product components, or modules,

that can be assembled into a large number of different products. To the customer, it appears there are a great number of different products. To operations, there are only a limited number of basic components and processes (Schroeder, 2000).

Overall, the delivery process can be simplified by reducing the number of suppliers, and shortening the distance and number (and complexity) of transactions between the supplier and the end customer.

Designing the service is as important as designing the product. Services that are allowed to just "happen" rarely meet customer needs (Russell and Taylor, 2000). The basic steps involved are the same as for design for manufacturing and assembly, namely standardisation, simplification and modularisation. A well-designed service system is consistent with the strategic focus of the firm, user-friendly, robust in that it is able to cope with surges in demand (or, conversely, a drop-off in demand), easy to maintain, cost-effective, and visible to the customer. A well-designed manufacturing, service and delivery process will lead to the development of a competitive, sustainable company.

CONCLUSION

Before the process of manufacturing and/or delivery of a new business venture is designed, it is imperative to understand the entire "process of making". The process involves inputs, a transformation process, and outputs. A good, well-designed process will "delight the customer" and lead to greater market share, greater profitability, and sustainability. It is also important to understand the impact of volume, nature of the product/service, design of product/service, and involvement of the customer in the design and location of the facility.

QUESTIONS

1. Explain what is meant by the term "process of making".
2. Specify the transformation process and what it means to an entrepreneur establishing a manufacturing business.
3. Detail the five major ways of adding value to a product.
4. How does the design of a process differ between products and services?

5. Describe the basic factors affecting the design of a process.
6. Give a detailed account of the operational issues that would need to be considered when establishing a health club.
7. "Location is critical to the success of a manufacturing business." Discuss.

USEFUL WEBSITES

www.amtmag.com
www.benchmarking.co.uk/
www.bmpcoe.org/
www.ceia.ie
www.enterprise-ireland.ie
www.excellence-ireland.ie
www.fas.ie
www.iei.ie
www.iitd.ie
www.isme.ie
www.mel.nist.gov/
www.sebic.ie
www.sfa.ie
www.smartgroup.org
www.sme.org/
www.software.ie
www.wceb.ie

CHECKLIST FOR CHAPTER

After reading this chapter, check that you understand and appreciate:
• The "process of making"
• The supply chain and the transformation process
• Process and process types
• Design for manufacturing (DFM), service, and delivery
• The impact of customer requirements on the design of a process
• The impact of product/process design on the design of process and delivery
• The importance of considering location.

REFERENCES

Amrine, H.T., Ritchey, J.A. and Hulley, O.S. (1982) - *Manufacturing Organisations and Management* - Prentice Hall, New Jersey.

Chase, R.B., Aquilano, N.J. and Jacobs, F.R. (2001, 9th Ed) - *Operations Management for Competitive Advantage* - McGraw Hill, New York.

Dilworth, J.B. (2000, 3rd Ed) - *Operations Management: Providing Value in Goods and Services* - Dryden, U.S.

Drucker, P.F. (1990) - *Manufacturing* Renaissance - Harvard Business Review Books, Boston.

Drucker, P.F. (1992) - The New Society of Organisations - *Harvard Business Review*, Sept-Oct, pp. 95-104.

Ho, S.K.M. (1999) - *Operations and Quality Management* - Thomson Business Press, UK.

Loch, C. (2000) - Tailoring Product Development to Strategy: Case of a European Technology Manufacturer - *European Management Journal*, Vol.18, No.3, pp. 246-258.

Meredith, J.R. and Shafer, S.M. (1999) - *Operations Management for MBAs* - John Wiley, U.S.

Naylor, J. (1999) – *Management* - Financial Times, U.S.

Naylor, J. (2002, 2nd Ed) - *Introduction to Operations Management* - Prentice Hall, UK.

Russell, R.S. and Taylor, B.W. (2000) - *Operations Management* - Prentice Hall, U.S.

Samson, D. (1991) - *Manufacturing and Operations Management* - Prentice Hall, Australia.

Schroeder, R.G. (1993) - *Operations Management: Decision-Making in the Operations Function* - McGraw Hill, U.S.

Schroeder, R.G. (2000) - *Operations Management: Contemporary Concepts and Cases* - McGraw Hill, U.S.

Skinner, W. (1985) - *Manufacturing: The Formidable Competitive Weapon* - John Wiley, New York.

Slack, N., Chambers, S. and Johnston, R. (2001, 3rd Ed) - *Operations Management* – Prentice Hall, UK.

Smith, A. (1776 - Reprint 1991) – *The Wealth of Nations* - Prometheus Books, New York.

Sule, D.R. (1988) - *Manufacturing Facilities, Location, Planning, and Design* - PWS-Kent, Boston.

Yankee, H.W. (1979) - *Manufacturing Processes* - Prentice Hall, New Jersey.

CHAPTER 10

HUMAN RESOURCE MANAGEMENT

*Dermot Rush**

LEARNING OBJECTIVES

- To understand the core contribution of Human Resource Management to firm success
- To know what aspects of human resource management make the critical difference in high performance organisations
- To learn how to structure and focus recruitment and selection practices
- To learn how to ensure that training and development activities add real value
- To comprehend how to build robust performance management and development processes
- To understand the importance of establishing an open and involving company culture.

INTRODUCTION

Human Resources Management (HRM) is concerned with optimising the ways in which human resources are acquired, organised, developed, and

---

* Dermot Rush is a director of The Performance Partnership, a Human Resources Management consultancy based in Galway.

motivated to add value to the enterprise. HRM has evolved through three main streams of activity (Armstrong, 1989):

- **Personnel administration and welfare:** Activities primarily concerned with administering the recruitment, contracting and deployment of staff including contracts, payroll and benefits, provision for sickness, and other support arrangements
- **Promoting excellence in performance:** Activities concerned with how to organize staff and develop performance. Here, the focus has been on getting the organisation structure right and providing training and development activities
- **Industrial and employee relations:** Activities concerned with the resolution of disputes and the building of a climate conducive to staff morale.

A more contemporary approach to HRM builds on the foundation of these activities and adds value by ensuring that critical aspects of "people-related practices" within the company are aligned closely with the business strategy and goals. This approach gives a more proactive and business-focused dimension to HRM and is arguably better suited to the dynamic nature of many new venture companies.

The late 1990s saw an upsurge in research on the human resource management practises that contribute to more successful firm performance, as measured by indices such as ROI, shareholder value and customer satisfaction levels (Becker and Huselid, 1998). This research clearly identified the need to ensure that human resources practices are directly aligned with the current and future-facing strategies of the firm. Put simply, the key human resourcing practices of a research and development-focused start-up will differ considerably from those of a firm intent on cost-efficiencies in a saturated market. Nevertheless, the same set of core human resource activities underpin high performance in most commercially-orientated ventures.

These key HR drivers or factors are:

- Recruitment and selection practices
- Training and development practices
- Building a strong employee involvement culture
- Operating a robust performance management system.

Successful companies use regular measurement processes that track the efficacy of each of these factors. This chapter will demonstrate how these drivers relate to the development of a new venture.

RECRUITMENT AND SELECTION
PRACTICES

A challenge for Irish employers during times of economic prosperity is finding the right person for a particular position. Indeed, anecdotal evidence suggests that there has been an increasing difficulty for Irish employers in finding any staff (good or bad) during the economic prosperity of the early years of the new millennium. The key challenges therefore in recruitment include attracting the right candidates, selecting the candidates with the best fit to the positions required, and setting the appropriate performance expectations in the process. The recruitment process is illustrated in **Figure 10.1** below:

FIGURE 10.1: THE RECRUITMENT PROCESS

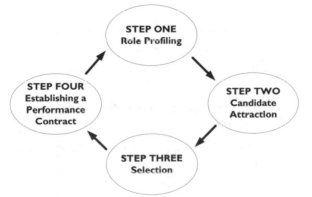

Step One – Role Profiling:

A simple start to role profiling involves answering the following questions:

1. Why is this role needed and what objectives will it fulfil?
2. What other roles will it interface with and to what level of interdependence?
3. What are the main tasks in this role? Which are most frequent and which are most critical?
4. What are the main types of interaction in the role?
5. What knowledge, skills, or special qualifications are required for role performance? Distinguish between what is an initial role requirement and what can be learnt on the job.

6. What aspects of the role need to be done absolutely right first time, to what standard?
7. What are the most critical things that can go wrong in this role and what personal characteristics might contribute to this?
8. How do really excellent performers do this role, what distinctive style do they use?
9. What type of demand levels can be expected in the role? What will be the main pressure points?
10. How is the role likely to evolve over time?

The answers to these 10 questions will allow the entrepreneur to define the selection criteria for the job or role. Typically, selection criteria will break out along the following dimensions:

- Knowledge base and formal qualifications
- Prior experience level required
- Skills level required
- Competency profile (defined as the distinctive personal attributes or behaviours required to do the job well)
- Personal engagement, motivation and availability for the role.

Step Two – Sourcing and Attracting Talent

The next step is to sell the company and the role profile to the right candidate pool. Suffice it to say that the options here are typically to advertise the role in the appropriate media and/or to retain the services of recruitment specialists (DBM Ireland, 2001).

Remember that advertisements should embody what is unique or distinctive in the company brand or proposition and cannot contain any of the discriminatory prohibitions mentioned in **Chapter 6**.

Step Three – The Selection Assessment Process

Research on high-performance organisations identifies the use of validated selection tests as a key-differentiating factor at the recruitment stage. This is supported by other HR research that recommends the use of more than one assessment method for any critical roles. **Table 10.1** below indicates the relative effectiveness of the main assessment methods used in selection:

TABLE 10.1: THE PREDICTIVE POWER OF SELECTION METHODS

0.65	Assessment Centres (Promotion)
0.54	Work Sampling
0.53	Ability Tests
0.43	Assessment Centres (Development)
0.39	Personality Questionnaires
0.38	Biodata
0.23	References
0.19	Interviews

Smith, 1988

The mistake that many companies make in recruitment is to assume that experience equals competence. A sound selection assessment will go beyond "what" the candidate has done and establish "how well" they have done it. The recommended approach is to prioritise the selection criteria developed using the 10 questions format above and then choose the assessment methods that best measure these criteria. A simple rule of thumb is to use a more objective test or assessment exercise in combination with a structured interview. The interview is also a critical opportunity for the entrepreneur to sell their vision for the business in a compelling and engaging way to the right candidate.

Step Four – Establishing the Performance Contract

The final step in the selection process is establishing the psychological contract. At the point of making a job offer, it is crucial to spell out the performance expectations that the business will have of the individual and the support, recognition and reward that it will provide in return.

While many owner-managers complain of the difficulty in finding the right people, it is interesting to note how some organisations always appear to attract those who share the values of the organisation. The entrepreneur sets the tone for the organisation by way of their values and business beliefs, and that is demonstrated on a daily basis through the staff that they are willing, or unwilling, to employ.

TRAINING AND DEVELOPMENT PRACTICES

A new venture should have some element of uniqueness or quality that will give it an initial competitive edge in the marketplace. The question then arises as how to sustain and develop further this position of superiority. The level and quality of training and development for both new and experienced staff is a second critical determinant of high performance organisations, with the more successful companies providing over three times more training than their less successful cohort. It is not simply a question of quantity either, as the more successful companies typically adopt a more focused approach to their training and development activity, ensuring that the bulk of training is concentrated on areas directly linked to tangible performance improvement. This approach requires identification of the critical performance factors that will give the company a distinctive performance advantage (See the 10 questions approach that was used for role profiling earlier). Put simply, an entrepreneur must identify the specific behaviours or competencies that underpin the performance of really effective individuals and teams. It is in these areas that the training and development spend should be concentrated. The *caveat* here is that performance-enhancing training may often need to be preceded by baseline training covering induction, process skills or certification training.

There are a number of support schemes to help organisations to benchmark their development activities against best practice, including the Excellence Through People scheme promoted by FÁS.

Finally, it makes good sense to regularly track and review the effectiveness of training activities. The five-level approach highlighted in **Table 10.2** is a useful format to follow, as it looks at training impact from a number of different perspectives.

The level of spending by Irish firms on training is generally quite low. Many entrepreneurs believe that it is a waste of limited firm resources to train a person who may leave the company subsequently, taking their expertise to another organisation. But what is the option – not train them and keep them for life?

TABLE 10.2: FIVE LEVEL EVALUATION FRAMEWORK FOR A TRAINING PROGRAMME

Level	Evaluation Activity	Source of Evidence	Key Questions to ask
5	Cost Benefit analysis	Not possible to get a current measure of tangible benefit that could be directly linked to the programme. But business performance data in relevant areas will be the ultimate criterion versus the costs of the training investment	Does the relative "on the job" benefit justify the overall costs of the programme?
4	Generalisation of skills and knowledge back onto the job	Field interviews with participants and their direct managers	Have improved skills, awareness or knowledge been demonstrably applied on the job?
3	Participants' level of skills acquisition	Self and manager evaluation on a structured competency questionnaire. Pre- and post-programme measures	What new skills were learnt? To what level are they being applied?
3 – 2	Materials and methods review	A critical review of the course coverage, materials and learning methods effectiveness	Are the right areas of competence being covered? Are the learning materials and methods effective?
2	Knowledge and Awareness acquisition	Feedback from participants to the programme providers or to the external evaluation	What did you learn? What new knowledge do you have? What awareness was raised?
1	Participants' immediate perception of each model (The "feel good" factor)	Completion of model evaluation forum at the end of each module	How did you feel about the programme? What went well and less well?

Training staff generally brings a win-win scenario. Staff are more productive for the firm because they are better skilled to do their job and they feel better about themselves because their company is taking an interest in their personal development. Thus, the entrepreneur has a happier and more skilled workforce, with better productivity and lower costs as a result – which is how effective training and development pays for itself.

BUILDING AN EMPLOYEE INVOLVEMENT CULTURE

High performance organisations elicit a greater sense of ownership and commitment from employees, evidenced by higher job satisfaction ratings, leading in turn to enhanced productivity or service levels.

The three ways that companies develop this involvement are by:
- Ensuring that employees understand the broader business goals and get a clear message that their personal contribution is valued
- Symbolic behaviours by leaders, including a deliberate attention to encouraging the right type of management style
- A practical emphasis on developing and sustaining teamwork and group problem-solving.

Companies that are informative with regard to their goals and results, and inclusive of their employees in terms of decision-making, will inevitably perform better, since they are operating as a team and not as individuals employed by an owner/manager. For example, customer care is the responsibility of everyone in the organisation and therefore each employee should understand their role in developing the image of the company through enhancing the satisfaction that a customer gets when doing business with the organisation. The receptionist is the first point of contact for many customers and will give them an immediate impression (true or false) of the type of company with which they are doing business. The production personnel are manufacturing products that should not come back for customers who will return. To build an employee involvement culture, Irish owner-managers should share information, responsibility, accountability, and rewards with their staff, if they truly want to have them operating as a united team.

PERFORMANCE MANAGEMENT PRACTICES

Given the vagaries of human nature, it is unlikely that an entrepreneur will get consistently high performances from individuals across a company unless a formal and well-structured performance management system is put in place. Such systems typically include the four Fs detailed below:

- **Focus:** Focus each individual on the key result areas in their job. This includes defining output or outcome standards, as well as other essential behaviours or competencies such as effective communication, customer service, or teamwork

- **Feedback:** Ensure that each individual gives and gets feedback on how well things are going. In these times of fast-paced work, it is essential to develop in all employees an awareness and discipline around the need to regularly update their manager on the status of work-in-progress. Equally, the onus is on managers to be well-informed in order to give employees specific and timely feedback on what is going well and what needs improving

- **Frequency:** Put in place processes and disciplines so that performance is reviewed and encouraged on a frequent and regular basis. All the evidence indicates that it is frequency of feedback and review, not duration or formality, which makes the difference in effective performance management. It is recommended that reviews take place at least quarterly as a basic ingredient of performance management (a format should be followed, issues explored and records kept)

- **Follow-through:** Put in place financial or other tangible benefits that reward excellent performance in an equitable and structured way. Increasingly, organisations are moving away from long and complex pay scales to simpler and more flexible pay systems that embody fixed and variable elements linked to individual or team performance. In general terms, the fixed pay element should be sufficient to retain staff and recognise competent core job performance, while the variable element should reward excellent performance differentially.

The other dimension to managing performance is building an environment where coaching and mentoring becomes a normal part of workplace behaviour. There are many excellent guides to performance coaching (for example, Whitmore, 1992) with the common themes summarised below:

- **Coaching** is about: Keeping responsibility for performance with the person being coached while the coach provides a structured process to facilitate:
  ◊ Goal setting in an area identified for improvement;
  ◊ Establishing clarity about the performance gap
  ◊ Developing ways to perform better or differently
  ◊ Making a committed effort to progress the improvement plan
  ◊ Monitoring and reviewing progress in a disciplined way.
- **Mentoring** is a process whereby more experienced staff give the benefit of their expertise or wisdom to less experienced staff. Mentoring can vary on a continuum from *ad hoc* and informal arrangements to a more formalised system where mentors are formally assigned in specific circumstances.

Small businesses, because of the close working relationship between the owner/manager and staff, are ideally suited to the use of coaching and mentoring as a means of staff training and development.

CONCLUSION

The point was made at the start of the chapter that HRM in entrepreneurial new ventures differs significantly from HRM as practised by larger organisations (and as recorded in textbooks). Since the key driver to success for these ventures, after the quality of the entrepreneur/management team, is usually the quality of the staff, this chapter has focused on recruitment and selection, training and development, building an employee involvement culture ands performance management techniques. In addition, regard must be had to the increasingly complex requirements of labour law (see **Chapter 6**).

QUESTIONS

1. What is meant by human resource management?
2. Describe the recruitment process.

3. "Attracting the right people for a position is the principal HRM challenge for Irish owner-managers." Discuss.

4. In your last work position (part-time or work experience), what steps should the manager have taken to make you feel more involved in the organisation? Why would these steps have made a difference to you?

5. Using the recruitment process outlined in this chapter, select three people in the class to find the right person for the position of class representative.

6. Evaluate the importance of training and development in building the turnover and profits of a venture.

USEFUL WEBSITES

branchwebs.cipd.co.uk/ireland/
www.iitd.ie

CHECKLIST FOR CHAPTER

After reading this chapter, check that you understand and appreciate:

- The core contribution of Human Resource Management to firm success
- What aspects of human resource management make the critical difference in high performance organisations
- How to structure and focus recruitment and selection practices
- How to ensure that training and development activities add real value
- How to build robust performance management and development processes
- The importance of establishing an open and involving company culture.

REFERENCES

Armstrong, M. (1989) - *Personnel and the Bottom Line* - Institute of Personnel Management, London.

Becker, B. and Huselid, M. (1998) - High Performance Work Systems and Firm Performance: A Synthesis of Research - *Research in Personnel and Human Resources Management*, Vol.16, pp 53- 102.

DBM Ireland (2001) - *The Irish Recruitment Directory 2001* - Hillgate Publishing, Dublin.

Phillips, J. (1997) - *Return on Investment in Training and Performance Improvement Programs* - Gulf Publishing Company, Houston, Texas.

Whitmore, J. (1992) - *Coaching for Performance* - Nicholas Brealey, London.

CHAPTER 11

FINANCE FOR NEW VENTURES

*Anthony Foley**

LEARNING OBJECTIVES

- To develop an understanding of the role of finance in new venture creation
- To know the different types of finance
- To be familiar with the situation for new venture finance in Ireland, the availability of finance, and how to access finance
- To determine how new venture promoters can estimate their finance needs
- To know the role and means of efficient financial management.

INTRODUCTION

The three key financial issues for new ventures are:
- How much finance is needed to establish and maintain the venture
- What types of finance will be used in the venture (this will also determine the sources of the finance)
- The management of the finances.

The element of finance is crucial for new and existing ventures because ultimately the criterion for success is a financial one. The generation of

---

* Anthony Foley is a senior lecturer in economics and enterprise at Dublin City University Business School.

sufficient revenue (or inward financial flows) to cover the outward flows such as expenditures on materials, plant and machinery, staff, insurance, premises and other expenses and to cover the required profits is the main financial task of the venture.

Entrepreneurs will have different perspectives on what constitutes adequate returns. A new venture may provide psychological benefits and rewards to the entrepreneur. It may provide much needed employment. It may meet the needs of the community. But, if it does not generate sufficient funds to meet the costs of investment and operation, then the venture will not be sustained. And, if the required initial finance is not available, or is inadequate, the new venture will either not commence or will cease quickly.

The financial aspects are important also because other stakeholders, such as banks or investors, assess the venture mainly on its projected financial flows and financial structure. The American Accounting Association summarised the importance of financial factors as follows:

> *Accounting reports provide the information by which millions of investors judge corporate investment performance and by reference to which they make investment decisions. Every day, decisions concerning the allocation of resources of vast magnitude are made on the basis of accounting information.*

There are many types of new ventures. Differentiating factors include the legal structure of the venture, the sector/industry in which the venture will operate, the scale of finance needed and the potential of the new venture. A promoter of a new venture might be forgiven for expecting financial support for their venture from State agencies such as Enterprise Ireland, the City/County Enterprise Boards or Shannon Development. However, support is determined by the sector in which the project belongs and the scale of the project. Generally, State support is available only for projects in manufacturing and in what are defined as "internationally traded services". This latter classification is unique to Ireland and refers to certain services that are defined in legislation. The definition governs the aids and incentives that the support agencies can provide to enterprises. Consequently, not all enterprises or new ventures are eligible for assistance. It is wise not to presume that State financial support will be available but clearly a new venture promoter should check out whether their new venture is eligible for support.

In addition, State agencies are moving away from grants towards various forms of repayable support and also away from capacity support to capability support.

THE ROLE OF FINANCE IN NEW VENTURE CREATION

Festervand and Forest (1991) reviewed the causes of small business failures and concluded that "finance related issues appear to be the number one cause of small business failure". They reported research that 80% of all new business failures are due to under-capitalisation, which basically refers to ventures having insufficient financial resources to sustain them. The unavailability and/or high cost of long-term financing was identified as a serious problem. O'Neill and Duker (1986) reported that small firms have excessive debt finance, the management of which is expensive and time-consuming. The review also noted that cash flow problems were extensive and significantly influenced the survival or failure of new ventures. New venture promoters often underestimated start-up and operating costs that caused cash flow problems ,even in the very early stages of a new venture. Financial control and cost control are also areas of weakness for new ventures.

Overall, the three critical financial problems were:
- Under-capitalisation
- Cash flow
- Financial and cost control.

Storey (1997) reviewed evidence on business failures and contrasted the opinions of entrepreneurs with those of the official receivers. While the official receiver regarded mismanagement as the main source of failure, entrepreneurs blamed financial issues such as under-capitalisaton, inadequate working capital, and bad debts.

The Task Force on Small Business (1994) noted that "with the possible exception of taxation, the issue of finance has been the subject of more study and analysis than any other topic (relating to small business) covered in this report" (page 50). Only a small proportion of those who dream of setting up a business actually do so. In many cases, this is because of a lack of funding. Overall, funding or finance is:
- An important determinant of actualising the dream of starting a business

- An important determinant of business success and failure.

Without adequate financing, products or product ideas cannot be developed or brought to market.

The Forfás Report, *Shaping Our Future – A Strategy for Enterprise in Ireland in the 21st Century* (1996), noted that Irish enterprise needed access to new sources of finance to fund growth. It argued that the key financing issues were:

- The operation of the Irish capital markets
- The interaction between banks and industry
- Sources of venture capital.

Under capital markets, Forfás argued that there was a serious equity gap for companies seeking up to €380,000 (IR£300,000). It noted that, at present, the equity market was irrelevant to the financing needs of the vast majority of businesses. On banking, the Forfás report noted that the enterprise sector believed the banks were unwilling to extend long-term finance on reasonable terms, demanded too much security, and had excessive profit margins. However, banks argue that there must be prudent management of funds lodged by depositors. Forfás argued that banks should be more pro-active in providing long-term finance and should develop better relationships with companies.

The Forfás Report refers to the improvement in the availability of venture capital since the mid-1990s, primarily through measures in the Operational Programme for Industry. The growth in the scale, range, and type of venture capital available in Ireland since the mid-1990s is striking. Details of many of these venture capital funds are available in the 2002 report of the Seed and Venture Capital Measure of the 1994-1999 Operational Programme (available on the Enterprise Ireland web site in the "Finance for Growth" section under "Access to Third Party Funding"). This EU-supported Seed and Venture Capital Measure was set up to provide early stage small and medium-sized growth-oriented enterprises with equity capital. Additionally, there has been significant growth in the number of funds – the first was launched in May 1996, and by 2000 there were 16 funds.

The importance of finance is reflected in the range of public policy interventions that exist in Ireland to improve the scale, type and conditions of finance for new ventures and existing small and medium-sized enterprises. The policy statement of the Department of Enterprise,

Trade and Employment (1999) on Enterprise Ireland noted that, with regard to finance:

> *A key market failure is the provision of affordable equity and working capital to small and fast growth firms and the element of risk adversity exhibited by the financial institutions in their lending policies. This is a particular problem for start-up and fast growth firms, especially those operating in international services and technologically-intensive sectors.*

The justification for use of taxpayers' money (whether European or Irish) to support start-ups and other SMEs follows a reasoned logic. New and growing small firms are a vital source of dynamism, innovation, and structural change in an economy and significant risk attaches to new ventures. Lending institutions may be unwilling to provide finance because of the high risk, or the cost of the finance may be prohibitive, and consequently there should be policy interventions to assist in the generation of the required flow of new ventures. In effect, the economy needs new ventures, market sources may not provide the required financing, and therefore intervention is needed.

While there are substantial public policy interventions in financing new ventures and existing small firms, there is, as noted by the Task Force on Small Business, no unanimity of view about the severity of financing gaps. Some argue that the problem is mainly a shortage of good quality projects in which to invest, as opposed to a shortage of finance for reasonable projects. However, the Task Force concluded that there were finance gaps for:

- First-time entrepreneurs requiring seed capital to develop an idea before commencing operations
- First-time entrepreneurs needing general start-up capital
- Small firms needing equity capital
- Start-up and early stage venture capital
- Rapid growth firms.

Therefore, finance is an important determinant of new venture failure and survival and the principal problems arise in the areas of under-capitalisation, cash flow, and cost control. Because of the importance of the finance issue, there have been significant public policy interventions in recent years to improve the availability of finance to small firms and new ventures. However, the inadequate provision of finance for new ventures may be due to market failure or due to the poor quality of projects and business ideas, depending on the viewpoint adopted.

TYPES AND SOURCES OF FINANCE

This section outlines the different types of finance and the desirability of each type. Usually, entrepreneurs do not have sufficient finance from their own resources (such as savings, income flow from other sources, or wealth/assets that can be sold to finance the new venture). Therefore, they have to obtain funds from other sources.

The main alternative sources are borrowing from banks or others and money provided by external sources as equity, that is investment in the new company. "Bank borrowing" here includes all financial institutions including the main retail banks, smaller banks, building societies and credit unions. Some new ventures may receive grant finance. A breakdown of the main types of finance is given in **Figure 11.1**.

Borrowing

The advantage of loan finance or borrowing is that the entrepreneur retains complete ownership of the new venture and has to repay only the amount borrowed and the interest charges, even if the new venture performs excellently, generating high profits and increasing the value of the company or enterprise. On the other hand, debt is a commitment to pay back funds, regardless of how the business performs. Even if the performance is poor, there is the obligation to repay the capital sum and the interest charged. If the borrowing is from a bank, it will probably have been secured by assets, which must be given up if the loan cannot be repaid.

The main advantage of debt financing is that, after the debt and interest are paid, the lender has no further claim on the business. The main disadvantage is that the loan has to be repaid, even if the business performs badly.

In addition, the repayments may be a serious drain on the venture's finances in its delicate early stage of operation. However, some lenders may negotiate a moratorium on repayments.

If borrowing is a large component of capital, the new venture is more vulnerable to temporary events such as cash flow difficulties, bad debts, economic downturn or unanticipated expenditure than firms with a low level of borrowing.

FIGURE 11.1: TYPES OF FINANCE

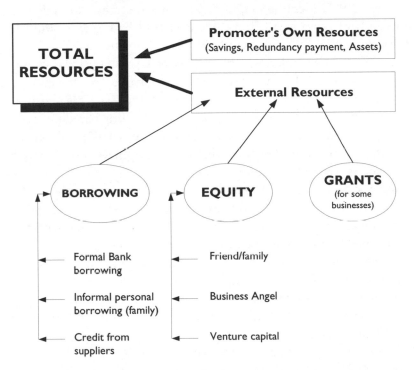

Loan finance may be difficult to obtain for new ventures. Lenders lend in the expectation that the loan will be repaid as agreed. They would rather avoid regular renegotiations of loans. They would rather receive repayment than realise security or chase after loan guarantees. Consequently, banks prefer to lend to low-risk borrowers. They prefer proven established businesses to new untried higher-risk enterprises. While banks are often criticised for excessively prudent lending that inhibits entrepreneurs, such behaviour is perfectly rational. A bank makes its profit from the difference between deposit rates and lending rates, less the cost of providing the service. A small ratio of bad debts would eliminate the profit. Bank lending to small businesses and new ventures is more risky than lending to larger firms. In addition, a bank will not get a return in excess of the loan and interest, even if the new venture is very successful. The bank does not have high return projects to compensate for projects that default on loans. In contrast, the venture capitalist expects to encounter failures and low returns but expects that these will be compensated by other projects that generate very high returns.

Storey (1997) identified eight factors that underline the relationship between banks and small firms. These should be borne in mind when approaching banks for new venture finance. They are:

- **Asymmetric information:** Entrepreneurs in small business know more about their business than the lending bank. This can make a bank wary of lending to small businesses. However, this may not be true in the case of new ventures where the lending bank may have a more informed view of the venture's survival potential, based, for example, on knowledge of the sector or previous ventures, than the inexperienced entrepreneur

- **Agency issues:** While the bank advances the loan, it cannot control the actions of the new firm. The entrepreneur acts as an agent for the bank that wants to ensure that the loan is repaid. Consequently, the bank needs to have confidence in the entrepreneur

- **Higher risk:** Small firm and new venture lending is more risky than lending to big firms. Banks deal with this in three ways:
  ◊ Make loans only to firms with a low probability of failure
  ◊ Ensure security/collateral is available to provide a return in the case of failure
  ◊ Charge higher interest rates to compensate for the risk

- **Monitoring and assessment costs:** The costs are substantial for small firms/new ventures when expressed as costs per project or costs per amount of loan advanced

- **Competition between banks:** There are additional elements in the impact of competition between banks apart from interest rates, such as collateral requirements, repayment holidays or contract charges

- **Variability of entrepreneurs:** It is difficult for a bank to judge entrepreneurs, because their ability and motivation are not uniform. If all entrepreneurs were identical in a perfectly competitive market sense, the banks would not have problems in assessing their worthiness for loans

- **Entrepreneurs gain from increase in project/venture valuation**

- **Banks only gain from repayment, regardless of success of project**.

The various lending bodies give useful guidelines on applying for finance (for example, see the AIB website). A bank will want to see the business plan, which should include financial information such as forecast profit and loss accounts for three years, cash flow forecast, breakeven analysis, 12 months of business (if not a new venture) and/or personal bank statements and tax compliance information.

The bank will also assess issues of character, capacity, collateral, conditions and capital. Full details of these are on the website but a brief summary is given here:

- **Character:** Is the borrower honest and reliable? Has the borrower a good credit history? Has the borrower met his/her commitments in the past?
- **Capacity:** What is the capacity of the business and/or borrower to repay the loan?
- **Collateral:** Can the loan may be secured on assets that could be sold to repay the loan if the borrower defaults?
- **Conditions:** The entrepreneur has no control over external conditions and national and sectoral economic trends but the lender will expect the entrepreneur to have a strategy for dealing with these issues and for dealing with competition
- **Capital:** Most lenders will be unwilling to advance money for a business unless there is evidence that the promoter is willing to risk his/her money. As a new business is riskier than an established business, the entrepreneur may be expected to provide a higher percentage of needed capital than for an established business.

In short, a lender wants favourable answers to the following questions:
- Is there good evidence that repayment is likely?
- Is there sufficient collateral?
- Is there sufficient equity and personal funds as evidence of commitment and risk sharing?
- Is there confidence in the entrepreneur?

Collateral can be a major problem for new ventures, particularly in certain sectors. Borrowing for the purchase of plant and machinery generates assets that can be sold to part-repay the loan should the business fail. However, if the business is in software development, there may be few saleable assets. The borrowing may be needed to finance salaries for staff to develop the product. If the business fails, there will be no assets to finance repayment of a loan. Intellectual capital may not be as attractive to lenders as physical capital. Collateral or security may have to come from other sources, such as insurance policies or other property.

In the past, it was argued that banks discouraged new venture formation by expecting that the private residence of an entrepreneur be used as collateral. In the past decade, the Government encouraged the banks to introduce special "Enterprise Loans" which do not include the residence collateral requirement for certain sectors, again primarily manufacturing and international services. Of course, the security problem is related to the level of finance. The greater the borrowing, the greater the banks requirement for security, although equipment can be rented or leased which reduces the need for direct bank borrowing. Small sums generally do not have collateral requirements.

New venture promoters should be committed and determined, and confident about the potential of their project. Sometimes, this can lead to an expectation that funds should be forthcoming because, in the entrepreneur's view, the project is wonderful. The bank does not have the some "ownership" of the project, does not receive a big return if the project is very successful, is wary of failed debts (even a small proportion can be very significant), likes the notion of collateral and ultimately must be convinced of the safety of the loaned capital. It is important to note that using one's own resources to part-finance a new venture gives a strong signal of confidence and commitment. Why should someone be keen to invest their money in a project, if the project promoter is unwilling to risk a significant part of their own financial resources? Even non-entrepreneurial people might be willing to initiate new businesses, if all the risk is borne by someone else.

Over the past decade, the Irish banking system has greatly improved its range of loan products to reduce some of the gaps between the attractions of equity over loan finance. Several products include moratoriums on capital repayments for a period and others allow flexible repayment systems. Both fixed and variable interest rates products are available. However, while the range and type of loan products have expanded, the entrepreneur must bear in mind the earlier comments that banks lend in the expectation that repayment will occur with as little risk as possible. It is a very useful initial step to consult the websites of the lending institutions before making enquiries.

Equity

Many of the issues that arise in obtaining debt financing also arise with externally-sourced equity. The new venture promoter seeks to convince some external source to invest in the project. The external source may be a friend, family member, business angel (private investor) or formal venture capital fund. The big attraction of equity financing is that there is no obligation to repay funds, if the business fails or generates poor profits. The negative aspect for many entrepreneurs is that external equity financing effectively means selling an interest in the business and losing part of the control of the business.

The price of the equity is the link between the percentage share of the business being acquired and the finance being provided. To an entrepreneur, equity financing is expensive if he/she feels that an excessively high portion of the company is being transferred for the equity finance. To the equity investor, the price is high if he/she feels too much money is being invested in return for the percentage share of the company received in return. The details of the price and the share, and also the degree of day-to-day involvement in management, depend on the specific negotiations. At a minimum, the original promoter may continue to be the sole day-to-day manager but no longer owns all the company or the future flow of profits. In other cases, especially with formal venture funds, the investor may expect a substantial say in management and strategy. Indeed, the infusion of additional management and strategic skills is often seen as an attractive feature of bringing venture capitalists on board.

Equity investors are exposed to greater risk so they expect a greater return than loan providers. They have no guarantee of repayment of the equity. There is no guaranteed interest payment. In the event of a business failure, creditors will be paid before owners of equity. Even whether equity investors can sell on their share of the business to a third party depends on the agreement entered into at the initial equity participation.

Equity can come from the entrepreneur's own resources, from formal venture capital funds, from informal investors or business angels, or from people whom the entrepreneur knows. Enterprise Ireland maintains a database of business angels (see its website).

Except for First Step (see below), the venture capital funds focus on projects, which require large amounts of capital. This will exclude many new ventures. Also, the funds tend to be interested in only those new ventures that have excellent growth potential and several are focused on manufacturing and international services. These features will exclude many new ventures. Once again, the important message is not to get carried away with the broad publicity material relating to the availability of venture capital. The availability of venture capital has grown greatly over the past decade; there are many funds; and there are many business angels but this does not necessarily mean that a particular project/new venture will be eligible, attractive, or supported even if it is eligible.

In practice, most new ventures will be financed by the entrepreneur's personal equity and loan finance from the banks. Some will be supported by private loans or private equity from friends or family. A proportion will get Enterprise Board, Shannon Development, or Enterprise Ireland support. Only a small number of new ventures with high potential growth will get venture capital fund support. The scale of the venture capital funds' activities is shown below in **Table 11.2**.

The 98 start-ups supported over the period 1996-2000 involved a total of €24.3m or an average of €248,000 per start-up. This gives an indication that relatively large amounts of equity per project is involved. The number getting start-up equity from the venture capital funds can be related to the number of new indigenous manufacturing establishments starting up each year. There were 454 new Irish-owned manufacturing start-ups in 1998, in 1997 it was 413, and 1996 it was 303.

Venture capital funds each have their own criteria for project acceptability. A few examples will illustrate this point:

- **ACT Enterprise Limited Partnership:** Investments in the range €317k to €1.3m in start-ups, early-stage and existing companies in software and technology; duration of investment is between five and seven years

- **AWG Investment Fund Limited:** Investments in the range €63k to €635k in start-up or established SMEs in manufacturing, tourism, and certain traded services; duration of investment five to seven years

- **Bank of Ireland Entrepreneurs Fund Limited Partnership:** Investments in range of €127k to €1.3m in early-stage or high potential start-ups in the technology and food sectors

- **First Step Limited:** Advances up to €6k in start-up small or micro enterprises; mainly geared at projects that fail to raise funds through the banking system or State support agencies.

Full details of all the venture capital funds and their criteria are available from the Seed & Venture Capital Measure Annual Report.

Clearly, there are many more start-ups in manufacturing than get venture capital support. The Task Force on Small Business (1994) stated that about 14,000 new VAT registrations accrued each year and that there were about 14,000 new company registrations each year (see also Foley and Hogan, 1996). The Revenue 2000 Statistical Report states that the number of new businesses registrations for VAT was 19,061 in 2000 (page 10). Overall, there are thousands of new ventures each year, only a small proportion get grant-aided, and a tiny proportion get venture capital fund equity. The vast majority depend on personal equity, bank borrowing and, to a lesser extent, on informal external funds of both loans and equity.

TABLE 11.1: INVESTMENT ACTIVITY VENTURE CAPITAL FUNDS 1996 TO 2000 (15 FUNDS[8])

TYPE Total No. of Investments	Start-ups	Early Stage	Development
214	98	91	25

SECTOR Total No. of Investments	Software	Comms.	Life Sciences	Manuf'g	Food	Mix
214	98	40	24	37	6	9

As noted above, the attraction of equity is that the return on the capital depends on the performance of the venture, there are no loan repayments, and the equity investor may be more interested in and committed to the venture. The disadvantages are that the entrepreneur ceases to have full ownership and possibly full management control; there may be disagreements on strategy; there will be a requirement to involve accountants and solicitors because of the complexity of bringing in new equity which, of course, carries a cost and the promoter/ entrepreneur surrenders part of the profit flow and growth in value of the venture. On the plus side, equity can be used to leverage bank borrowing (that is persuade the banks to lend). The higher the amount of equity, the higher the amount of borrowing that lenders will consider.

---

8 Excluding First Step, which provides small levels of funding to many micro enterprises. While Enterprise Ireland includes First Step in its venture fund classification, it is primarily engaged in providing loans rather than equity.

Grants

Only a small proportion of new ventures are eligible for financial support from government agencies.

The Enterprise Boards provide three types of grants:
- Feasibility study grant
- Capital grant
- Employment grant.

The feasibility grant assists in assessing the viability of a business idea. This can also include prototype production test-marketing, consulting, financial projections and the preparation of a business plan. A maximum of 50% of the cost, subject to a maximum level of €5,080 is available.

A capital grant is available for purchase of equipment and machinery and refurbishment or outfitting of premises. Purchases of buildings are not eligible. A grant of 35% of cost up to a limit of €63,500 is available.

An employment grant is available in two parts, the first when the person is taken on and properly registered for PRSI and income tax and the second part after six months, if the person is still in employment.

It should be noted that there is often a time lag between expenditure and receipt of grants. Cash flow and other financial projections should take account of this time lag.

Enterprise Boards can also take preference shares or equity in the larger of their client companies.

It is important to repeat the "health warning" that has been given throughout this chapter. Projects are not automatically entitled to Enterprise Board support. They are eligible to be considered. They may be approved or rejected. They may or may not get the maximum level of support.

The Dublin City Enterprise Board's website identifies a number of activities that would not receive financial support. These include:
- Retail outlets
- Professional services (including consultancies)
- Builders
- Hairdressers
- Cafés, pubs, hotels
- General printers and trades.

The Enterprise Boards must ensure that assisted enterprises will not displace existing businesses.

Enterprise Boards generally deal with enterprises with 10 or fewer employees. Manufacturing or internationally traded services are dealt with by Enterprise Ireland. New ventures with significant growth and sales potential within the eligible sectors are dealt with by Enterprise Ireland, while lower potential projects fall to the Enterprise Boards.

Enterprise Ireland (and Shannon Development/Údarás na Gaeltachta in the appropriate regions) gives grants for capability (actions that develop business competence) and capacity (measures that increase production capacity). The funding is available only to eligible projects. It is not an automatic entitlement and it is paid in arrears. With certain projects, Enterprise Ireland will insist on an equity stake. Enterprise Ireland tends to focus on those new ventures that have high growth potential (high potential start-ups – HPSUs), with expectations of significant sales, employment and exports. The Enterprise Boards deal with the new ventures that have lower expectations. Of course, a new venture that begins with Enterprise Board support can move to the Enterprise Ireland /Shannon Development/ Údarás portfolio, as it moves into a new stage of high growth.

The criteria for Enterprise Ireland support of HPSUs generally are:

- The business is in manufacturing or internationally traded services
- It is based on technological innovation or exploitable market niche opportunity
- It has credible projected sales of at least €0.95m and 10 jobs by Year 3
- It has longer term potential to significantly exceed these levels
- It has export potential
- It is established by experienced managers, academics, or technical graduates.

Other financing

There are other sources of finance, or more precisely, there are other methods of financing the inputs needed for a new venture. Equipment can be leased instead of purchased. Clearly, the business must be in a position to pay the lease charge each month/quarter if it is to continue to use the equipment. Leasing replaces the upfront requirement of cash for equipment purchase and ownership of the asset with regular smaller payments over the period of the lease. If one cannot get access to sufficient initial funds, leasing may be the only option available.

The process by which a business sells its outstanding invoices to a financial house at a discount relative to the face value of the invoices is called *factoring* and is another resource of funds. It is clearly of more interest to businesses that are up and running and have generated outstanding invoices. The basic trade-off between factoring and the entrepreneur collecting the bills relates to the discount relative to the value of the invoices and the opportunity cost of using equity or bank borrowing to finance the time lag between selling the product and collecting the payment plus the cost of collecting the due payments. Clearly, not all businesses benefit from factoring. Cash sale and retail businesses do not generally generate invoices. There is no delay between sales and receipt of revenue. Business-to-business operations usually operate an invoice/delayed payment basis and factoring may be relevant.

Trade credit is an additional source of finance. Suppliers may be willing to provide inputs and wait for payment over a period. Of course, a new venture may find it difficult to get credit from suppliers as it has no track record of good payment. Depending on market conditions, suppliers may be willing/unwilling to extend credit terms to a new venture.

The www.startingabusinessinireland.com website identifies a wide range of sources of equity finance, of loan finance, and of grants. Possible additional sources of grant finance, depending on the type of enterprise, are available from the Arts Council, Bord Glas, Bord Iascaigh Mhara, and Bord Fáilte. However, heed the health warning that a particular project may not be eligible for funding.

If there is a choice between two methods of financing, the entrepreneur should give careful consideration to the costs and benefits associated with each. However, in reality, for most entrepreneurs the issue is not deciding on the ideal mix and level of finance, it is more making do with the levels and the types that are available for the particular project.

ESTIMATING FINANCING NEEDS

The amount of money that is needed upfront to start a business varies greatly, depending on the nature of the business. A manufacturing business requires plant and machinery that frequently requires substantial amounts of capital before the business can begin to trade. A new software firm may require a long period of product development and testing before revenues start to flow, with substantial amounts of capital are needed to finance operations over the non-revenue generating periods. On the other hand, opening a new shop may quickly result in reasonable revenue flows. Even here, initial capital will be needed for fittings, lease, rent deposit stock, insurance, and other expenses. The investment capital needed will also depend on whether equipment and premises are leased or rented instead of purchased. The amount needed can range from a few thousand to millions of Euro.

Generally, entrepreneurs tend to underestimate the amount of money needed for a new venture. This is understandable because the entrepreneur is passionate about the business or product. He/she will be enthusiastic and confident about the viability of the project. The larger the amount of money needed, the less likely it is that the venture will commence. Therefore, there is a natural tendency to understate the amount of money that is needed. In addition, it is not easy to get money so, again it is understandable that the requirements are understated. Nonetheless, it is important to identify realistically and fully the financial requirements of the business. It is also necessary to allow for mismatches between financial outlays and revenue inflows. Basically sound businesses can be plunged into trouble through not allowing for the time lag between buying raw materials/financing production and payments by customers.

Costs estimation can be divided into three elements:

- Start-up costs
- Operating costs
- Personal remuneration of the owner/manager.

There is a link between operating costs and personal remuneration. From an economics perspective, the full range of resources used by the firm should be taken into account and priced at their opportunity cost. The labour and managerial inputs of the entrepreneur, and also unpaid family labour, should be included in operating costs. This would then include personal remuneration and a separate category would not be needed.

Usually, however, the entrepreneur prices his/her input at a zero value in calculating the operating costs. Therefore, money is needed to cover the personal needs of the entrepreneur such as living expenses, accommodation, household expenses, and family bills. Over time, hopefully, the new venture will generate a profit flow that will provide the income for the entrepreneur. On an accounting basis, new ventures do not include the cost of free family labour.

The level and type of start-up costs depend on the new venture. A retail new venture is illustrated below:

START-UP COSTS (Retail business)

- Decorating, remodelling
- Fixtures, equipment
- Installing fixtures, equipment
- Services, supplies
- Inventory
- Legal, professional fees
- Licenses, permits
- Telephone and other communications
- Insurance
- Signs
- Advertising
- Other expenses (for example, work clothes, professional fees)
- Unanticipated expenses
- Premises deposit or purchase.

Source: *Checklist for Going into Business*, www.bizoffice.com/library/files/chklist.txt

The www.startingabusinessinireland.com website suggests that the entrepreneur should make an initial "wish list" of the desired inputs and then prune this down to an "essentials" list. Of course, the entrepreneur must ensure that the pruning does not go so deep as to make the business unattractive to customers. The standards that might satisfy the entrepreneur may be insufficient to meet customer needs. The start-up checklist should relate to the expectations of the target customers. The entrepreneur should allocate a great deal of time to deciding on the items needed for the business.

It is strongly advised that the entrepreneur should research the physical resources and equipment required for the setting up of the venture by checking out similar operators, if any. In most cases, entrepreneurs set up business in activities in which they have some experience and so are familiar with the input requirements, but even here the tendency is to understate financial needs.

The entrepreneur next must estimate the operating costs, which include supplies, rent, leasing payments, loan repayments, commercial rates, advertising, electricity, heating water, accountancy fees, employee wages and employee indirect costs, vehicle, insurance, maintenance, unforeseen costs (broken front windows), burglary and other items (contribution to charity). This list does not include personal expenses.

It is likely that the new venture will not generate remuneration for the entrepreneur for a period of time until the business is developed. The financial resources must be able to support the entrepreneur's living expenses over this period.

The general rule of thumb is that entrepreneurs underestimate start-up costs and are too optimistic about how quickly the new venture will generate adequate personal remuneration. This is what is meant by under-capitalisation. Too often, the new venture is initiated with less than the necessary level of financial resources to cover the above items. For example, a new venture might need six months before the volume of business is sufficient to generate adequate remuneration to the entrepreneur.

Cost estimation must allow for realistic assessment, while avoiding unnecessary items or excessive quality. Of course, it is possible that a new venture promoter may have plenty of money relative to the needs of the business. This is very much a minority situation and, in any case, investment should be sensible and relative to the business potential.

A new venture will require resources prior to the start-up phase. The project has to be researched and assessed. Feasibility has to be examined and equipment and suppliers have to be sourced. A business plan will be needed, if bank finance is being sought. Finance at this stage is very risky because the as yet unfinished evaluation may give a very negative assessment of the potential and the new venture may not proceed.

The financing assessment must take into account the phasing of payments and receipts. Payment for products or services sold will occur after the expenses incurred in producing the output. Finance must be in place to support this temporal mismatch.

While the cost of inputs has a reasonable degree of certainty attached to its estimation, the overall financial requirements also depend on revenues, the projection of which can be very uncertain. Maybe sales take longer to take off than envisaged, maybe prices have to be lowered. Even if cost projections are reasonably accurate, unfulfilled revenue projections can result in unanticipated financing problems. The estimation of financial needs includes a strong element of uncertainty. Good planning can reduce the uncertainty but it will not eliminate it. It also involves a risk assessment of the decision to go ahead, based on the available resources relative to seeking additional finance. This is one of the creative aspects of starting a new venture. There can never be certainty about the future, the accuracy of the financing needs, the adequacy of the resources and the revenue flows. Ultimately informed judgement is required.

A risk assessment of the financial needs is important. Avoid taking the most optimistic scenarios that the entrepreneur might naturally be tempted to do. Identify the impact of costs being 10% or 20% higher; or prices being 10% lower; or if the business did not generate a return for the entrepreneur for six months instead of three.

The projections may be very sensitive to reasonable alternative scenarios. Bigger start-ups are more likely to be influenced by the alternative scenarios because they may involve venture capital fund involvement or because very large amounts of bank borrowing are required. Small amounts of external funding (family or bank) will probably be forthcoming even if the venture is sensitive to alternative scenarios.

Ultimately, however, the entrepreneur will have to do with whatever finance is available, even if he/she recognises the desirability of larger levels of capital. Entrepreneurs must be confident and optimistic but they must also be realistic in estimating financing needs. A balance between optimism and realism is needed.

FINANCIAL MANAGEMENT

There are two aspects to the financial management issue. First, there are the details that must be included in the financial plan. These are crucial because external sources of finance will examine them critically before agreeing to support the project. Additionally, these financial details are the summary of the economic/commercial viability of the project and are an important source of enlightenment for the entrepreneur as to whether the project is worth pursuing.

The business plan should include profit and loss accounts, projected balance sheet and cash flow projections. Of course, these projections are based on assumptions of sales volumes, prices, cost of inputs, bad debts, and the best one can do is to make realistic estimates. Many businesses begin with only a brief reference to the above items. However, if bank or other external finance is needed, the providers will require more information. If substantial funds are required, the level of detail required will increase and full sets of financial projections will be required.

The financial plan items are the "glamorous" aspect of the financial management. It is about starting the project, it is about proving the projects commercial viability, and it is the means of persuading external sources of finance.

The second aspect is the mundane and often boring careful recording of the venture's financial information as it operates. Good management of the ongoing finances and good accounting systems and practices are essential to ensure the project's survival. It is all too easy to ignore recording transactions and accounting and financial paperwork to concentrate on marketing and production. But, without proper monitoring and controls, it is easy to go beyond bank lending limits unintentionally, to allow excessive credit to develop, to fail to provide for tax payments, to mismatch financial receipts and outflows and to generate excessive costs.

Use of an accountant is strongly recommended. In some cases, it is a legal requirement. Very small businesses that are not limited companies, such as those in self-employment, may manage without using an accountant but generally it is advisable to use professional accounting services if the financial aspects of the business go above the very basic level. The tax authorities will require annual accounts to determine the tax liability.

Even if an accountant is used, the entrepreneur should be careful to maintain good day-to-day accounting and recording practices. Most new ventures would not be of a sufficient scale to employ a book-keeper or accountant. Even where these are employed the entrepreneur should have up to date information on the financial flows of the project. The Immink/O'Kane *Starting Your Own Business* guide gives a good and brief summary of the accounting requirements. These include:

- Recording transactions
- Appropriate classification of transactions
- Provision for tax
- Bank balance data
- Credit and debt control.

Extracts from the guide appear in an Appendix at the end of this chapter.

The importance of cash flow and credit management cannot be over-stressed (Roberts, 1997). Slow payments by customers have a strong negative impact on new ventures. Roberts suggested a strong active approach to credit management and makes the accurate observation that a customer who does not pay is not really a customer. In the attempt to build the market of a new venture that advice is often ignored.

In short, the accounting data should provide the entrepreneur with full details of what is being sold, what is being purchased, how much money is flowing in, how much is flowing out, what is owed and what is due, how much tax is due, what is the bank balance, and what is the balance sheet of the venture.

Cash flow planning is vital. As noted earlier in the chapter, inadequate cash flow causes many new firms to go out of business. Even profitable businesses can be adversely affected by cash flow problems. For example, a payment may be expected that will cover wages or other expenses. Let us assume that the customer will eventually pay, the problem is solely one of timing. In a world with perfect knowledge, this generally should not cause a problem for the firm. The entrepreneur would approach the bank to raise its borrowing limit temporarily, the wages would be paid, the firm would continue, the cheque would eventually arrive and the increased borrowing would be paid off. One difficulty, even in the perfect knowledge scenario, is that the borrowed money has an interest charge whereas the cheque arriving on time has no charge. Therefore, this scenario imposes an extra cost on the firm, which could affect its profitability. The world does not operate with perfect knowledge. The firm can not guarantee the future receipt of the cheque. The bank manager is not sure additional borrowing will be repaid and is unlikely to approve it. And that's how firms fail.

Inadequate cash flow can also be indicative of fundamental flaws in the business. For example, the market may turn out to be less receptive than projected and revenue flows may be correspondingly lower. While the entrepreneur may be confident that the market will improve in the near future, external sources of finance may not share that optimism and will not advance any additional finance. In effect, such a business cannot prove its potential profitability to the satisfaction of external providers of finance.

CONCLUSION

Every new venture needs finance to commence and continue. Only on very rare occasions does the entrepreneur have sufficient resources of their own to provide the required finance. Consequently, there is normally a need for external sources of finance. This means that the entrepreneur must persuade outsiders to provide finance. Generally, outsiders will be less certain of the project's commercial viability than the entrepreneur, who naturally will be confident and committed.

The main outside sources of finance are equity or loans. There are a large variety of sources of each. However, the vast majority of new ventures depend on the entrepreneur's own resources and bank financing. Many projects may be supported by family, who provide equity or loans. Manufacturing, international services and some other sectors are eligible for financial support from the State development agencies, but these constitute a small number of total new ventures. A very small number of high potential start-ups receive equity finance from the formal venture capital organizations. For many ventures, however, the bank is the significant source of finance.

For most potential entrepreneurs, the issue is not deciding on the ideal mix and level of finance, it is making do with what is available, which is usually obtained only after much persuasion and effort. The amount of money needed upfront to start a business varies greatly, depending on the nature of the business and whether equipment is purchased or leased. Entrepreneurs normally underestimate the level of finance needed. Because of the entrepreneur's enthusiasm to get started, there is a natural tendency to understate the financing difficulties. Overall, however, there should be a well-judged balance between optimism and realism in identifying the financing requirement.

Good management of the project's finances and sound accounting systems are essential to ensure the new venture's survival. It is all too easy to neglect the boring recording, accounting and financial paperwork and concentrate on marketing and production. This is a recipe for disaster. Without proper vigilance, it is possible to go beyond bank lending limits, to allow excessive credit to develop, to fail to make provision for tax payments, to mismatch the outgoing and incoming financial flows, and to run up excessive costs. Use of an accountant is generally desirable. In some cases, it is legally required. Sound financial management and accounting practices from day one are essential.

QUESTIONS

1. Discuss the difficulty in accessing finance for a new venture in Ireland.
2. Evaluate the different sources of finance available to an entrepreneur.
3. Describe the role of support agencies in offering financial assistance to a new venture.
4. Using the Internet, detail the support available from your local County Enterprise Board.

5. "The banks hinder the development of entrepreneurship in Ireland". Discuss.
6. Why is financial management so important to the success of a new venture?
7. Use statistics from the Revenue Commissioners, the Census of Industrial Production, Enterprise Ireland and the Enterprise Boards to identify the numbers of new ventures that get grants.
8. What sort of projects are most likely to be successful in accessing venture capital?

USEFUL WEBSITES

www.aib.ie
www.bankofireland.ie
www.dceb.ie
www.entemp.ie
www.entemp.ie/syob/index.html
www.enterprise-ireland.com
www.startingabusinessinireland.com

CHECKLIST FOR CHAPTER

After reading this chapter, check that you understand and appreciate:
- The role of finance in new venture creation
- The different types of finance
- The situation for new venture finance in Ireland, the availability of finance, and how to access finance
- How new venture promoters can estimate their finance needs
- The role and means of efficient financial management.

REFERENCES

American Accounting Association (1971) - *Report of the Committee on Establishment of an Accounting Commission* - American Accounting Association.
Dept. of Enterprise Trade and Employment (1999) - *Policy Statement on Enterprise Ireland* - Dept. of Enterprise Trade and Employment.
Divilly, M. (1997) - Financing Your Business in *Running Your Business: Success Strategies for Small Business* – Allied Irish Bank.

Festervand, T.E. and Forrest, J.E. (1991) - *Small Business Failures: A Framework for Analysis* - hpttp://www.sdaer.uca.edu/research/1991/SBIDA/91sbi271.txt

Forfás (1996) - *Strategy for Enterprise: The Way Forward* – Forfás, Dublin.

Forfás (2000) - *Enterprise 2010: A New Strategy for the Promotion of Enterprise in Ireland in the 21st Century* - Forfás, Dublin.

Hogan, T. and Foley, A. (1996) - *The Financial Structure of Fast Growth Firms in Ireland: An Empirical Investigation* - Paper presented at the 2nd Entrepreneurship Research Conference, University of Ulster Belfast.

Immink, R. and O'Kane, B. (2001) – *Starting Your Own Business: A Workbook* (2nd edition) – Cork, Oak Tree Press.

O'Neill, H. and Duker, J. (1986) - Survival and Failure in Small Business - *Journal of Small Business Management*, Vol.21, No.1, pp 30-37.

Roberts, D. (1997) - Financial Control and Management - *Running Your Own Business*.

Storey, D.J. (1997) - *Understanding the Small Business Sector* - International Thomson Business Press, London.

Task Force on Small Business (1994) – *Task Force on Small Business Report* - Oireachtas Committee, Stationary Office.

APPENDIX*

RECORDING TRANSACTIONS

First, identify what transactions must be recorded. Most small businesses have:

- Purchases on credit
- Sales for credit
- Receipts – Cash into the bank account
- Payments – Cash out of the bank account
- Petty cash.

Let's start with these. For each transaction, it's necessary to record:

- The date
- The type of transaction
- The other person involved
- The amount involved.

If a separate page is used for each type of transaction, it is not necessary to record the type of transaction – the page it is recorded on will show what type it is.

ANALYSING TRANSACTIONS

Next, it is necessary to analyse the transactions to provide information.

---

* Reproduced with permission from *Starting Your Own Business: A Workbook*, 2nd edition (2001), Ron Immink & Brian O'Kane, Oak Tree Press: Cork.

Take purchases on credit. The transactions might be analysed under the following headings:

- **Fixed assets:** Items not for resale
- **Stock:** Items for resale
- **Overheads:** Expenses incurred in running the business (analyse these further into categories – Staff, Production, Premises, Transport, Sales and promotion, General expenses and Finance – these can be further subdivided if necessary to show the detail you need)
- **Miscellaneous/Sundry:** Items for which there is no other obvious category or which happen so seldom that it's not worth setting up a separate analysis of them.

Sales on credit might be analysed by product/service type.

Cash into the bank account might be analysed by source, one of which will be debtors paying for goods/services bought earlier on credit. Other sources will include cash from cash sales (which should tie up on a daily basis), loans to the business, VAT and miscellaneous items.

Cash out of the bank account might be analysed by destination, one of which will be creditors from whom the business bought goods/services on credit earlier. Goods and services bought and paid for by cheque also need to be analysed, as do overheads. Small items of expenditure can be recorded as Petty cash expenses.

Value Added Tax

If the business is registered for it, recording VAT is the next step. With certain exceptions, VAT paid on purchases is recoverable, while the business must account to the Revenue Commissioners for VAT charged on sales. This means that, if the amount paid for purchases includes VAT, the cost to the business of those purchases can be reduced by the VAT amount. Similarly, VAT charged on sales must be deducted before accounting for them in the business, since this income does not belong to the business.

The "books"

Below are the very basic "books" that a business must keep, although most businesses keep accounts that are much more sophisticated.

Accounts Pages: Purchases on Credit

Date	Supplier	Total	Net	VAT	Staff	Production	Premises	Transport	Selling	General	Financial	Other
Total												

Accounts Pages: Sales on Credit

Date	Customer	Total	Net	VAT	A	B	C	...	X	Y	Z	Other
Total												

Accounts Pages: Receipts

Date	Received From	Total	Net	VAT	Debtors	Cash Sales	Loans	Other
Total								

Accounts Pages: Payments

Date	Paid To	Total	Net	VAT	Suppliers	Staff	Production	Premises	Transport	Selling	General	Financial	Other
Total													

Accounts Pages: Petty Cash

Date	Paid To	Total	Net	VAT	Postage	Stationery	Office Exp.	Transport	Other
Total									

INTERPRETING THE FIGURES

The next step is interpretation. Most of this is common-sense, for example:

- If the bank balance is always overdrawn, the business is spending more than it is bringing in – and the owner will need to schedule another meeting with their bank manager
- If purchases are high, and sales are low, stocks will begin to build up – and worse, stock held for a long time may become unsaleable because it might be perishable, go out of fashion or become damaged
- If overheads are high, the owner may be spending money on unnecessary items, like fancy office stationery and equipment, instead of on more productive items.

Business owners should talk to an accountant about the kind of information they need to manage their business and make sure that their system of recording and analysis provides it.

Regular accounts

Every business is effectively required to prepare accounts once a year – some because they are limited companies and are required to do so by law, others because the tax authorities will need them to determine how much tax the business should be paying. But annual accounts in the form of a profit and loss account and balance sheet prepared according to accounting standards and company law are not much help in running and managing a business because:

- They are too infrequent – A year is a long time not to know what is happening to the finances of your business
- They are prepared to a different format – One that often is not helpful for decision-making.

So more regular accounts are required. Monthly accounts may be too much of a burden for a start-up or smaller business but quarterly accounts are essential.

CONTROLLING

Controlling is the process of making sure that the financial outcome planned for in the budget becomes the financial results shown in the annual accounts. It's most a matter of day-to-day attention to detail.

For example, credit control. The first element here is sending out accurate invoices on time. If a business does not send out accurate invoices, customers will complain and delay paying. Equally, if it does not bother to invoice customers as soon as a job is done, it suggests that there is no great hurry for payment – and customers again will delay paying.

A simple credit control system might operate like this:

- Always invoice as soon as a job is done. Don't wait for the end of the month
- Make sure the invoice clearly states the date on which it is due to be paid
- File invoices in the order in which they are due to be paid, to be able to see at a glance which invoices are overdue
- Check every week for overdue invoices. Telephone to ask when a cheque can be expected. Get the name of the person who are speaking to and ask for them the next time you phone
- After three or four phone calls, write. Say that the account will be put into the hands of solicitors and/or cut off supplies. But only threaten to cut off supplies when you really mean it.

KEEPING BOOKS AND RECORDS FOR TAX PURPOSES

A business must keep full and accurate records sufficient to enable it to make a proper return of income for tax purposes. These records must be kept for six years. Failure to keep proper records or to keep them for the necessary six years, where chargeable to tax, is a Revenue offence, punishable by fines and/or imprisonment.

The records kept must include books of account in which all purchases and sales of goods and services and all amounts received and all amounts paid out are recorded in a manner that will clearly show the amounts involved and the matters to which they relate. All supporting records such as invoices, bank and building society statements, cheque stubs, receipts etc., should also be retained.

CHAPTER 12

PLANNING FOR GROWTH

Colm O'Gorman[*]

LEARNING OBJECTIVES

- To understand the "stages of development" in new ventures
- To know the key entrepreneurial, organisational, and strategic transitions that characterize high growth new ventures
- To analyse the strategies that are associated with high growth in new ventures
- To establish the barriers to growth in new ventures
- To know the sources of assistance available for high growth new ventures in Ireland.

INTRODUCTION

Talk to an entrepreneur about the creation of a new venture and, typically, they will tell a story that describes a period of apparent unstructured chaos peppered with opportunistic decisions and sometimes heroic actions that created what is now a successful business. The entrepreneur may reveal how they survived on meagre financial resources, bootstrapping their way to success. Further, the story may provide insights into the naivety of the entrepreneur's initial assumptions about starting a business and the lack of knowledge they

---

[*] Colm O'Gorman is a lecturer in entrepreneurship at UCD Business School, University College Dublin.

had about the market they sought to enter. Such a story may be the antithesis of "good" management practice, certainly of the type written about in management texts, but it is not untypical of successful start-ups.

Ask the entrepreneur to describe how the business is now managed and the entrepreneur whose venture has achieved significant growth will describe a business that is characterized by plans, budgets, systems, controls and reporting procedures, that is managed by an experienced "professional" management team, and that probably has attracted finance to fund further growth.

This provokes two interesting questions:

- How does an unplanned, *ad hoc*, reactive start-up transform itself into a planned, organized, managed growth business?
- What strategies, if any, are associated with the growth and development of a new venture?

This chapter will seek to explore these issues, and in the process outline the key entrepreneurial, organizational, and strategic imperatives facing entrepreneurs as they seek to grow and develop their new venture.

THEORETICAL BACKGROUND

Research by Storey (1994) in the 1980s and 1990s suggested that the vast majority of new businesses do not grow. His research showed that nearly all new ventures stay small; of those that survive the start-up period, the majority will employ few, if any, employees 10 years later. His research suggested that as few as 4% of all start-ups achieve high levels of growth, as measured by growth in employee numbers. However, these 4% make a disproportionate contribution to the local economy. Interestingly these high growth businesses are found in a diverse range of sectors (for example, the fastest-growing businesses in the UK in 2001 included two coffee shop chains, a financial advisory firm, a publishing firm, and a retailer of leather furniture), and are in no way confined to high technology businesses.

There are several explanations for the apparent lack of success for most new ventures, though growth should not always be regarded as synonymous with success; there are many successful firms that are small but highly profitable and conversely, many unsuccessful large firms that struggle to create value. The most important reason for the lack of growth is that growth is not a strategic objective for most entrepreneurs.

Many entrepreneurs start businesses to provide employment for themselves and do not wish to grow and develop the business beyond a self-employment type of business. Another explanation is that many entrepreneurs adopt a growth strategy of multiple new ventures rather than trying to grow one business. These entrepreneurs are not captured in the methodology used by Storey, as he focused on the growth of individual businesses rather than the growth of a portfolio of business interests by an entrepreneur.

Even though the majority of new businesses do not grow, there is much research on the small number that do. Several perspectives have been taken to the study of new businesses that do achieve high levels of growth. Of most importance are the "stages-of-growth" process models, research that explores the barriers to growth in new businesses, and research that has sought to identify the strategic characteristics of high growth ventures.

"STAGES-OF-GROWTH" MODELS

The "stages-of-growth" perspective suggests that there are common patterns to the development of all new ventures. Each stage of growth is characterized by specific managerial, organizational, and strategic challenges. Knowledge of these patterns allows an entrepreneur to anticipate problems and react in advance. Models by Churchill & Lewis (1983) and Kazanjian (1988) typify this perspective.

Churchill & Lewis (1983) suggested a five-stage model:
- **Stage 1:** Existence
- **Stage 2:** Survival
- **Stage 3:** Success-Disengagement or Success-Growth
- **Stage 4:** Take-Off
- **Stage 5:** Resource Maturity.

The model suggests that growth is not a natural process and that the most typical growth and development pattern consists of Existence, Survival and Success-Disengagement. This common pattern describes the entrepreneur that survives start-up but doesn't grow and develop the business. Many of these ventures are only marginally financially viable, but survive because the entrepreneur has no alternative or values the non-financial benefits of self-employment. Others are what are referred to as "life-style" businesses, businesses where the entrepreneur uses the proceeds of the business to support other activities.

The critical transition point in their model is therefore the choice to grow the business, producing the following pattern: Existence, Survival, Success-Growth, Take-Off, and Resource Maturity. The model emphasizes how key managerial and organizational issues change as the business grows. For example, they highlight how the role of the entrepreneur must change from "doer" at start-up (the hands-on managerial style necessary to start a business) to "manager" at later stages of the model. Research on small businesses suggests that many entrepreneurs find this transition very hard to make.

The model also highlights how the organization structure of the new business will become more formal and hierarchal as the business develops. At start-up, new ventures are characterized by a lack of structure – the entrepreneur covers all functional areas such as finance, production, sales, hiring new staff, promotions, etc. At later stages of development, an organization structure may emerge. Furthermore, the model emphasises how a focus on cash management typifies the early development of a new business but, as a business matures, cash management becomes less of a critical concern, with a solid customer base providing repeat business and dependable cash flow. However, should the entrepreneur choose to grow the business, cash resources once again become critical and, frequently, the entrepreneur will seek external resources from private investors, banks or (for a small majority) from venture capitalists.

Intensive levels of activity characterise two stages of the model. They are the Existence stage, when the business is initially created, and the Take-off stage, when the business begins to experience significant levels of growth. The model suggests that, for this growth to occur, systems and controls must be developed, the owner must delegate activities and that growth requires high amounts of financial resources – cash to fund new personnel, new premises, product and market for development, etc.

Kazanjian's model focused explicitly on the development of high technology new businesses (1988). He suggested a four-stage model:

- **Stage 1:** Conception and development
- **Stage 2:** Commercialisation
- **Stage 3:** Growth
- **Stage 4:** Stability.

The evolution of the business can be explained in terms of specific strategic challenges and associated "solutions" to these issues. The first key problem is resource acquisition and technology development. The key focus of activity during the second stage is on producing the new product and getting initial market support. The focus of activity in the third stage shifts to generating sales and coping with the emergence of an organization. Finally, the fourth stage of development is characterized by an emphasis on profitability, the implementation of organizational controls, in particular financial controls, and the development of a base for future growth.

There are several deficiencies in the "stages-of-growth" perspective to understanding growth in new ventures. First, many of the models are normative, meaning that they are developed without any research evidence to support the model. Second, individual stages cannot be defined explicitly in terms of sales, employee numbers, or number of years of existence. Businesses develop differently depending on industry context. In some industries, such as basic engineering, an entrepreneur may be able to manage a business of 50 to 100 employees with a relatively simple organizational structure, while a software business with a similar number of employees will typically be characterized by a much more complex organizational structure with developed reporting relationships and extensive internal controls, procedures, and systems. Third, there is some evidence that successful entrepreneurs anticipate growth. So, rather than reacting to crises that typify the transition from one stage to the next, as suggested by many "stages-of-growth" models, some entrepreneurs build organizational structures, systems, procedures, managerial competences, entrepreneurial skills, and resources in advance of actually needing them (Hambrick & Crozier, 1985). Fourth, the emergence of new technologies and business systems have allowed some businesses to be "born global", that is progress from start-up to being a global business in a very short space of time (Knight & Cavusgil, 1996). These businesses do not appear to exhibit many of the traditional stages described by "stages-of-growth" models. Nonetheless, they may still experience many of the same generic entrepreneurial, organizational and strategic challenges.

Can entrepreneurs get any practical benefit from stages-of-growth models if the models don't allow them to anticipate when their business will experience a transition from one stage to another? It can be argued that a broad awareness of how businesses grow and develop may be useful to an entrepreneur, though many entrepreneurs argue that, if they had known in advance the amount of work involved in starting and growing a business, they might not have started the business! Also, experience suggests that entrepreneurs have a preference for specific information about business development at the time they encounter a given problem. This is in keeping with the problem-solving managerial style of many entrepreneurs.

BARRIERS TO GROWTH

The "stages-of-growth" perspective suggests that growth is not an automatic outcome for all organisations. In what is now regarded as a seminal work in the study of organisations, Penrose (1956) argued that a firm's ability to grow was limited by the combined effect of three factors:

- What she termed the "productive opportunity" of the firm
- The firm's resources and capabilities
- The ability of the firm's management and organisation structure to match these two elements profitably.

Specifically, "productive opportunity" refers to the extent to which a firm is able to see opportunities for expansion, is willing to act on them, or is able to respond to them. Penrose argued that firms could be competently managed but not necessarily entrepreneurially ambitious, and therefore might not grow.

The most common reason for lack of growth in new businesses is that the entrepreneur does not have growth as a business objective. However, there are other reasons why a new venture might not grow. The barriers to growth reported by entrepreneurs include the following:

- Difficulty in accessing external finance
- Low levels of product and market innovation
- Difficulty in attracting experienced staff and management
- Poor managerial systems and controls
- The small size of the Irish market and the difficulties and costs associated with expanding into foreign markets.

Hambrick & Crozier (1985) have suggested that the key managerial and organisational problems facing high-growth new businesses are:

- **Instant size:** This can create problems of disaffection, inadequate skills, and inadequate systems

- **A sense of infallibility:** This may result from the success of the strategies and plans employed by the organisation in order to bring about growth. Such organisations can become complacent in monitoring the environment for changes and new competitors
- **Internal turmoil:** This is created by the strain of growth. An influx of new people results in a mix of staff, some of who are not all that familiar with each other or the culture of the company. Turf battles abound, decision-making suffers and people burnout or leave
- **Extraordinary resource needs:** Often quickly-growing businesses are cash-starved.

One important barrier, not reported by entrepreneurs but suggested by research, is that the entrepreneur may in fact be a barrier to the growth of the new venture. The fact that the skills and managerial styles of the entrepreneur may retard the growth of the new venture is not necessarily a criticism of the entrepreneur. It is merely a recognition of the fact that the skills and attributes needed to start a business differ from those needed to grow and develop a business. Examples of how the entrepreneur is the barrier to growth include:

- The entrepreneur might resist sharing responsibility. This "need to be in control" trait may have encouraged the entrepreneur to start the new business, but may subsequently prevent them sharing responsibility with staff. A lack of delegation means that the entrepreneur has neither the time nor the skills to grow the business
- The "desire to be in control" may prevent the entrepreneur from sharing equity and thereby raising the funds needed to fund growth
- The lack of business experience that is common among entrepreneurs may mean that the entrepreneur may not have the managerial skills that are necessary to manage a growing business. Many entrepreneurs resent the increased formalisation that is associated with growth. This has led some researchers to suggest that "the founder must go, if the business is to grow".

In summary, there are many barriers to growth in the new venture, but some entrepreneurs successfully manage the transition from start-up to high growth business. This is frequently done by augmenting their own skills at start-up, by involving people with a range of skills in the start-up team, by creating a board of advisors of experienced managers who act as an informal board of directors for the entrepreneur, or by attracting so-called "grey hair", experienced managers, into the new venture by offering share options.

Other entrepreneurs recognise that their skills and interests are in starting, and not growing, businesses, and therefore put their energy into new businesses and projects rather than growing any one business.

But where the entrepreneur cannot make the transition in managerial style necessary to manage growth, the business may miss out on growth opportunities, lose market position to businesses that do grow, and in the process weaken their strategic position and endanger their prospects for survival.

STRATEGIC CHARACTERISTICS OF HIGH GROWTH VENTURES

The discussion above has suggested that growth, or the lack of growth, in new ventures can be explained in terms of organisational and entrepreneurial issues. However, it can also be argued that growth in new ventures is the outcome of superior competitive strategies. This is the approach that is more commonly used to explain growth and success in more established businesses. What constitutes superior competitive positioning in a new venture?

The strategic challenge facing entrepreneurs managing high growth new businesses relates to:

- The identification of an opportunity
- The exploitation of the opportunity through consistently excellent implementation of basic business functions, such as sales and customer service.

The choice of market has a significant impact on the growth prospects of a new venture. A survey of successful Irish companies revealed that there are common strategies pursued by successful companies (O'Gorman, 2001). The study analysed 131 small and medium-sized enterprises (SMEs) in the manufacturing and services sectors. "Success" was defined as the ability of the company to grow consistently over a five-year period. The study suggests that those small companies that wish to be successful must pay special attention to the decisions they make with regard to both market choice (industry, sector, segment) and competitive strategy.

With regard to "market choice", the results of this research suggest that the choice of market determines the likelihood of success and growth. If the "wrong" market is chosen, success will be limited or unachievable. However, the market-choice decision is not a choice that is, or can be, subject to frequent change. Market selection will always be constrained by the entrepreneurs' experiences. Furthermore, choosing a growing market is not a sufficient condition for successful growth. Other decisions will influence whether a business achieves success in its market. In particular, many businesses might experience initial growth when a new market emerges but, as the nature of competition changes as a market grows and matures, frequently only a few competitors will continue to be successful, with many initially successful businesses experiencing a loss of market-share and some being forced to exit from the market.

Research by Bhidé (2000) suggests that the key characteristics of markets that will result in a greater number of high growth new businesses are uncertainty and turbulence. He argues that, where there is market uncertainty and turbulence, established businesses will not be able to quantify potential returns and therefore will delay investing in the market opportunity. This creates a situation where new ventures are not at a competitive disadvantage relative to established businesses. Bhidé suggests that new entrants to such markets have what he calls a "lottery ticket", meaning that some will achieve significantly high levels of growth. It is important to note that uncertainty and turbulence is not limited to high technology markets and that it is not only the result of changing technology. For example, changes in competitive dynamics, social trends, changes in competition and licensing legalisation can result in market uncertainty and turbulence.

The survey of Irish companies referred to above also identified a number of competitive and growth strategies that characterize successful high-growth small and medium-sized businesses. High-growth SMEs:

- Do not necessarily pursue focus strategies. They pursue a strategy of a broad product line, though this may be in a narrower product-market niche than their competitors
- Pursue strategies of differentiation and uniqueness by differentiating their products from those of their competitors
- Are characterised by innovation. High growth SMEs continually introduce new products and, over a period of five years, will significantly change and improve their product portfolio
- Compete by emphasising product quality, customer service and by introducing new and improved products

- Invest in their future by expanding capacity and by up-dating plant and equipment
- Grow in related areas of business by building on their existing strengths. They are likely to be involved in exporting or in export markets
- Successfully combine high profitability with high growth.

It is important to remember that these strategic characteristics are the outcome of the successful daily implementation of good business practice. Many high growth entrepreneurs attribute their success to the exceptional implementation of a relatively "mundane" business idea (Bhidé, 2000).

To achieve growth, entrepreneurs must successfully attract resources into the business – not just financial but managerial and technical resources also; they must generate sales and, in particular, sales revenues; and they must be able to "unmake" and "remake" the new venture's market-offering in response to market fluctuations.

So, in seeking to create a new venture that has significant growth potential, the strategic challenge for the entrepreneur is to position the new venture in a market that has significant growth potential. However, this does not mean that high growth entrepreneurs produce better business plans that identify the market opportunity and outline the new venture's competitive positioning and advantage. What high growth entrepreneurs appear to be good at is identifying a market characterised by market uncertainty and modifying their business idea in response to market requirements. The consequence of market uncertainty is that typically there will be no dominant or established competitor, though there may be many competitors. This means that the entrepreneur who best meets the emerging needs of the market may experience very high levels of growth.

PRACTICAL INFORMATION ON DEVELOPMENT OF BUSINESSES IN IRELAND

In seeking to start a new venture with high growth potential, the entrepreneur might avail of a number of supports offered by private and public organisations in Ireland. Typically, these supports address one or more of the following needs:

- For initial seed finance to start the business and for venture capital to fund subsequent growth
- To develop and professionalise management capabilities
- For physical factory and office space
- To sell into international markets.

However, it is important to remember that many entrepreneurs successfully start and grow their new venture without availing of any of these supports. What follows are summary descriptions of some of the programmes and supports that entrepreneurs may wish to access (in complying this information, the research was drawn heavily from the websites of the agencies providing the support). The various agencies tend to offer support across a number of the above four categories.

Financing High Growth New Ventures

Enterprise Ireland offers grants (employment and/or capital) to new ventures that have high growth potential. These firms must be of a minimum size and must be engaged in manufacturing or internationally traded services (for example, software) and must have the objective of selling overseas and of growing quickly. Many of the businesses funded under this programme are software or technology businesses. In addition, Enterprise Ireland offers supports in these functional areas:

- Business planning and information
- Research, development and design
- Production and operations
- Marketing and business development
- Human resource development.

Shannon Development has specific responsibility for the development of Irish indigenous industry in the Shannon Region. It has a particular interest in supporting technology and knowledge-intensive high growth businesses. Financial and development supports include employment, research and development, and management development grants. Shannon Development has a venture capital unit that invests directly in businesses. Údarás na Gaeltachta provides similar supports in the Gaeltacht regions.

High growth new businesses can raise funds through the Business Expansion Scheme (BES), which allows investors to buy equity in an approved business (the Department of Finance develops the rules governing eligible businesses) and set the investment against their tax liability. For certain investments, an appropriate development agency must certify that the business is eligible for BES funding. The Project Development Centre and the Bolton Trust (allied to Dublin Institute of Technology) operates a designated Business Expansion Scheme called the Small Enterprise Fund. The fund invests in growth-orientated businesses. The fund typically makes investments of less than €300,000 in a single company. Many private accountancy firms also operate Business Expansion Schemes for their clients. There are also a number of seed capital funds that will support high growth potential businesses. Examples include the Dublin Seed Capital Fund; The Enterprise 2000 Fund; and the Irish BICs Seed Capital Fund.

All the major banks offer finance and business supports for high growth new ventures. For example, Bank of Ireland have a special unit called the Enterprise Support Unit (ESU), which works closely with a business to assist in providing the right financial package to allow the company to grow. The objective of the ESU is to identify start-up and developing businesses with a distinct competitive advantage that can demonstrate viability and have the capacity to create jobs. They require a comprehensive business plan; tangible promoter commitment by way of personally-sourced capital; and that the entrepreneur demonstrates the viability of the project. Enterprise Support's normal lending range is from €60,000 to €200,000. It offers a complete guide to writing a business plan in a publication available from the bank's website (*Starting your Business*). Similarly, AIB Bank offers finance and business supports for new and growing businesses. They advise entrepreneurs to bring a business plan and a completed application pack (available from the website) to their local branch.

First Tuesday is an informal community of entrepreneurs, business angels, and venture capitalists, and providers of services to entrepreneurs operating in the new economy. The "community" supports entrepreneurs by facilitating networking, through events such as open forums and their website. First Tuesday provides the entrepreneur with access to support services that assist in the management of growth. For service providers, First Tuesday provides a forum for accessing the opinion leaders and the entrepreneurs that are driving the new economy in Ireland. At their meetings, First Tuesday labels attendees as follows: "green dots" are entrepreneurs and start-ups, "red dots" are potential investors such as venture capitalists or private angel investors, and "yellow dots" are service providers ranging from design and marketing companies to head-hunters, all interested in selling support services to new ventures.

Business Innovation Centres (BIC) operate in a number of regions in Ireland. BICs assist and provide advice to entrepreneurs and access to seed capital for selected enterprises. BICs are funded from both public sector funds (including EU funds) and private sector funds. For example, Dublin BIC assists and provides advice to selected early stage innovative and technology-based business ideas/projects. It supports entrepreneurs through the various start-up stages and continues to assist the business through the first three/five years of business. Their activities complement the assistance and services provided by the State agencies and the private sector.

The County Enterprise Boards (CEBs) are a Government-funded initiative to support enterprise creation in every county in Ireland. They support a wide range of businesses, including manufacturing and service businesses, and tourism businesses. They provide grant assistance for feasibility studies, capital equipment purchases, and employment creation. They also provide business information, business advice, counselling, and training and mentoring.

Developing Managerial Capabilities

Enterprise Ireland offers a free mentoring service to young and small to medium-sized enterprises. Mentors provide the entrepreneur with strategic guidance, practical advice, and emotional support. In addition, Enterprise Ireland will seek to match entrepreneurs with business angels (private investors interested in investing equity in start-ups and growing businesses).

In a development of its traditional mentor service, Enterprise Ireland, now offers, in conjunction with Shannon Development and Ernst & Young, a new programme called Excellerator. To avail of the Excellerator programme, entrepreneurial companies must:

- Be located in the regions
- Be primarily export-focused and be preparing to grow quickly
- Be 12-18 months or older
- Have a turnover of over 1 million euro
- Employ 15 or more staff
- Be a knowledge and/or manufacturing business in one of four key industry sectors: informatics, health and life sciences, digital media, and e-business.

The Excellerator programme seeks to address specific skills and knowledge gaps that are common to entrepreneurs. One unique aspect of this programme is that Excellerator has created a group of "champions", comprising some of Ireland's leading entrepreneurs, to act as mentors to the new companies (for example, Denis O'Brien and Chris Horn).

PLATO is a European Union initiative that supports business-to-business networks. Entrepreneurs can join a local Plato group that usually meets monthly for a two-year period. Two business people from large companies in the local region chair the monthly meetings. The meetings are a forum for entrepreneurs to discuss their specific business development concerns and for sharing information and ideas.

The Institute of Technology, Tallaght, offers potential entrepreneurs a one-year training and support programme – the M50 Enterprise Platform Programme. The programme assists participants in making the "leap" from employment to the full-time operation of a business. The programme offers training on all the key aspects of business start-up and operation; access to incubation facilities; funding support; one-to-one business mentoring; and peer counselling through an "enterprise support network". Other third level institutions offer variations of this programme.

The Project Development Centre (PDC) offers a "Fast Growth Programme" to businesses that are between three and 10 years old, have achieved a turnover of at least €300,000, and are presently on the verge of major growth. These companies must operate in one of the following sectors: manufacturing, internationally traded services, or services to industry. By participating in the programme, the entrepreneur can expect the following benefits:

- Help in developing a three-year strategic business plan
- Improved business capabilities across all functions
- Support in identifying and creating a balanced management team
- Assistance with financial issues, and an investment prospectus where appropriate
- The opportunity to access Business Expansion Scheme funding
- The opportunity to meet potential investors.

The major consulting firms also offer services to high growth potential new ventures. For example, PriceWaterhouseCoopers offers specialist advice that can assist entrepreneurs in growing the new business. The firm offers advice across a range of areas, including helping to develop a business strategy, developing business plans, preparing financial projections and related forecasts, raising finance, optimal tax structures for the business, protecting intellectual property, and incorporating the business.

Accessing "Space"

Enterprise Ireland operates a number of business parks across the country that provide factory space to entrepreneurs. Shannon Development operates an Innovation Centre in the National Technological Park in Limerick, which offers two stage levels of business accommodation: "Business Starter Units" and "Business Expansion Units". As projects develop and grow, they may progress from a Business Starter Unit to a Business Expansion Unit.

The universities and Institutes of Technology offer entrepreneurs from within their own community (students, graduates, academics, etc) incubator space and enterprise training and support. For example UCD, through the University Industry Programme, seeks to facilitate the commercialisation of UCD research and services. It offers advice in the areas of patents, licensing and protection of intellectual property; training and supports for entrepreneurs and campus companies; and incubator space. The TCD Innovation Centre (Trinity College) offers incubator space for campus companies during their initial stages of development. The centre seeks to support the commercial development of research products carried out in TCD, and to manage intellectual property and patenting issues.

There are also private providers of incubator space. For example, Dublin BIC manages an Incubation Centre within the Guinness James' Street complex. The Guinness Enterprise Centre has 77 incubator units for new and established small businesses, primarily in software services, small-scale manufacturing, light hi-tech engineering and internationally traded/technology services. The centre is equipped for hi-spec communications facilities and e-commerce, and offers shared services such as secretarial, telephone answering, video conferencing and access to conference and boardrooms.

Internationalising

Enterprise Ireland provides extensive supports for indigenous businesses wishing to internationalise and to export from Ireland (the former Irish Trade Board is now part of Enterprise Ireland). Enterprise

Ireland operates offices in most of Ireland's key export markets, where its staff can provide information and introductions (to potential customers, distributors, strategic partners) in the local market. They can also help Irish businesses access appropriate local business and legal advice and office space.

The Business Innovation Centres (BICs) can provide international marketing assistance to entrepreneurs through their membership of the European Business and Innovation Centre Network of 140 BICs throughout Europe.

Irish entrepreneurs are in the very fortunate position of having a vast array of support available to them through a broad spectrum of agencies. When growing a venture, it is beneficial to access these resources as they provide knowledge, expertise, and support of varying kinds that will assist the process of successfully building a business. For a more detailed record of the many sources of assistance that are available, check out the website www.startingabusinessinireland.com.

CONCLUSION

Achieving high growth is not a strategic objective of the vast majority of all start-ups. However, the small number of start-ups that do achieve high levels of growth make a significant and disproportionate contribution to the economy. The process of growing a new business involves:

- The successful implementation of the business idea, frequently in a market characterized by uncertainty and turbulence
- Anticipating and managing transitions – in the role of the entrepreneur, in the organisation, and in strategy.

However not all entrepreneurs can manage the process successfully and in some cases the entrepreneur needs to be replaced if the business is to realise its growth potential.

In terms of actually starting a new venture with high growth potential, what are the key lessons from this chapter? There are a number of questions that the entrepreneur should seek to answer:

- **Is the entrepreneur motivated to grow the new venture?** Lack of motivation to grow the business is most likely the biggest obstacle to growth. The lack of a clear "exit strategy" may also reduce the motivation for the entrepreneur to grow the business. Exit strategy refers to how the entrepreneur and investors intend to realise the value of their investments (examples are trade sales, selling the business to a competitor or customer; "floating" the business on the stock exchange, what is known as an IPO or an initial public offering)

- **Is there growth potential in the chosen market?** While it may not be possible to quantify or assess fully growth potential in advance of creating the new venture, there is strong evidence that markets characterised by uncertainty and turbulence offer a higher probability of growth. Paradoxically, the nature of these markets make them harder for the entrepreneur to survey in advance of new venture creation, and therefore it is harder to produce a meaningful business plan. But this attribute often means that more established and better-resourced firms may delay investing in these markets, providing the entrepreneur with a short-term lead on competitors

- **Is there competitive space for the new venture?** Does the new venture possess similar resources and skills to those of its competitors? This is frequently the case in emerging markets, as all new entrants typically have the same resource constraints and all suffer from the lack of an established market reputation. Where there are established competitors, with good market reputations, it may be difficult for the new venture to capture market share. It is easier to grow in a market that is growing rather than trying to grow by taking market share from competitors

- **Does the entrepreneur have the skills to sell the new product/ service?** The critical management capability in new ventures appears to be the ability to sell the product/service. In many high growth ventures, the entrepreneur is actively involved in selling the product/ service to customers. The ability and motivation to engage in this activity will be critical to the venture establishing itself in the market. Entrepreneurs should have some knowledge of customers and their requirements, be persistent in trying to establish contact with potential customers, and have a strong belief in their product/ service's superiority

- **Does the entrepreneur have managerial capabilities to grow the new venture?** There is evidence that entrepreneurs who have access to a network of business people, such as potential customers, suppliers, business angels, accountants, solicitors, etc, are more likely to grow their business. While formal management training and/or detailed management experience is not a necessary prerequisite to new venture growth, a business network provides the entrepreneur with access to skills and expertise beyond their own experience. Starting a new venture with a team of entrepreneurs, rather than as a solo-entrepreneur, is one way of increasing the network of contacts and resources that the new venture will be able to exploit.

Note that these are not definitive requirements for growth, they only provide a general indication of the likely growth potential inherent in the entrepreneur and the new venture.

QUESTIONS

1. "For the firm to grow, the founder must go". Discuss.
2. How can growth be incorporated into the business plan of a new venture creation?
3. Detail the key entrepreneurial, organisational, and strategic transitions that characterise high-growth new ventures.
4. Describe the "stages of growth" models.
5. Using the Internet, identify the principal sources of assistance for enterprises in your region.

USEFUL WEBSITES

www.dbic.ie
www.deloitte.ie
www.enterprise-ireland.com
www.firsttuesday.ie
www.guinness-enterprisectr.com
www.it-tallaght.ie
www.itw.ie/exporter
www.pdc.ie
www.plato.ie
www.pwcglobal.com
www.sfa.ie
www.shannondevelopment.ie
www.startingabusinessinireland.com
www.tcd.ie/research_innovation
www.ucd.ie/uip

CHECKLIST FOR CHAPTER

After reading this chapter, check that you understand and appreciate:
- The "stages of development" in new ventures
- The key entrepreneurial, organisational, and strategic transitions that characterize high growth new ventures
- The strategies that are associated with high growth in new ventures
- The barriers to growth in new ventures
- The sources of assistance available for high growth new ventures in Ireland.

REFERENCES

Bhidé, A. (2000) - *The Origin and Evolution of New Businesses* - Oxford University Press.

Churchill, N. C. and Lewis, V. C. (1983) - The Five Stages of Small Business Growth - *Harvard Business Review*, Vol.61, No.3, pp 30-39.

Hambrick, D. and Crozier, L. (1985) - Stumblers and Stars in the Management of Rapid Growth - *Journal of Business Venturing*.

Kazanjian, R. K. (1988) - Relation of Dominant Problems to Stages of Growth in Technology-Based New Ventures - *Academy of Management Journal*, Vol.31, No.2, pp 257-279.

Knight, G. and Cavusgil, S.T. (1996) - The Born Global Firm: A Challenge to Traditional Internationalisation Theory - *Advances in International Marketing*, Vol.8, pp11-26.

O'Gorman, C. (2001) - The Sustainability of Growth in Small and Medium-Sized Enterprises - *International Journal of Entrepreneurial Behaviour and Research*, Vol.7, No.2, pp 60-75.

Penrose, E.T. (1959 - reprinted in 1995) - *The Theory of the Growth of the Firm* (3rd Edition) - Oxford, Basil Blackwater Publishing.

Storey, D. J. (1994) - *Understanding the Small Business Sector* – Routledge, London.

CHAPTER 13

REVIEWING THE BUSINESS PLAN

Ron Immink* and Brian O'Kane**

LEARNING OBJECTIVES

- How to prepare financial projections for a start-up
- The techniques used to review the process of business planning
- How to use these review techniques as dynamic, not static, tools
- How to review a business plan document
- How to tailor a business plan document for different audiences.

INTRODUCTION

At this stage, the entrepreneur has (almost) completed the process of business planning, having considered a range of issues from finding the business idea (**Chapter 2**), through intellectual property (**Chapter 5**), legal issues (**Chapter 6**), marketing research (**Chapter 4**) and marketing (**Chapter 8**), HR issues (**Chapter 10**) and the management team (**Chapter 7**), operations (**Chapter 9**) and finance (**Chapter 11**). They may even have

---

* Ron Immink is new business director of Oak Tree Press.
** Brian O'Kane is managing director of Oak Tree Press.

begun planning for exceptional growth, with all the stresses that brings (**Chapter 12**).

The entrepreneur will now be ready to prepare financial projections – profit and loss account, balance sheet and cash flow, plus supporting information – based on the plans already developed. These projections will reflect in financial terms the underlying business, showing its viability (or otherwise), its strengths and vulnerabilities, and the resources required to sustain it. Of course, initial projections are often subject to change, as grandiose schemes are tempered by the acceptance of commercial reality.

FINANCIAL PROJECTIONS

Ideally, the financial projections will have grown out of the process of business planning. The exercises that have been undertaken through the planning should have generated numbers for input into the financial projections. Where financial planning takes place separate from the process of business planning, the resulting numbers are rarely dependable.

The critical inputs for financial projections are:

For the projected profit and loss account
- Sales (volumes or values)
- Costs of Sales
- Fixed overheads
- Variable overheads

For the projected balance sheet
- Fixed asset acquisitions and depreciation
- Inventory
- Working capital
- Financial structure of the business

For the projected cash flow
- Credit terms – received and given.

From these inputs, and an understanding of the business model, financial projections can be developed to whatever level of detail and sophistication is appropriate. Micro-businesses can manage with single-page statements of no more than a few lines each, trading loss of detail for ease of comprehension. Larger, more complex businesses require greater detail, often summarised into appendices.

It is the accepted norm that three years' projections are prepared although, increasingly, venture capitalists and other frequent readers of business plans dismiss the later years' data as little more than conjecture. Nevertheless, the exercise of thinking through the future financial consequences of current actions is educational for the entrepreneur and/or management team. Sample projection formats are shown in **Figures 13.1** and **13.2** (see the Appendix to this chapter). In addition, since this is critical for a start-up, it is usual to prepare a schedule showing the business' need for funding and the proposed sources of same as shown in **Figures 13.3** and **13.4** (see the Appendix to this chapter). These initial financial projections represent a first effort at reflecting the as yet unproven business model on which the start-up is to be based.

REVIEWING THE PROCESS

The financial projections encapsulate the thinking of the entrepreneur. However, before the process can be considered complete, it needs to be reviewed in some depth, to identify gaps and challenges before these are allowed to cripple the new venture. Usually, this review is financially-directed and mimics the type of review that a banker or investor will carry out when considering the plan for lending or investment. However, the entrepreneur is in possession of a great deal more information than the banker or investor, has a better knowledge of the linkages between parts of the plan and is, at this stage, at least in a position to make quite radical changes if necessary without loss of face or, worse, loss of confidence on the part of the banker or investor.

The techniques used to carry out a financial review of an almost-completed business plan include:
* Profit and cash flow review
* Break-even analysis
* Ratio analysis
* Sensitivity analysis
* Quantification of risk.

Profit and Cash Flow

The aim here is to review both the profit and loss account and cash flow projections for acceptability under normal investment criteria. Ideally, one is looking for:

- Profit (or an acceptable level of losses, with profitability in sight) to be achieved within the period of the projections
- Positive cash flow (or positive cash flow in sight) within the period of the projections
- Explanations of sharp fluctuations in monthly profitability or net cash flow
- Explanations for significant impacts on profit or cash flow in specific months.

Rarely will the projections for a new venture show acceptable profit and/or cash flow on a first try. So, the aim of this technique is to review the projections for corrections that can be made to improve the projected financial position of the business. Typical areas to consider are:
- **Sales:** Can these be increased, whether in value, volume or mix?
- **Purchases:** Can cheaper alternative suppliers or raw materials be found?
- **Credit terms:** Both debtors and creditors.
- **Overheads:** Can any be cut, reduced or postponed?

When analysing overheads, it may be helpful to classify them as:
- **Stable:** These are predictable – for example, insurance, rent and rates, audit fees, etc. Some options here involve "shopping around", negotiation and exploring the potential for changing environmental or work practices to reduce costs – for example, disposing of unused space, better records or preparation of records to reduce unnecessary audit and accounting fees, and improved safety practices to reduce insurance costs
- **Dependant:** These are overheads that arise from decisions made elsewhere – for example, depreciation, which results from decisions on investment, leasing charges and loan interest. These overheads cannot be considered in isolation from the factors that determine them
- **Volatile:** These are overheads requiring careful budgeting and control – for example, travel, motor expenses, maintenance costs, telephone and electricity, and promotion and advertising.

A positive cash flow is one of the most critical elements of the business, and failure to monitor the situation may lead to financial difficulties. While not every entrepreneur will be familiar with accountancy techniques, it is their responsibility to understand their monetary position at any given time.

Break-even Analysis

Calculating a business' break-even point is an elementary, though often overlooked, review tool. The size of the gap between current turnover and break-even turnover may be too great to be bridged and an alternative, less ambitious, venture may need to be considered. In most cases, however, a small boost is all that is needed to get a business over the break-even hurdle point.

Areas to consider that may affect the achievement of break even include:

- **Sales price:** Can this be increased?
- **Sales volume:** Can this be increased?
- **Cost of sales:** Can this be reduced?
- **Overheads:** Can this be reduced?

The break-even figure is normally sought by those investing or giving loan finance to the enterprise.

Ratio Analysis

Modern finance offers a wide range of ratios for calculation, some of which are set out below:

Profit (Loss) ratios
- Gross profit : Sales %
- Net Profit : Sales %
- Net Purchases : Sales %
- Overheads : Sales %.

Liquidity ratios
- Current ratio (times)
- Quick ratio (times)
- Stock Turnover (days)
- Debtor days
- Creditor days.

Investment ratios
- Net Profit: Total Assets %
- Net Profit : Capital Employed %
- Sales : Total Assets (times)
- Sales : Fixed Assets (times)
- Sales : Current Assets (times).

Gearing
- Debt : Equity %
- Equity : Total Assets %
- Net Profit : Interest (times).

Accountants and bankers look at these ratios as a static analysis of the relationships between key figures within the projections and use them to measure the business against industry norms. A more dynamic approach links the relationships to key figures with the underlying business activity and suggests that, if the ratios are unacceptable, changes in the underlying business activity are required. Thus, if a ratio is x%, when y% is desired, then by identifying the underlying business activities whose relationship is reflected in the ratio, the entrepreneur can tackle bringing the ratio back into line. Key drivers in this context are price, volume, product mix, and seasonality. Each of these has consequences, in terms of costs, or market perception, or manufacturing, and these must be taken into account in deciding what action should be taken to bring the ratio to the desired level. But the ratios provide a means of working back dynamically to a desired performance, by altering the underlying business activity.

Figure 13.5 shows how these ratios combine to direct attention to increased profitability.

FIGURE 13.5 HOW RATIOS COMBINE

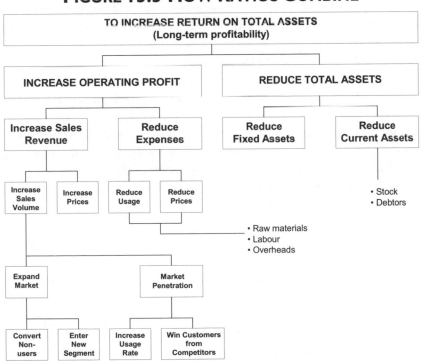

Source: Clarke, 2002

Sensitivity Analysis

In any business, a small number of critical factors have an undue influence on its success (or lack of it). For example, because of high fixed costs, a business may have a high break-even point although, once past that point, profits flow steadily in. Such a business could be vulnerable to changes in market conditions that reduce turnover below the break-even point. Identifying these critical factors, and their impact, is sensitivity analysis. Bankers and investors use sensitivity analysis to identify areas of potential weakness in a business plan by asking: "What would happen if ...?". It is wise, therefore, to perform the analysis oneself – and wiser still to use it to develop a stronger business plan.

Quantifying the Risk

It is important for an entrepreneur to consider the risks to which they and their business are (or may be) exposed. With this insight, the plan can be adjusted to account for these exposures; without it, the business continues to be exposed without warning of likely incidence. When the risks have been identified, the entrepreneur can:

- Reconsider the business plan and look at alternatives
- Review their insurance situation (personal and business)
- Review their dependency on particular customers, suppliers, or staff.

Finance has been used as the driver of the business planning review process. An entrepreneur should also look to the text of their business plan, to consider whether it fairly reflects their efforts at planning the development of the business. In addition, a re-run of SPOTcheck (see **Chapter 3**) or the Key Questions outlined in that chapter will always prove helpful.

It should be noted that, in reviewing the process of business planning, it is important to take a holistic approach, recognising that decisions made in one area may have an impact in other areas. For example, it is unlikely that sales can be significantly increased in the short-term without significant additional marketing expenditure or other costs. If the aim of increasing sales revenue is thus to boost profitability, account must also be taken of the negative profit effect of increased expenditure on marketing. Also, the capacity of the production systems and the chosen channels of distribution need to be checked, to ensure that they can cope with the proposed increased sales volume – and so on, until the plan as a whole is back in balance again.

REVIEWING THE OUTPUT

As emphasised repeatedly in this chapter and in **Chapter 3**, the business plan is the output from the process of business planning – it is the proof that planning has been done.

The traditional format of business plan is a document that comprises:

- **Executive Summary:** A single page that encourages further reading
- **Introduction:** Basic information about the business and the purpose of the plan
- **Promoter(s):** Who you (and your team) are and your qualifications for starting and running the business
- **Project Overview:** A description of the business, its mission statement, trends in its industry, targets, employment (actual and potential) and the legal status of the business
- **Marketing:** A summary of your marketing plan, backed up by a market overview, details of your customers, competition, products/services, price, distribution and promotion strategies and a sales forecast
- **Process & Resources:** Your products/services in more detail, how they are made/delivered, how you will make sure of quality, what staff you will need and how they will be organised
- **Finance & Funding:** A summary of your financial projections, with your funding requirement (and your own contribution) highlighted
- **Appendices:** Including financial projections – profit and loss account, balance sheet, cash flow projections – and other relevant information.

The entrepreneurs' aim is to be able to answer the following questions quickly and easily from the business plan document – the questions reflect a reader's immediate concerns about the viability of the start-up and go to the heart of the business model. They are:

- Who are you?
- What is your product or service?
- Who are your customers?
- Why will your customers buy my product or service?
- What price will your customers pay for your product or service?
- At this price, how many products/services will your customers buy?
- How many products/services can you make?
- How much does it cost to make/deliver each unit of product/service?
- How much start-up investment does the business need?
- Is this a viable business?

As the output of the business planning process, the business plan document has three basic outputs:

- Text
- Evidence
- Numbers.

Text

The text elements of the business plan are important in attracting – and keeping – the reader's attention. This is so whether the reader is a potential investor, a banker, a supplier, or a key member of staff. In drafting the text element of a business plan, the entrepreneur should remember that professional readers of business plans receive far more plans to read than they have time to do so. So they make snap judgements, often based on no more than the physical impression given by the plan and perhaps a few minutes' reading. Therefore, the Executive Summary, the first part of the business plan document to be read, should be the last to be written and should have a disproportionate amount of writing time lavished on it. That is what sells the plan – that is where the entrepreneur's attention must focus.

Evidence

The missing link in most business plans is evidence. An entrepreneur who has diligently completed the process of business planning should be capable of producing and providing evidence that supports the targets, strategies, decisions, and resulting text and financial projections that make up their business plan. All of it builds up into a "Book of Evidence" that supports the business plan document and provides immediate answers to queries raised by readers of the plan.

Table 13.1 shows the critical questions that readers of a business plan may ask and shows where the answers ought to lie within a business plan (using the traditional format) and what evidence ought to back up those answers.

TABLE 13.1: CRITICAL QUESTIONS, ANSWERS AND EVIDENCE

Questions	Answers in the business plan ...	... backed up by external evidence ...	... or internal evidence
Promoters Can you show that you and your colleagues are suited to this particular venture?	Promoter(s)	Previous experience in similar ventures	CVs Personal circumstances Commitment
Organisation Can you show that you have completed all the relevant legal requirements to set up your business?	Project Overview, *Business status*	Legal status Taxation Licensing Trade mark registrations and patent applications	
Organisation Can you show that you have an appropriate organisation structure in place to manage your business?	Project Overview, *Organisation*		Organisation structure Information systems
Sales Can you show where will your sales come from?	Marketing, *Summary of Marketing Strategy* Marketing, *Market Overview* Marketing, *Customers*	Market research Letters of comfort/forward orders	Marketing plan Promotion budget
Sales Can you show that you will be paid as quickly as you expect?	Marketing, *Price*	Market research Letters of comfort/forward orders (inc. agreed credit terms)	Credit terms

Questions	Answers in the business plan ...	... backed up by external evidence ...	... or internal evidence
Sales Can you show that you have established the resources and activities that will be needed to generate, handle and meet your projected sales and that you have a plan to put them into place?	Project Overview, *Organisation* Marketing, Summary of *Marketing Strategy* Marketing, *Place* Marketing, *Promotion* Process & Resources, *Process*	Quotations for fixed assets required showing price, terms and availability Deeds or Lease to premises Evidence of compliance with planning and other legal requirements for premises External research showing availability of suitable staff	Marketing Plan Promotion budget Order processing and other selling functions Production process Logistics/ Distribution Organisational structure Workload
Purchases Can you show that you can secure supplies when you need them and under the terms assumed?	Process & Resources, *Process*	Contracts or letters of comfort from suppliers specifying prices, minimum order quantities, and payment terms Supplier price lists	Purchasing function Credit terms
Administration Can you show that you have a realistic plan for the administration and running of the business?	Project Overview, *Organisation* Process & Resources, *Process*	Quotations for services referred to in your overhead budget	Administration Analysis of the overheads required to run the business
Funding Can you show that you have clearly calculated the funding required?	Finance & Funding Financial projections		Break-even analysis Ratio analysis Sensitivity analysis What If analysis
Funding Can you show that you will be able to finance your business as planned?	Finance & Funding Financial projections	Letters confirming external equity, loans, leases, etc, if not already paid in Valuations of any assets you are transferring to the business	Financial projections "Ownership" of the financial implications of your business plan

Numbers

Business planning requires that the business' activities and expected results are not only described in words but are also translated into figures. For many entrepreneurs, this is the most difficult part of the business plan to prepare. Some abdicate the responsibility for it to their accountants, exposing themselves to a critical lack of knowledge about their own future. But, unless the entrepreneur fully understands the financial element of their business plan, they cannot really understand their own business. They may be a superb craftsperson, retailer or engineer, but they will never make a successful entrepreneur.

Whether the numbers are prepared on paper, on a spreadsheet or using financial modelling software, it is important that the entrepreneur is comfortable in explaining the figures and knows the source of every figure within the projections. In a presentation to potential investors, nothing strikes a wrong note faster fumbling over figures.

Failings of Business Plans

The typical failings of business plan documents, as perceived by professional readers, include:

FAILING	
1	The document does not look professional and inviting; first impressions do count.
2	Executive Summary does not engage or excite -- it must apply the AIDA (Attention – Interest – Desire – Action) principle.
3	The document is written from the entrepreneur's perspective, rather than from the perspective of the reader.
4	The document is full of hot air and has no grounding in the real world.
5	The document is too marketing-driven without a solid financial grounding.
6	The document lacks credibility, due to lack of evidence.
7	The document is too long.
8	The document is boring; a business plan describes a new venture, a journey into the unknown – it should be exciting.
9	The entrepreneur has not applied basic publishing techniques to the document; for example, clear layout, correct grammar and spelling, etc.
10	The document creates no visual images in the reader's mind that will hold their attention.

With the extensive availability and use of computers and word processing, poor presentation is no longer acceptable to professional readers. If the entrepreneur does not take the time to present a good business plan, then why should the reader use their valuable time to analyse the proposal. Failing to work on the detail in a plan could indicate a failing in taking care of detail with the business.

The Plan as a Live Document

The business plan reflects all of the changes in thoughts and directions since the entrepreneur started the process of the business plan. What appears in the business plan document is the end result of the process – the proof that the entrepreneur has planned the start-up. But it's not the 'final' plan. A business plan must reflect the business. As it changes direction, so too must the business plan. The two are inextricably linked. That's why so much emphasis has been laid on the process of business planning, because a process is on-going. Business planning never ends. It is always happening and the business plan document needs to be reviewed and updated regularly as a routine part of the management of the business.

The focus of the business plan document will change over time, adapting to the stage of the business life cycle in which the business finds itself at the time (see **Figure 13.6**).

FIGURE 13.6: BUSINESS LIFE CYCLE

1. **Existence and survival**
   - Owner is the business
   - The key problem is finding customers and managing cash flow.
2. **Consolidation and control**
   - Developing systems
   - The key problem is to generate repeat sales and to maintain financial control.
3. **Control and planning**
   - Taking on staff
   - Focus on management
   - The key problem is fighting competition, development of new markets and control of margins and costs.
4. **Expansion**
   - Delegation and decentralisation
   - Market expansion (new products and/or markets)
   - Tight financial control.

Tailoring the Plan for the Reader

Thus far, the discussion has centred about a single "business plan document". However, in reality, there will probably be several different documents representing the business plan, across a spectrum from an operational manual to a fund-seeking document. Each document needs to be tailored both to its audience and its purpose. The operational manual-type business plan document will be lengthy, detailed and effectively a turn-key manual for implementing the development of the business. It will show step-by-step how the business plans to achieve its targets. On the other hand, the fund-seeking document will be much shorter (perhaps more than a dozen pages), will be focused on the reader's needs and will explain what funding is required, how it will be used, what results are expected and how the reader will benefit from investing in the business.

Different audiences have different information needs, each with their own perspective:

- **The entrepreneur:** To manage the business
- **Management team and key staff:** To understand their roles in implementing it
- **Bankers:** To assess any loan applications you make
- **Investors:** To judge the risk/return potential of your business
- **Advisers to the business:** To let them quickly "read in" to your business strategies
- **Customers or suppliers:** In certain special circumstances, you may circulate parts of the plan to important customers or suppliers, to gain their support.

As in any communication situation, the key to the style and emphasis of the document is determined by:

- Why does the entrepreneur want the person to read the document?
- The level of detail they require to make a judgement
- The level of confidentiality needed and offered.

The Executive Summary is critical. It must:

- Jump at the reader, grab them and hold their attention (if that is not achieved, there is no point going any further)
- Persuade the reader that the idea is good, to encourage them to read on – many readers of business plans never go beyond the Executive Summary because it fails to excite them

- Summarise the company, its objectives, and why it will be successful
- Describe the products, the market, critical financial information
- Outline the finance required -- how much, in what form and when
- Assume that its reader is not expert in your industry and knows nothing about your business
- Be short and easy to read.

The rest of the document must explain:
- How much funding (if any) the business requires
- How much the entrepreneur has contributed
- How much has already been secured from other sources (identify the sources)
- How much is still to be raised and what form it is expected to take (equity, debt or subsidies).

In presenting a business plan, the entrepreneur must show:
- Credibility
- Willingness to work and prepare
- Ability to sell
- A positive attitude
- Professionalism.

Remember, the only objective evidence that an entrepreneur can show at this stage is the thoroughness with which they have completed the business planning process.

CONCLUSION

At this stage, you should have a sound understanding of business planning and the business plan document. The important points to remember are that:
- The process of business planning and the business plan document itself are separate things. One leads to the other.
- Before the business plan can be said to complete, a thorough review, using a variety of techniques, need to be done in order to ensure that all possible factors have been considered in a holistic and dynamic manner.
- The business plan document must be tailored for its audience and addressed to the needs of that audience.

And then it's down to implementation. There are no guarantees of success, though all the research shows that good planning improves the likelihood of success significantly.

QUESTIONS

1. Explain the distinction between the process of business planning and the business plan document.
2. "The plan doesn't matter, it's the planning that counts." Discuss.
3. What are the stages involved in reviewing a business plan? How do they help an entrepreneur to improve his/her plan.
4. Explain the importance of evidence as part of a business plan. What sorts of evidence might you expect to find in a typical business plan?

USEFUL WEBSITES

www.bplans.com
www.startingabusinessinireland.com

CHECKLIST FOR CHAPTER

After reading this chapter, check that you understand and appreciate:
- How to prepare financial projections for a start-up
- The techniques used to review the process of business planning
- How to use these review techniques as dynamic, not static, tools
- How to review a business plan document
- How to tailor a business plan document for different audiences.

REFERENCES

Clarke, P. (2002) - *Accounting Information for Managers* - 2nd edition, Oak Tree Press, Cork.

Immink, R. and O'Kane, B. (2001) – *Starting Your Own Business: A Workbbok* - 2nd edition, Oak Tree Press: Cork.

Immink, R. and O'Kane, B. (2002) - *TENBizPlan: Dynamic Business Planning for Start-Ups* - 2nd edition, Oak Tree Press: Cork.

APPENDIX

FIGURE 13.1: PROJECTED PROFIT & LOSS ACCOUNT

BUSINESS NAME			
PROFIT AND LOSS ACCOUNT *			
	Year 1 €	Year 2 €	Year 3 €
Sales			
Cost of Sales			
Gross Profit			
Gross Profit %			
Overheads			
Staff			
Production			
Premises			
Transport			
Selling and promotion			
General expenses			
Finance			
Depreciation			
Total overheads			
Net Profit/(Loss)			
Tax on profit/(loss)			
Profit retained in business			

FIGURE 13.2: PROJECTED BALANCE SHEET

BUSINESS NAME			
CASHFLOW PROJECTIONS: SUMMARY **			
	Year 1 €	Year 2 €	Year 3 €
Opening balance			
Cash sales			
Debtors			
VAT refunds			
Other income			
Total income			
Initial investment			
Cash purchases			
Creditors			
Overheads:			
Staff			
Production			
Premises			
Transport			
Selling/promotion			
General expenses			
Finance costs			
Loan repayments			
Personal drawings			
Fixed assets			
VAT payable			
Other taxes			
Other expenses			
Total expenses			
Net cash flow			
Closing balance			

FIGURE 13.3: INITIAL INVESTMENT: SUMMARY

BUSINESS NAME INITIAL INVESTMENT: SUMMARY	€	€
1. Fixed assets		
Property		
Renovations		
Fixtures and fittings		
Transport		
Machines and equipment		
Goodwill, security deposits		
Other		
Total fixed assets		
2. Current assets		
Stock of raw material		
Stock of finished goods		
Work in progress		
Debtors		
Other		
Total current assets		
3. Liquid assets		
Cash		
Bank		
Other		
Total liquid assets		
4. Start-up costs		
Prepaid expenses		
Promotion, opening		
Other		
Total start-up costs		
5. Margin for unforeseen costs		
INITIAL INVESTMENT		

FIGURE 13.4: INVESTMENT INVESTMENT: SOURCES OF FUNDING

BUSINESS NAME		
INITIAL INVESTMENT		
PROPOSED SOURCES OF FUNDING		
	€	
INTERNAL		
Personal assets available		
Fixed assets		
Car		
Additional private mortgage		
Savings		
Deferred loans (family)		
Other		
Total personal assets		
Introduced as:		
Equity		
Loans		
TOTAL INTERNAL FUNDING		
EXTERNAL		
External equity		Agreed?
Source		Y/N
External debt (Long/medium-term)		Agreed?
Mortgage		Y/N
Loan		Y/N
Leasing		Y/N
Other		Y/N
Total long/medium-term debt		
External debt (Short-term)		Agreed?
Overdraft		Y/N
Suppliers' credit		Y/N
Payments received in advance		Y/N
Other		Y/N
Total short-term debt		

BUSINESS NAME		
INITIAL INVESTMENT		
PROPOSED SOURCES OF FUNDING		
Subsidies/grants		Agreed?
Agency		Y/N
Enterprise Board		Y/N
Area Partnership Company		Y/N
Other		Y/N
		Y/N
Total subsidies/grants		
TOTAL EXTERNAL FUNDING		
TOTAL FUNDING		

*   It will usually be appropriate to prepare back-up schedules, explaining the calculation of most of the figures in the projected profit and loss account and cash flow.

**   It is also usual to prepare the projected cash flow in greater detail – usually, monthly – for the first year, with quarterly or annual figures for the later years.

Source: www.startingabusinessinireland.com

CHAPTER 14

ENTREPRENEURSHIP IN
DIFFERENT CONTEXTS

Thomas M. Cooney[*]

LEARNING OBJECTIVES

- To demonstrate how entrepreneurship can take place in different contexts
- To develop an understanding of corporate entrepreneurship (intrapreneurship), mediated entrepreneurship, public sector entrepreneurship, and social entrepreneurship
- To analyse how each of these forms differ from the traditional concept of entrepreneurship
- To examine the entrepreneurship process for each of these contexts.

INTRODUCTION

The origins of entrepreneurship theory stem from an economics background. A review of the literature normally incorporates the notions of the entrepreneur as risk-taker, innovator, supplier of financial capital, decision-maker, industrial leader, co-ordinator of economic resources, employer of factors of production, and proprietor of an enterprise.

[*] Thomas M Cooney is a lecturer in entrepreneurship and marketing at the Dublin Institute of Technology and a director of Optimum Results.

In more recent times, the work has diversified to include differing schools of thought that have their foundations in areas such as management, psychology, and sociology. Gartner (1989) altered the traditional discussion from a focus on the person to an examination of the behaviour of the entrepreneur. He contended that an entrepreneur was someone who located a business opportunity, accumulated resources, marketed the product or service, and created an organisation. Bygrave and Hofer (1991) extended this contention by highlighting the notion of entrepreneurship as a process. They argued that an entrepreneurial process involves all functions, activities, and actions associated with perceiving opportunities and the creation of organisations to pursue them. They further suggested that entrepreneurship does not occur unless there is a risk of losing personal capital. But the primary interpretation of entrepreneurship as the creation of a new venture is very narrow and maintaining its significance has diminished the potential for expanding entrepreneurship into other areas of activity.

Schumpeter (1934) described entrepreneurship as "creative destruction", whereby established ways of doing things are destroyed by the creation of new and better ways. He suggested that an entrepreneur seeks to reform or revolutionise the pattern of production by exploiting an invention or, more generally, an untried technological possibility for producing a new commodity or producing an old one in a new way, by opening up a new source of supply of materials or a new outlet for products. He believed that an entrepreneur was someone who gathered resources, organised talent, and provided leadership. Timmons' (1994) three driving forces of entrepreneurship (opportunity, resources, and team) are not dissimilar to Schumpeter's concept of an entrepreneur. Likewise, Drucker (1985) viewed entrepreneurship as occurring when resources are redirected to progressive opportunities, not to ensure administrative efficiency. When one considers these interpretations, then entrepreneurship is not so tightly bounded by the act of a new venture being created and, thus, entrepreneurship can occur in many different contexts that to date have received limited discussion in the literature.

Some authors and researchers are now beginning to observe entrepreneurial behaviour in many different fields of activity beyond new venture creation. Thompson (1999) demonstrated how entrepreneurs could be found in many walks of life, not just business, and explained that they are responsible for creating social and artistic capital as well as financial wealth. He observed that people who behaved entrepreneurially demonstrated 10 key characteristics:

- Entrepreneurs are individuals who make a difference
- Entrepreneurship is about spotting and exploiting opportunities
- Entrepreneurs find the resources required to exploit opportunities
- Entrepreneurs add value
- Entrepreneurs are good networkers
- Entrepreneurs have "know-how" and "know-who"
- Entrepreneurs create capital (financial, social, artistic, etc)
- Entrepreneurs manage risk
- Entrepreneurs are determined in the face of adversity
- Entrepreneurship involves creativity and innovation.

When these characteristics are examined, entrepreneurship is not about the creation of a new venture but about a mindset, a way of thinking and doing that is beyond simply managing that which already exists. If one accepts this interpretation, then the world is full of entrepreneurs and entrepreneurial behaviour. It could be argued, for example, that the Gaelic Athletic Association (GAA) has behaved entrepreneurially in the redevelopment of Croke Park, a state-of-the-art stadium that cost in excess of €100 million. There are many, many more such examples in Irish society from sports, to the arts, to the public sector, and even into large organisations that behave entrepreneurially. Employing this expanded interpretation of entrepreneurship, this chapter explores entrepreneurship in different contexts and examines how they contrast to the traditional interpretations of entrepreneurship.

CORPORATE ENTREPRENEURSHIP (INTRAPRENEURSHIP)

Once a business has been established, the general ambition is to bring it through a period of growth that enables it to achieve sustainability and survival. Having reached this plateau, a different attitude might prevail. After a period of little change, management may seek to maintain the *status quo* and change may be resisted or avoided. But in a dynamic environment where change is a constant and there is a continual need for renewal, the necessity to sustain entrepreneurial behaviour is ever more critical.

Over the past decade, management of large organisations are understanding more fully the benefits of using entrepreneurship within the context of corporate life. But frequently it is not the organisation that is behaving entreprenurially but an individual within that organisation.

It was Pinchot (1986) who first coined the term "intrapreneur". He suggested that intrapreneurs were entrepreneurs within large organisations who "bootlegged" company resources and time to develop their own initiatives and make things happen while those taking the official route were still waiting for permission to begin. As Gibb (1988) observed, an intrapreneur is an employee of a large organisation who has the entrepreneurial qualities of drive, creativity, vision and ambition, but who prefers, if possible, to remain within the security of a large organisation. These individuals continually seek new opportunities, gather resources, build project teams to develop new possibilities, and take risk instead of managing existing assets. But to enable intrapreneurs to flourish, the organisation must develop a culture that promotes such activity since, unlike new venture creation, it is being done within the realms of an existing enterprise.

The process of intrapreneurship is very similar to entrepreneurship. Hornsby *et al* (1993) proposed a framework of how organisational and individual characteristics combine with a precipitating event that leads to a decision to act that, in turn, leads to business/feasibility planning, from which resource availability and the ability to overcome barriers is analysed before the idea is implemented. This framework is broadly similar to the framework for entrepreneurship proposed by Gartner (1985) and Bygrave (1989). It is multidimensional and is not concerned with events happening in isolation but with the successful interaction of several activities. But, as Carrier (1994) suggested, for such a process to occur, there must be a climate within the organisation that engenders such activity, since large organisations differ in context in terms of structure, strategy, relationships, and rewards.

Jones-Evans (2000) identified eight factors for creating the right climate within a large organisation. These are:

- Sponsors and champions throughout the organisation who not only support the creative activity and resulting failures but have the planning flexibility to establish new directions and objectives as needed
- The continuous involvement of the original intrapreneur whose enthusiasm and energy maintains the drive to succeed with the opportunity

- The autonomy of the intrapreneurial team to have control over the destiny of their particular idea
- Willing individuals within intrapreneurial teams, regardless of functional specialism, must modify the traditional boundaries between different parts of the organisation to encourage multi-disciplinary teamwork and participation
- Management must have a tolerance of risk, failures and mistakes, accepting such occurrences as part of the price of developing an entrepreneurial culture within the organisation
- A company must be prepared to establish a long-term horizon for evaluating the success of individual ventures as well as the overall intrapreneurship programme
- Organisations need to make available resources to intrapreneurs in order that these ideas reach the marketplace more quickly
- The energy and effort expended by the intrapreneurial team in the development of the new opportunity needs to be appropriately rewarded.

Similar to Jones-Evans are the factors put forward by Luchsinger and Bagby (1987), who suggested that for an entrepreneurial climate to exist, an organisation should focus on results and teamwork, reward innovation and risk-taking, tolerate and learn from mistakes, and remain flexible. As Bridge *et al* (1998) noted, while policies, practices, and appraisals assist innovation, innovative ideas and their commercialisation are generated by people. Since behaviour is influenced by context, the organisational context must support innovative behaviour. Engendering a climate of entrepreneurship within an organisation leads to continual self-renewal and enables firms to update their portfolio of activities more fluidly. Rather than being viewed in a threatening sense, intrapreneurship should be accepted for the many benefits that it brings to an organisation as well as enhancing the personal development of employees through the opportunity to express themselves in an innovative capacity.

While intrapreneurship may be of significant benefit to an organisation, many barriers exist to such activity. These barriers are traditionally due to a resistance to change, management attitude, and organisational procedures that have been developed as the company grew. In discussing intrapreneurship, Jones-Evans (2000) identified seven barriers to intrapreneurship within a corporate culture. These are:

- The traditional hierarchical nature of large corporations is not conducive to entrepreneurial behaviour as there is considerable distance between the top layers of management and the lowest level of the workforce with each layer having the potential to reject the proposal
- The corporate culture of established reporting systems, lines of authority, and control mechanisms support the existing management structure and generally do not promote creativity and innovation
- The short-term performance standards imposed by large organisations may adversely affect the long-term nature of intrapreneurial projects
- The planning procedures requiring paperwork and reporting standards may take precedence over entrepreneurial and innovative behaviour
- The intrapreneur will have difficulty in retaining total ownership of the idea, from its developmental stage to its final marketing, due to the functional nature of management within a large organisation
- The mobility of managers within a large organisation may lead to a lack of commitment to specific projects as priorities may alter with different managers
- There are frequently inappropriate methods to compensate creative employees as rewards are normally based on improvements in strict performance measures laid down by management.

There is a tendency in large organisations towards short-termism, incrementalism, and conflicting priorities. There exists an attitude towards managing that which is already there and improving it gradually without taking a great deal of risk, rather than dreaming of that which might be possible. In any operation, barriers will arise but the entrepreneurial organisations will see these as challenges to be overcome and not as excuses for not making something happen.

Intrapreneurship can take a number of different forms. It can be about the development of an overall climate of entrepreneurship at corporate level, the creation of new ventures within an existing organisation to stimulate or develop new products, or it can be the encouragement of initiatives by employees to undertake something new that brings additional value to the organisation. However one considers intrapreneurial behaviour, what is clear is that the characteristics that are considered entrepreneurial in the creation of a new venture can also be applied within the context of a large organisation. It is about a way of thinking and doing. To be truly entrepreneurial, an organisation should be moving from where it is now to where it could be in the future.

MEDIATED ENTREPRENEURSHIP

An increasingly popular form of business start-up is mediated entrepreneurship. This form of entrepreneurship involves establishing a venture through an idea that already exists or through a business that already is in practice.

The principal forms of mediated entrepreneurship include:
- Buying or licensing a patent belonging to someone else and creating a venture from it
- Taking a distributorship or agency to sell an existing product (for example, Ford cars)
- Getting a license to manufacture and sell an existing product (for example, Budweiser made under license by Guinness)
- Availing of business format franchising (for example, McDonald's, Body Shop).

These forms of entrepreneurship allow a potential entrepreneur to identify an existing idea, product, or service and develop it into their own business in return for a fee and royalties to the original owner.

Mediated entrepreneurship is generally not given the same recognition as traditional entrepreneurship, because there is a perception that there is a reduction of risk. This is not quite true since the entrepreneur still risks his or her own capital, and there is also the cost of lost opportunity in pursuing this venture. However, there is a reduction of risk in that the possibility of success is far greater in undertaking a concept that has already been proven in the marketplace and failure rates are lower than in non-mediated ventures.

Another argument made by traditionalists against mediated entrepreneurship is that there is little independence for the entrepreneur since, in reality, the business is a managed outlet using the business patterns of a larger, independent organisation. This point offers little credit to the entrepreneur who operates the business at a local level and adapts the pattern to suit local needs.

It is also worth noting that the entrepreneurship process involved in exploiting the concept is similar to that which has already been identified earlier in this chapter (opportunity recognition, gathering of resources, building a team, initiating venture). Therefore, mediated entrepreneurship should be welcomed for the additional entrepreneurial activity that is stimulated within an economy rather than criticised for its lack of purity in an entrepreneurial sense.

The exploitation under license of a patent requires characteristics and processes that are very similar to traditional entrepreneurship, except that the original concept was generated by the inventor/patent-holder. Having negotiated the cost of taking the patent and developing it for oneself, and also agreeing what royalties or profit share the inventor should receive, the remainder of the activity remains the same for the entrepreneur.

But the other forms of mediated entrepreneurship (which could come under the general heading of franchising) have advantages and disadvantages that differentiate them from the usual form of new venture creation. As Barrow (1993) identified, there are numerous benefits to franchising for the franchisee (entrepreneur), including:

- The use of a name that has widespread recognition
- Publicity, both direct and indirect, undertaken by the franchisor (original owner of the concept) that benefits the franchisee
- Direct and close assistance and training during the start-up period
- A set of standard management, accounting, sales and stock control procedures incorporated in an operating manual
- Better terms for centralised bulk purchase negotiated through the franchisor
- The benefit of the franchisor's research and development activity
- The protected or privileged rights to the franchise within a given geographical area.

These advantages enable the entrepreneur to pursue a business opportunity, while guided by an organisation that already has experience in the chosen market. But Barrow (1993) also identified a number of disadvantages that the franchisee may experience. These disadvantages may include:

- There is little opportunity for initiative by the franchisee in terms of product, service or design
- There is a royalty (or management fee) to be paid to the franchisor based on turnover or profit levels
- Territory agreements may be difficult to enforce in practice
- The franchisee may have to buy the goods and services exclusively from the franchisor at monopoly prices

- If the franchisor suffers bad publicity, it may affect all franchise operations
- The failure of a franchisor may leave the franchisee unable to operate in isolation.

While these disadvantages are primarily concerned with the power that the franchisor holds over the franchisee, it should be remembered that there are also many disadvantages to an independent entrepreneur establishing their own venture. In entering into a franchise agreement, potential entrepreneurs should examine the historical performance of the franchise and the ethical practices of the franchisor to satisfy themselves that many of the disadvantages mentioned can be minimised. A prospective franchisee should undertake due diligence to establish that they are no hidden concerns and that they are comfortable with the organisation and the type of agreement into which they are entering. Due diligence is not an act of mistrust but sensible behaviour that will enhance the legal protection of the prospective franchisee in the event of difficulties arising.

While mediated entrepreneurship is attractive from many perspectives, it is not necessarily less expensive or more profitable than establishing an independent business. While it is potentially less risky, it will still require the entrepreneur to spend long hours developing the business, personal commitment and many of the other characteristics that are associated with independent entrepreneurs. The most fundamental difference is that an independent entrepreneur is autonomous and can determine their own strategies while a mediated entrepreneur enters into a contractual agreement that places boundaries on their decision-making and restrictions against selling the business when they wish to do so. Nevertheless, in the same fashion as traditional entrepreneurship, the success of the venture is dependent upon the abilities and determination of the entrepreneur.

PUBLIC SECTOR ENTREPRENEURSHIP

While being conceptualised as having captive demand, guaranteed sources of funding, and being immune from the influence of most stakeholders, the public sector has in recent years increasingly faced cutbacks in funding and simultaneously a greater demand for services offered. Health boards, local authorities and educational institutes, for example, are being challenged to become more flexible and adaptive to environmental change despite limited budgets and resources. The traditional public sector model of centralised control, rigorous administration, and hierarchical structures is being viewed as outdated, while the private sector model of responsiveness to customer needs is being touted as the way forward for all organisations. While the term entrepreneurship was once used exclusively with regard to the private sector, it is now finding increasing employment within the public sector as the challenges of today's environment has required management within the public sector to be more innovative, proactive, and risk-orientated. But public entrepreneurs must complement their institutional roles with the democratic values of the public for whom they are responsible. According to Bellone and Goerl (1992), there is conflict between entrepreneurial autonomy and democratic accountability, public entrepreneurial vision and citizen participation, entrepreneurial secrecy and democratic openness, and between entrepreneurial risk taking and democratic stewardship. However, as in corporate entrepreneurship, entrepreneurial behaviour can still occur through a variety of avenues in a continuous attempt to recognise new opportunities, use resources more effectively, and build strong management teams that behave entrepreneurially.

In examining public sector entrepreneurship, Morris and Jones (1999) recognised a process that was broadly similar to that identified by Bygrave (1989). They suggested that, within the public sector, the entrepreneurial process involves identifying an opportunity, developing the concept, assessing the required resources, acquiring the necessary resources, and then managing and harvesting the venture. However, they did suggest that, while some of the tools and concepts were equally applicable in the public sector (opportunity recognition, leveraging resources), others needed to be adapted (criteria for evaluating resources, harvesting strategies), while others still are not really applicable (entry strategies, sources of finance). They additionally noted that innovativeness in the public sector will tend to be more concerned with novel process improvements and new services, that risk-taking means the non-delivery of services rather than potential bankruptcy, and that pro-activeness involves anticipating and preventing problems before they occur. Therefore, while entrepreneurial behaviour can exist within the public sector, it may not be characterised in the same manner that traditional entrepreneurship demonstrates.

While the comparison between corporate entrepreneurship and public sector entrepreneurship is immediately obvious, a number of substantial distinctions exist between these two forms of entrepreneurship. As Morris and Jones (1999) observed, some key differences include the fact that public sector organisations:

- Do not have a profit motive but are guided by social and political objectives
- Have less exposure to the market and its incentives for cost reductions, operating economies, and efficient resource allocation
- Receive funds indirectly from an involuntary taxpayer rather than directly from a voluntary customer
- Have difficulty in recognising their "customer", as there are a number of different publics being served
- Produce services that have consequences beyond those immediately involved
- Are subject to public scrutiny and transparency
- Face risk/reward trade-offs that strongly favour avoiding mistakes.

These fundamental differences have led many commentators to question whether entrepreneurship can really take place in such an environment. Ramamurti (1986) identified six barriers common to public entrepreneurs:

- Goal ambiguity
- Limited managerial autonomy and political interference
- High visibility
- Disincentives for risk-taking
- Short-term orientation
- Rigid personnel practices.

But he also noted that the public entrepreneur is able to deal with these challenges successfully, just as an independent entrepreneur or an intrapreneur overcomes the challenges that they face. A public entrepreneur, he argued, is one who undertakes purposeful activity to initiate, maintain, or augment public sector organisations. More recently, researchers and writers in the area of public sector entrepreneurship are intensifying the perspective that, while public sector entrepreneurs face unique challenges, they still display similar entrepreneurial characteristics and behaviour as found in other entrepreneurship contexts.

While operating in a stable environment, hierarchical structures may be the most appropriate organisational form (Burns and Stalker, 1961). But when the environment is changing rapidly, funding is no longer assured, social and political pressures are demanding more for less, and a whole range of other discontinuities regularly present themselves, then a more entrepreneurial approach is not merely advisable but essential for public sector organisations. If one accepts the general thrust that entrepreneurship is a general construct and not preciously concerned with new venture creation, then entrepreneurship can equally occur in the public sector since the process and fundamental characteristics are basically the same as found in traditional entrepreneurship. It is acknowledged that differences exist in terms of goals, constraints, approaches, and outcomes but then that is true of entrepreneurship in any context that one may examine. What is relevant is that entrepreneurial behaviour can flourish in the public sector and, instead of public sector entrepreneurs being viewed as "loose cannons", they are now becoming more valued for the entrepreneurial approach that they bring to their work and to the organisation.

SOCIAL ENTREPRENEURSHIP

For centuries, individuals have been working to improve the environment of communities, attempting to offer a better way of life for others less fortunate. Frequently, individuals would establish charitable organisations for the enhancement of society. The entrepreneurial behaviour of these individuals led to the development of social enterprises and activities from which communities suffering a wide variety of human needs could benefit. Those who initiated these ventures were not motivated by profit in these circumstances but by broader social objectives.

In contemporary times, there has been greater recognition of the contribution by social entrepreneurs to the economy and to the social needs of any country. Some have initiated well-established organisations such as Children At Risk in Ireland (CARI), while others have initiated events that have raised money for those in need. For example, Bob Geldolf behaved entrepreneurially when organising the Live Aid concerts that helped raise millions of pounds for famine victims in Africa. But how does entrepreneurship differ in this context from other forms of entrepreneurship?

Defining social enterprise is fraught with difficulty. Many commentators simply view it as any not-for-profit organisation and thereby include the public sector. But social enterprises are significantly different to the public sector where organisations are larger, funding comes from government, and the taxpayer is the boss. Social enterprises need to be established in the same way as profit-orientated ventures, they need to generate income from a variety of sources, and the risk of bankruptcy and closure is constant. Defining a social enterprise is additionally complicated by the legal status that it may take since the options include a charity, trust, co-operative, private company, or public company. The variety of legal and operating structures used by social enterprises contributes to the challenge of identifying how many exist and to the deeper understanding of their characteristics. A social enterprise in this chapter is taken to mean any not-for-profit organisation, excluding the public sector.

The process of social entrepreneurship is again broadly similar to those processes that were examined in other entrepreneurship contexts. Campbell (1998) identified the stages as:

- Gauge the commitment
- Develop the infrastructure
- Generate and screen ideas
- Conduct feasibility studies
- Plan the venture.

Campbell also suggested that the social entrepreneur should establish a new venture team, develop a business plan, and determine sources of finance for the venture. These elements of the pre-start-up phase are particularly akin to those found in the pre-start-up phase of a for-profit venture.

The Small Business Service (2001) developed a more detailed process of developmental stages for social entrepreneurship. These stages were:

- The vision and the idea
- Identifying and enthusing the key stakeholders
- Identifying and marshalling appropriate partnerships, alliances and support
- Developing the idea to a workable plan
- Identifying and marshalling appropriate resources
- Turning the plan into reality
- Sustainability and survival.

As can be seen, social entrepreneurship follows a similar path to that found in other forms of entrepreneurship. But, as with the other forms, unique characteristics apply and these peculiar differences must be considered when initiating a social enterprise. For example, social enterprises frequently start from a point of having no assets and are unable to offer collateral for loans, and thus must access a range of non-traditional funds. Social enterprises often operate in complex partnerships with the private and public sector that may have a strong impact upon the developmental path of the organisation and that raise issues related to funding. Indeed, income will frequently come from a combination of commercial and non-commercial sources. The principal difference between social entrepreneurship and traditional entrepreneurship is that social enterprises reinvest the surplus income or use it for additional social purposes. The motives behind the venture are socially or community-driven.

A social entrepreneur, according to Thompson *et al* (2000), is an individual who is driven by a social vision, someone who has the leadership skills to operationalise that vision, and who will build something that will grow and endure. Social entrepreneurs build social, aesthetic and environmental capital, as well as the financial capital required to achieve the primary objectives of the social enterprise. Many of the characteristics of successful social entrepreneurs reflect those of entrepreneurs in the profit-seeking sectors. Leadbetter (1997) believes that their leadership and personal qualities are similar, that they are equally driven and ambitious, that they have a vision that they can communicate and sell to others, and that they have the capacity to bootleg resources. The vision is generally based on an opportunity where the current services to the community are weak. The social entrepreneur builds networks and relationships that bring credibility and co-operation to the organisation. The venture is normally financially fragile and the risk is high. Therefore, entrepreneurship can occur also in a not-for-profit environment. Indeed, how many sports clubs and hobby groups throughout the country have people behaving entrepreneurially on a regular basis? The new stand that was built at the local sports field to accommodate spectators – where did the idea come from, how were the funds gathered, was that not entrepreneurial behaviour? Throughout our communities, there are individuals demonstrating entrepreneurial characteristics everyday, except that people fail to recognise them because they have not established a profit-making venture.

CONCLUSION

This book began with a review of the literature addressing the question "What is entrepreneurship?". As always with this question, the answer is tightly bound about the traditional perspectives of entrepreneurship and particularly around the notion of a new venture being created. This limits both entrepreneurial thinking and the promotion of entrepreneurial activity.

If people understood that entrepreneurship was a way of thinking and of doing, that it was about behaviour that incorporated opportunity recognition, gathering resources, and building a team, then maybe more people would believe that they were capable of entrepreneurial activity. If people were not restricted to considering entrepreneurship being primarily concerned with creating a new venture but understood that entrepreneurship can occur within large organisations, public sector organisations, or for the benefit of the community, then maybe more people would believe that they could be entrepreneurial within their own endeavours. Many people believe that they are not creative and therefore could not come up with a good idea for a business. But if they knew that, through mediated entrepreneurship, there is a broad range of existing opportunities from which they can avail, then maybe more people would establish their own businesses.

It has been clearly established in this chapter that the process of entrepreneurship and the principal characteristics of entrepreneurial behaviour are broadly similar irrespective of the context. What differ are the goals, constraints, approaches, and outcomes. Moving beyond new venture creation enables people to understand these similarities and differences and allows them to appreciate the wonderful entrepreneurial activity that is happening all about them on a daily basis. It also encourages people to see these local heroes as people to be emulated. Entrepreneurial activity now becomes a daily choice as it can occur in many different contexts.

QUESTIONS

1. Differentiate between corporate entrepreneurship (intrapreneurship), mediated entrepreneurship, public sector entrepreneurship, and social entrepreneurship.
2. How does entrepreneurship vary in different contexts?

3. "Being entrepreneurial in a large organisation is more difficult than starting up a new enterprise on one's own." Discuss.
4. "Entrepreneurship and meeting social objectives are not compatible." Discuss.
5. Suggest ways in which Government Departments could become more entrepreneurial.

USEFUL WEBSITES

www.smallbusinessportal.co.uk

CHECKLIST FOR CHAPTER

After reading this chapter, check that you understand and appreciate:
• How entrepreneurship can take place in different contexts
• Corporate entrepreneurship (intrapreneurship), mediated entrepreneurship, public sector entrepreneurship, and social entrepreneurship
• How each of these forms differ from the traditional concept of entrepreneurship
• The entrepreneurship process for each of these contexts.

REFERENCES

Barrow, C. (1993) – *The Essence of Small Business* – Prentice Hall, Hemel Hempstead.

Bellone, C.J. and Goerl, G.F. (1992) – Reconciling Public Entrepreneurship and Democracy – *Public Administration Review*, Vol.52, No.2, pp 130-134.

Bridge, S.; O'Neill, K. and Cromie, S. (1998) – *Understanding Enterprise, Entrepreneurship and Small Business* – Macmillan, London.

Burns, T. and Stalker, G.M. (1961) – *The Management of Innovation* – Tavistock, London.

Bygrave, W.D. (1989) – The Entrepreneurship Paradigm (I): A Philosophical Look at its Research Methodologies – *Entrepreneurship Theory and Practice*, Vol.14, No.1, pp 7-26.

Bygrave, W.D. and Hofer, C.W. (1991) – Theorizing About Entrepreneurship – *Entrepreneurship Theory and Practice*, Vol.16, No.2, pp 13-22.

Campbell, S. (1998) – Social Entrepreneurship: How to Develop New Social-Purpose Business Ventures – *Health Care Strategic Management*, Vol.16, No.5, pp 17-18.

Carrier, C. (1994) – Intrapreneurship in Large Firms and SMEs: A Comparative Study – *International Small Business Journal*, Vol.12, No.3, pp 54-61.

Drucker, P. (1985) – *Entrepreneurship and Innovation* – Heinnemann, London

Gartner, W.B. (1985) – A Conceptual Framework for Describing the Phenomenon of New Venture Creation – *Academy of Management Review*, Vol.10, No.4, pp 696-706.

Gibb, A.A. (1988) – The Enterprise Culture: Threat or Opportunity? – *Management Decision*, Vol.26, No.4, pp 5-12.

Hornsby, J.S., Naffziger, D.W., Kuratko, D.F. and Montagno, R.V. (1993) – *Entrepreneurship Theory and Practice*, Vol.18, No.2.

Jones-Evans, D. (2000) – Intrapreneurship – *Enterprise and Small Business* (Eds. S. Carter and D. Jones-Evans), Pearson, Harlow.

Leadbetter, C. (1997) – *The Rise of the Social Entrepreneur* – Demos.

Luchsinger, V. and Bagby, D.R. (1987) – Entrepreneurship and Intrapreneurship: Comparisons and Contrasts – *SAM Advanced Management Journal*, Vol.52, No.3, pp 10-14.

Morris, M.H. and Jones, F.J. (1999) – Entrepreneurship in Established Organisations: The Case of the Public Sector – *Entrepreneurship Theory and Practice*, Vol.24, No.1, pp 79-91.

Pinchot, G. (1986) – *Intrapreneuring* – Harper and Row, NY.

Ramamurti, R. (1986) – Public Entrepreneurs: Who They Are and How They Operate – *California Management Review*, Vol.28, No.3, pp 142-158.

Schumpeter, J. (1934) – *The Theory of Economic Development* – Harvard University Press, Cambridge, MA.

Small Business Service (2001) – *Understanding and Supporting Social Enterprise* – Small Business Service, London.

Thompson, J.L. (1999) – The World of the Entrepreneur: A New Perspective – *Journal of Workplace Learning: Employee Counselling Today*, Vol.11, No.6, pp 209-224.

Thompson, J.; Alvy, G. and Lees, A. (2000) – Social Entrepreneurship: A New Look at the People and the Potential – *Management Decision*, Vol.38, No.5, pp 328-338.

Timmons, J.A. (1994) – *New Venture Creation* – Irwin, Chicago.

CHAPTER 15

ENTREPRENEURSHIP AND THE ROLE OF THE STATE

Dan Flinter[*]

LEARNING OBJECTIVES

- To understand the role of the State in promoting entrepreneurship
- To examine current Government policy
- To determine key areas of interest and future investment focus.

INTRODUCTION

The transformation in Ireland's economic fortunes over the past decade has been little short of remarkable. More than 700,000 new jobs have been created, the nation's finances went from chronic indebtedness to surpluses, and standard of living has improved significantly. Many reasons and factors have been advanced to explain this turnaround but one factor which is seldom given due credit is the emergence of a genuine culture of entrepreneurship in Ireland – one which had never really existed before. Ireland has moved from a culture that viewed entrepreneurs with scepticism to recognising their contribution to the country's economic growth. No longer are they "gangsters or chancers"

---

[*] Dan Flinter is chief executive officer of Enterprise Ireland.

but instead they are seen as local heroes who have demonstrated the courage and the capacity to leave the security of a "job for life" and have created successful enterprises that created employment for themselves and others.

But the success of Irish entrepreneurs has not just been in the Irish market, as increasingly Irish entrepreneurs have sought to conquer foreign markets. Such has been their achievement that Ireland now has a whole range of Irish-owned or Irish-led companies, including Iona Technologies, Parthus, Riverdeep and SmartForce, quoted on the Nasdaq and other international exchanges. What these companies, and others like them, have in common is the fact that they were all founded by Irish entrepreneurs whose ambitions and sights were set far beyond the horizons of the domestic market. While it would be invidious to claim credit for the State in the success of these companies and their founders, the fact remains that Government policies have had significant influence on the development of a new climate in which entrepreneurship can thrive.

THE ROLE OF STATE AGENCIES

Government policy in relation to enterprise and entrepreneurship is constantly evolving to meet changing sets of circumstances. In many ways, it can be said that Ireland has now moved on from what might be called the "climate creation" phase and has arrived at a point where access to finance is no longer the major problem it was for many start-up enterprises. The current policy is to work continually to identify and remove constraints and barriers to growth. For State agencies, this means taking a holistic approach to developing solutions for their clients. This approach takes into account all areas of business activity from design, through production to marketing and including the key areas of finance and human resource development. Solutions in each of these areas are designed to meet each client's specific needs and strategic requirements.

State agencies work in partnership with their client companies to meet shared growth objectives. In doing so, they are guided by a number of basic operating principles. They recognise that it is entrepreneurs in the private sector, not the State, that create successful businesses. The role of State agencies is to help create the environment in which people start businesses, to help them develop these businesses, and to explore new directions in terms of export market development, innovation, and internationalisation. In ensuring the long-term survival of businesses State agencies are more likely to succeed by responding to the dynamic inherent in them. Recognising that every company is different with its own set of needs, State agencies provide significant levels of hands-on support from business planning right through to in-market support, along with substantial direct equity investment.

While the only constant in today's business environment is change, Irish companies have shown themselves to be remarkably adaptable in coping with change over the past five years or more. This has been a crucial factor in the outstanding success of Irish enterprises over the period. In this light, there has also been a change in the overall view of financial assistance for companies. It is no longer necessary, nor desirable, to simply provide financial assistance to companies to support capacity-building in terms of employment and fixed assets. Instead, the focus is now on sharing risk and knowledge with companies as they build their capability to achieve competitiveness and export growth. Simply put, assisting firms to employ more people to output more products is no longer a sustainable practice. In no way does it assist a firm to become more competitive. In today's internationalised marketplace, those firms that do not become progressively more competitive will lose out. The focus is therefore to assist firms to innovate and internationalise in order to ensure long-term survival and growth.

IRELAND'S ENTREPRENEURIAL FUTURE

State support for entrepreneurship is clearly focused on the ongoing creation of new entrepreneur-led business entities with a solid base in intellectual capital and a capability of becoming internationally competitive within a short period of time. From the perspective of a State agency, such as Enterprise Ireland, there are three key deliverables:

- Ensuring a flow of intellectual property
- Providing business development support
- Accelerating the internationalisation of Irish businesses.

In relation to intellectual property, State investment is directed towards applied research both within companies and in the third level sector (where a clear focus on the marketplace is demonstrated). Ireland has already seen a number of significant businesses emerge from the university domain. While many of these have been in the electronics and software sectors, there are emerging opportunities in biotechnology – where Ireland already has a strong academic base. This base can provide the foundation for a new generation of campus companies. But they will require nurturing, not just through funding, but through hands-on support from State agencies that can advise and assist on the commercialisation of research efforts and on building a business capable of survival and growth away from its academic origins.

The vision of government is that the exploitation of technology innovation becomes a key driver in the internationalisation of Irish business. Ireland is positioning itself as a knowledge-based, technologically-sophisticated economy trading globally. Existing and new companies that invest in creating and applying innovation and technology to the development of new products, services and processes will be those that generate continued and sustained economic growth for Ireland. At the beginning of the 21st century, the global marketplace is predominantly comprised of business activity that is powered by advances and applications in science and technology. The clients of State agencies operate in this marketplace and technology innovation is crucial to their ability to achieve sustained growth by enabling them to respond to more sophisticated customer requirements, operate as efficiently as possible and, in so doing, gain competitive advantage. The most successful companies are those that invest in applying technology to add value to their products, services, or processes. This may be achieved by undertaking or collaborating in original research and development, by adapting and enhancing existing technology, or by procuring or transferring technology for the benefit of the company.

KEY INTERESTS

The State agencies provide a broad range of valuable assistance to Irish entrepreneurs. They possess expertise and knowledge of markets that entrepreneurs wish to enter. These agencies have differing objectives and remits but each are there to support Irish enterprise. For example, the key interests for Enterprise Ireland are:

- Working with clients to help them use technology to their advantage
- Commercialising research to get technology out of the research system and, where possible, into firms in Ireland.

The particular concern of Enterprise Ireland is to ensure that Irish businesses have access to appropriate technology solutions and that they have the capability to absorb and utilise the opportunities that technology can provide. The universities, the Institutes of Technology, research centres and other sources of technology generate ideas and products that have commercial potential. The aim is to help transform ideas into reality by supporting the transfer of commercially exploitable knowledge out of academia and into companies in strategic technology areas. This will lead to a direct transfer to firms in Ireland and to the creation of new, technology-based firms that will be the wealth creators of the future.

While problems with access to finance may no longer be of the same magnitude as they were some years ago, the funding requirements of Irish industry remain high and continue to grow. Finance is delivered to companies in a number of ways: directly by State agencies in the form of business development support with equity participation; and through a range of venture capital funds that are public-private partnerships. State investment in such funds has contributed to the creation of a vibrant, competitive venture capital market. Enterprise Ireland now works in partnership with a number of private sector venture capital companies to make new venture funds available in specific targeted market areas such as software, the food industry, electronics and so forth. More recently, Enterprise Ireland has become a partner in new funds specifically aimed at the life sciences and biotechnology sector.

State participation leverages private sector investment that might not otherwise be available for investment in relatively high-risk start-up ventures with large requirements for cash. On the other hand, the funds are commercially managed, with the State and the private sector partners sharing in the rewards of successful investments. The ambition must be to achieve an innovation-focused competitive venture capital sector of the scale necessary to grow a cadre of technology and knowledge-based Irish multinational companies.

CONCLUSION

The State's role in promoting and fostering entrepreneurship has changed greatly over the past decade. From a position of having to intervene in financial and capital markets and provide relatively high levels of financial support, we have now moved to a situation where the culture of entrepreneurship has taken firm root in Ireland. While the State can take some credit for putting in place the range of supports and other measures which helped the current crop of entrepreneurial companies to grow and flourish, the future now is one of facilitating those individuals who will be responsible for the development and creation of the next wave of internationally successful Irish-owned and Irish-led companies – a wave that we are already seeing emerge.

QUESTIONS

1. "Enterprise is now acceptable in Ireland." Discuss.
2. Evaluate the role of State agencies in enhancing new venture creation in Ireland.
3. How does Government policy engender entrepreneurship?
4. Using the Internet, examine the different supports offered to entrepreneurs by the various State agencies.
5. Discuss Ireland's entrepreneurial future.

USEFUL WEBSITES

www.enterprise-ireland.com
www.startingabusinessinireland.com

CHECKLIST FOR CHAPTER

After reading this chapter, check that you understand and appreciate:
- The role of the state in promoting entrepreneurship
- Current government policy
- The key areas of interest and future investment focus.

APPENDIX

State Support for New Venture Creation

State agencies that provide support for new ventures, in a wide variety of formats, include:

NATIONAL AGENCIES
- BASIS
- Enterprise Ireland
- FÁS
- Forfás
- Revenue Commissioners

REGIONAL AGENCIES
- Shannon Development
- Údarás na Gaeltachta

SPECIALIST AGENCIES
- Arts Council
- Bord Bia
- Bord Fáilte
- Bord Glas
- Bord Iasciagh Mhara
- Central Statistics Office
- CERT
- Coillte
- Comhar
- Companies Registration Office
- ENFO
- Environmental Protection Agency
- Food Safety Authority of Ireland
- Health & Safety Authority
- Marine Institute
- National Standards Authority of Ireland
- Office of the Director of Consumer Affiars
- Patents Office
- Registry of Business Names
- Registry of Friendly Societies
- Teagasc

LOCAL AGENCIES
- County Enterprise Boards (35)
- LEADER+
- Western Development Commission
- Area Development Management (which manages 38 Area-based Partnership companies and 35 Community Groups)
- Dublin Docklands Development Authority

For a complete listing of State agencies, see www.irlgov.ie.

For more information on how these agencies assist start-ups, see the individual agencies' websites or www.startingabusinessinireland.com.

OAK TREE PRESS

Oak Tree Press is Ireland's leading business book publisher. Increasingly, it is an international developer and publisher of enterprise training and support solutions.

Oak Tree Press has developed an extensive platform of pre-start-up, start-up growth and support content. The platforms include:
- **Publications**
- **Websites**
- **Software**
- **Assessment models**
- **Training**
- **Consultancy**
- **Certification**.

The platforms allow different levels of entry from the simple to quite complex, to meet different user needs.

Oak Tree Press' enterprise training and support solutions are in use in Ireland, the UK, Finland, USA and Eastern Europe and are available for customisation to local situations and needs.

For further information, contact:
Ron Immink or Brian O'Kane
OAK TREE PRESS
19 Rutland Street, Cork, Ireland
T: + 353 21 431 3855   F: + 353 21 431 3496
E: info@oaktreepress.com   W: www.oaktreepress.com